Talking
Hawai'i's
Story

A PUBLICATION OF THE

COLLEGE OF SOCIAL SCIENCES

center for oral history

UNIVERSITY OF HAWAIʻI AT MĀNOA

The Center for Oral History (COH), Social Science Research Institute, College of Social Sciences, University of Hawaiʻi at Mānoa, was established in 1976 by the Hawaiʻi State Legislature. COH preserves the recollections of Hawaiʻi's people through oral interviews and disseminates oral history transcripts to researchers, students, and the general community.

COH also develops books, articles, catalogs, brochures, photo displays, and videotapes based on oral histories; serves as a resource center for oral history materials; and trains groups and individuals in oral history research.

Talking Hawai'i's Story

Oral Histories of an Island People

EDITED BY

MICHI KODAMA-NISHIMOTO
WARREN S. NISHIMOTO
CYNTHIA A. OSHIRO

A BIOGRAPHY MONOGRAPH

PUBLISHED FOR THE BIOGRAPHICAL RESEARCH CENTER
BY THE UNIVERSITY OF HAWAI'I PRESS
2009

14 13 12 11 10 09   6 5 4 3 2 1

Library of Congress Cataloging-in-Publication Data
Talking Hawaii's story : oral histories of an island people / edited by Michi
Kodama-Nishimoto, Warren S. Nishimoto, Cynthia A. Oshiro.
    p.   cm.
  "A Biography monograph."
  ISBN 978-0-8248-3390-9 (softcover : alk. paper)
  1. Hawaii—Social life and customs—20th century—Anecdotes. 2. Hawaii—
Biography—Anecdotes. 3. Oral history. I. Kodama-Nishimoto, Michi.
II. Nishimoto, Warren S.   III. Oshiro, Cynthia A.
  DU627.5.T356 2009
  920.0969—dc22
                    2009004547

University of Hawai'i Press books are printed on
acid-free paper and meet the guidelines for permanence
and durability of the Council on Library Resources

Design and composition by Center for Oral History

Printed by Versa Press, Inc.

CONTENTS

ACKNOWLEDGMENTS

We express our gratitude to the Hawai'i State Legislature, the Social Science Research Institute, College of Social Sciences, University of Hawai'i at Mānoa, and the many individuals and organizations who have sustained our efforts for more than thirty years.

We thank present and former staff at the Center for Oral History, particularly research associate Holly Yamada and former director Chad K. Taniguchi.

We thank the Hawai'i Council for the Humanities for supporting this publication, in partnership with the National Endowment for the Humanities special initiative, "We the People."

We acknowledge Craig Howes and Stanley Schab of the Center for Biographical Research, University of Hawai'i at Mānoa, for their assistance. Their steady editorial guidance, advice, and support sustained this project through its months-long stop-and-go progress towards completion. The expertise and work of the University of Hawai'i Press are also noted and appreciated.

The narratives printed here first appeared in the Center for Oral History's newsletter, the *Oral History Recorder,* a publication largely underwritten by modest donations from hundreds of individuals who contribute year after year to the support of the Center's work. We are very grateful for their constant support.

Acknowledged also are the following organizations that generously funded individual oral history projects from which narratives were culled:

Castle & Cooke, Inc.
Center on the Family, University of Hawai'i at Mānoa
Civil Liberties Public Education Fund
Elsie Wilcox Foundation
G.N. Wilcox Trust
Hawai'i Council for the Humanities
Hawai'i Imin Shiryo Hozon Kai
Hawai'i State Department of Business, Economic Development, and Tourism
Hawai'i State Foundation on Culture and the Arts
Pālama Settlement
U.S. National Park Service
USS Arizona Memorial

And, to the interviewees, their families, and other members of our island community who entrusted the Center for Oral History with their stories, we extend a heartfelt thank you.

INTRODUCTION

The truth of a narrative is not necessarily to be discovered in its historical consistency, but rather in its ability to create common identity and shared values and to facilitate survival. . . . The validity of narratives must be evaluated not according to a foreign yardstick, but instead on the basis of their success in sustaining a culture that provides a system of coherent beliefs, nurtures a cohesive community, acknowledges the humanity of all members and ensures survival of a people.

—Robert Archibald

Talking Hawai'i's Story: Oral Histories of an Island People reflects the common identity, shared values, and survival of a unique culture that gave rise to and sustained a special sense of community in twentieth-century Hawai'i. Measured by standards suggested by historian Robert Archibald, this book holds truths and statements that readers can identify with and relate to as representations of a past still meaningful and relevant to the people of Hawai'i.

In this book are the experiences and observations of men and women who began their lives in the first three decades of the last century, and who speak not only of their own times and lives but of their parents' and grandparents'—reporting experiences and observations covering more than a hundred years and extending beyond the shores of our island state.

Featured are seventeen men and thirteen women: Faustino Baysa, Abigail Burgess, Lillian Cameron, Agnes Eun Soon Rho Chun, Severo Dinson, Henry K. Duvauchelle, Martina Kekuewa Fuentevilla, Ernest Golden, Alice Saito Gouveia, Venicia Damasco Guiala, Robert Kiyoshi Hasegawa, Lemon "Rusty" Holt, Jennie Lee In, Mae Morita Itamura, Emma Kaawakauo, Robert Kahele, Moses W. "Moke" Kealoha, Helen Fujika Kusunoki, Frederick P. Lowrey, Ernest A. Malterre, Jr., Stanley C. Mendes, Fred Ho'olae Paoa, Irene Cockett Perry, Alfred Preis, Alex Ruiz, John Santana, Etsuo Sayama, Willie Thompson, Kazue Iwahara Uyeda, and Edith Anzai Yonenaka.

They talk about the routines of everyday life—cooking, doing chores, going to school, and working—as well as special events and pivotal decisions and their consequences. They speak about family, neighbors, and friends. Persons prominent in their lives—teachers, supervisors, employers, mentors—are mentioned, as are the famous and notorious. Personal issues, family matters, and community concerns are shared. They talk about their homes, living conditions, foods, clothing, and means of transportation and communication. They describe their surroundings, both natural—mountains, valleys, streams, and shorelines—and built—villages, plantation camps, towns, and cities. They elaborate on their religious and cultural practices. Aspirations, expectations, triumphs, disappointments, and tragedies are recalled. Values and beliefs are openly discussed or conveyed in the telling of events.

These personal experiences and observations intersect with what many call the "historical record." The men and women who share their lives in this book lived through many key events and transformational periods of modern Hawai'i: the immigration of agricultural laborers to the islands, labor strikes, the Great Depression, two World Wars, statehood, the expansion of an American military presence in the Pacific, the growth of tourism, the demise of the sugar and pineapple industries, and the development of a multi-ethnic, culturally diverse island society.

This intersection of the personal and historical expands our knowledge of the past, adding the names and faces of largely anonymous people, together with their emotions, commentaries, and reflections, to the record. This intersection gives context to both the personal and historical.

For some readers whose memories may converge or coincide with those of the men and women featured here, the narratives will serve as mnemonic devices, rekindling and confirming remembrances that affirm the shared nature of their island experiences and observations. For these readers, the narratives easily settle into time and place.

For others lacking such remembrances, the narratives may serve as vehicles to revisit dissimilar experiences or to experience vicariously events of the last century. For these readers, the narratives will not settle into time and place so easily, and will require mediation by more of the historical record. Other works on the history of Hawai'i, and the project volumes that hold the oral histories on which these narratives are based, should be consulted.

The anthology's thirty narratives are selected from among sixty-nine originally published between Fall 1984 and Spring 2008 in the *Oral History Recorder,* the semi-annual newsletter of the Center for Oral History of the University of Hawai'i at Mānoa (COH).[1] Only after a thorough review of all sixty-nine narratives were these thirty selected for republication here. Others not selected have been republished previously or are slated for other use.

Although each narrative is not intended to be a comprehensive life history, together with its preceding biographical summary, each provides life details in a fuller context.

In the narratives are those aspects of local history, culture, and lifestyle seldom found in print and often irretrievably lost with the passing of older residents. As a collection, the narratives present a variety of life experiences in different island settings, and share the observations of persons from diverse ethnic and socioeconomic backgrounds.

First published in the *Oral History Recorder,* a six- to eight-page publication, the narratives are necessarily limited in length, and focused on specific topics determined by the projects of the Center for Oral History. When first published, the narratives showcased the results of recently completed projects, or highlighted subjects of upcoming projects discussed in other sections of the newsletter.

The oral history interviews on which these narratives are based were selected to be edited from transcripts to narratives for their potential to inform *Oral History Recorder* subscribers about a particular COH project, and for their portrayal of diverse experiences, documentation of historical events as experienced and perceived by individuals, articulation of feelings and values, and meaningful reflections. Also considered in the selection process were the completeness and length of responses, the interviewees' recall of events in a manner that lent itself to narrative treatment, and the interviewees' style of speech—with preference given to the more vivid, expressive speakers.

In editing the interviews into narratives, obscure statements, interviewers' questions, and portions of limited interest were removed. Topics were rearranged for readability and coherence. Added for fluidity were occasional conjunctive and transitional phrases or subheads; added for clarity were explanatory statements and definitions of non-English and other terms specific to Hawai'i. Except as mentioned, no words were added to the narratives.

Every attempt was made to reflect as accurately as possible the interviewees' recall of experiences and manner of speech. To the extent possible, the content and character of the narratives as well as the interviews were not compromised.

The narratives are based on oral history interviews from eighteen separate projects conducted by the Center for Oral History. Projects from which the oral history interviews were excerpted are identified in the biographical summary preceding each narrative. Developed in consultation with academic and lay community members, these projects, like others conducted by COH, focused on communities, ethnic groups, government, historical events, individual lives, and occupations. (For a list of COH projects, see the Appendix.)

All oral history interviews featured here were conducted by COH staff members who identified potential interviewees from research in written sources and contacts made within the community. Potential interviewees were evaluated in unrecorded preliminary interviews, where their depth and breadth of knowledge about the topics under study, their ability to articulate life experiences, and their willingness to participate were considered. COH then conducted interviews with each selected person on audiotape in two or more ninety-minute sessions. The majority of sessions were held at the interviewees' homes.

Because interviewees were asked to comment on experiences and incidents often specific to their lives, no set questionnaire was used. Instead, a life history approach was followed, creating biographical case studies centered mainly on the backgrounds of interviewees and the events that shaped their lives. Interviewees were asked to describe and comment on family and home life, community life, schooling, work, cultural practices, values, and other aspects of everyday living, as well as specific topics under study in a particular project.

COH staff transcribed the interviews almost verbatim. The transcripts, audio-reviewed to correct omissions and other errors, were edited slightly for clarity and historical accuracy. The transcripts were then sent to interviewees for their review and approval. Interviewees were asked to verify names and dates, and to clarify statements where necessary. Some interviewees edited statements—adding, deleting, or changing words. COH incorporated the interviewees' changes in the final transcripts; these include all statements the interviewees wish to leave for the public record.

The interviewees then read and signed a statement allowing the Center for Oral History and the general public scholarly and educational use of the transcripts. Published in bound volumes and/or CD-ROMs, and deposited in the University of Hawai'i and State of Hawai'i public libraries, the transcripts are the primary documents available for research purposes. Audio cassettes are in storage and not available for use, unless written permission is obtained from the Center for Oral History.

Since 1976 these transcripts and others produced by COH have been cited in works by various scholars. *Hanahana: An Oral History Anthology of Hawai'i's Working People,* based on COH oral histories, was published in 1984. In the decades that followed, except for the semi-annual newsletter narratives, the Center concentrated its efforts on recording and archiving oral histories.

Now, twenty-five years since its first monograph, the Center makes its newsletter narratives available to a wider audience in *Talking Hawai'i's Story.* Since many of the men and women featured here have passed away, and what we can know of the past is limited to what is left as a record, this book is an effort to share what might have otherwise gone undiscovered by present and future generations.

A collaborative effort of island residents and the Center for Oral History, *Talking Hawai'i's Story* represents continued sharing of an identity and values that still make the islands a special place.

NOTE

1. The Center for Oral History is a unit of the Social Science Research Institute, College of Social Sciences, University of Hawai'i at Mānoa. The only state-supported center of its kind in the islands, COH researches, conducts, transcribes, edits, and disseminates oral history interviews focused on Hawai'i's past. Since its inception in 1976, COH has interviewed more than 800 individuals, and deposited in archives and libraries a collection of over 36,000 transcript pages. In addition to providing researchers with first-person, primary-source documents, COH produces educational materials (journal and newspaper articles, books, videos, dramatizations, etc.) based on the interviews. The Center also presents lectures and facilitates discussions on local history, conducts classes and workshops on oral history methodology, and serves as a clearinghouse for oral history research relating to Hawai'i. For more information, visit the Center for Oral History website at www.oralhistory.hawaii.edu.

WORK CITED

Archibald, Robert. *A Place to Remember: Using History to Build Community.* Walnut Creek, CA: AltaMira, 1999.

FAUSTINO BAYSA

HAWAIIANO

They used to call bangō. That's the number given to you, and most time, they call you by the numbers. They say, "Hey, bayaw, you come here, 7488." And that was the thing I objected to. I tell 'em, "I have a name. I wish you'd call me by name." [But] the situation for you to think you're a human being was out of the question.

At age nineteen, Faustino Baysa left his native Ilocos Norte, Philippines, in 1927 to labor in Hawai'i's sugar cane fields. Assigned to Waialua Agricultural Company, Baysa worked in its cane fields, dairy, sugar mill; and from 1931 to his retirement in 1972, the plantation's hospital, where he received patients, dressed wounds, took X rays, and assisted in the morgue. In 1938, Baysa visited the Philippines, where workers returning from Hawai'i were dubbed *Hawaiianos*. On a later visit, Baysa met his wife Laurena. They made their home in Hawai'i and raised a family of six. Until his death in 1979, Baysa remained active in the Waialua community.

Vivien Lee, a COH researcher-interviewer, conducted over three hours of taped interviews with Faustino Baysa in the summer of 1976. Lee's notes include this description: "Mr. Baysa speaks very softly, is deeply tanned, and has an easy smile. He appears much younger than his sixty-eight years."

Faustino Baysa's complete interview transcript, from which the following narrative is edited, is part of COH's inaugural project, *Waialua and Hale'iwa: The People Tell Their Story*. This project documents lifestyles, cultures, physical surroundings, and ethnic relations on Waialua Agricultural Company's plantation and in Hale'iwa, a neighboring town located on O'ahu's North Shore. When Waialua plantation shut down in 1996, after a century in business, it marked the end of sugar cane production on O'ahu.

HARDENED PALMS

We had a family who did not have all the luxuries. We plowed our own fields. We planted our own rice, tobacco, corn, beans; and we harvested them ourselves. I was unable to continue my education. I wanted to go back to school badly. My parents could not afford it.

I made up my mind to come to Hawai'i, following my uncle. I expected to return sometime. But before then, I thought maybe if I earned enough money, I would go back to school. They [the Hawaiian Sugar Planters' Association] used to recruit only bona fide field workers. The procedure was to feel your hands, looking for calluses or things like hardened palms. I tried my best to make my palms hard enough by pounding rice, cutting firewood, digging [in the] garden. And they accept me.

This place was entirely different from where I came. My housemates were experienced because they were old-timers. Very few of the laborers in Waialua were younger than I was then. I was used to depending on my parents. I could cry when I found that I was not ready for [this] kind of place.

I remember three popular [Filipino] families in here when I came in. [Such families were rare at this time. The Filipino population was composed predominantly of men without families.] And some of the children were of our age. We were invited to join them on their activities and it made us feel good. And feeling at ease, [we] forgot [about] being homesick. Leaving the playground and back to our own homes, we were with the old people [older workers] and again became father and son to them.

My first work down here [paid] only dollar and ten cents a day. Weeding—hard work then. Turn out for work, early morning, at least six o'clock. Used to wake up about three o'clock in the morning, and then cook our own provisions, get ready for the train to come in. And if one don't wake up early enough, the train pass, and you are left behind. As soon as you reach there, except for lunch break, work until they call it pau hana at 3:30 p.m., time to go home.

A HUMAN BEING

Being new, and environment was not the same as where I was raised up, I objected [to] any ridicule. They used to call [the worker's identification number] bangō. That's the number given to you, and most time, they call you by the numbers. They say, "Hey, bayaw, you come here, 7488." And that was the thing I objected to. I tell 'em, "I have a name. I wish you'd call me by name." [But] the situation for you to think you're a human being was out of the question.

Not being used to it, my [work] speed was not the same as a regular farmhand's. So, as soon as I had the chance, I applied for another job. The plantation used to have a dairy. I landed up with tending to cows. We used to go and take care of the cows in the pasture right on the foot of the hills down here at Ka'ala Mountain. [But] the time came on a rainy day [when] I got tired of the cowboy work. I applied for factory [sugar mill] work doing all kinds of odd [jobs] inside there.

The sugar room was where I stayed most of the time. It's where the sugar juice [was] processed, limed, boiled in tanks, [and] passed through the evaporators. My immediate luna at the factory was Chinese. The other was Portuguese. They used to call me by first name. And then, I liked it. I felt like I was someone, a human being.

I used to love my work in the factory because there was something more than work. It was the attitude of my boss [Bill Ecklund] being friendly, showing us how to relax after work. He used to be a good tennis player, so he showed us how to play it. He must have been a well-known person in tennis because the people who used to play for the Davis Cup, whenever they pass [through] Hawai'i, he used to bring them as guest [to] the haole tennis court. Since we were guests of my boss, we were lucky enough to be called in to watch the game. We used to call it the haole tennis court [because] we used to have [a separate] tennis court for the laborers.

Very few of the Filipinos before I came in did socialize. They didn't go around and eat with the rest of the group. They had their own, and when

Plantation tennis players; Faustino Baysa, fourth from right (photo reproduced by courtesy of Dole Food Company, Inc.).

they invited guests it was their own kind. That was the routine way of living around here where [if] your group in there were mostly Filipinos, well, Filipinos eat together. The situation then was Japanese Club was just Japanese. The Haole Club was haoles.

We started making [i.e., participating in] that Cosmopolitan Social Club before. We had schoolteachers and plantation supervisors. But among the workers, they were either not willing to go in, or they were shy. Well, we joined in, and since we started playing together, play games, we began to understand that there was a gap. You go in there, and pick a little piece of paper, grab a subject, and supposedly talk about it, just to talk even if it were funny. We had to try our best, and since the intention was to socialize together and trying to know each other more, we began to like it.

THE CHALLENGE

They used to ask for volunteers to do odd jobs outside the factory. That's what happened on the off-season's time around October and November. So I was one of those volunteers to go out and do some dynamite work. We used to enjoy the blasting work. When you're young, you think you're capable of doing lots of things.

We were on one of the gulches down 'Ōpae'ula when the camp police came for me. The policeman came in and said, "The [plantation] boss wants to see you at the office."

I inquired, "What did I do?"

He said, "I don't know. He just wants you, the boss."

I dreaded the trip to the office. When the big boss came, he said, "Well, you didn't do anything wrong. I want you to go to the hospital. The office boy went for a vacation, and we don't have any help up there, so you help for maybe one month." It turned out that this man never came back, so I kept on relieving day in and day out.

In the first night, I had to do some unpleasant work. Somebody was blasted and so I had to help examine the corpse in the morgue, and I had to sew the remains. I was not used to it. The doctor [kept] urging, "Oh, keep on. You're doing all right. I'll stay with you." When we finished working and I went home, [I] could not sleep because I could see everything on my first experience [in my] imagination. So (laughs) my reaction in the morning was to resign.

[But] the challenge was there. Different jobs. We had to do clerical work, and we had to help in the dispensary. Those days, we didn't have adequate facilities for all, like your modern facilities now. Whenever we had an accident case, we took care of the accident.

Waialua Agricultural Company hospital staff; Faustino Baysa, far right (photo reproduced by courtesy of Dole Food Company, Inc.).

Most of it would be cane knives: cuts, lacerations, bruises, incised wounds, and abrasions. Clean, dress 'em up, took care of the paperwork, history of the accident, and made the accident report. Those were the things I was told to do.

In the beginning, before mechanization, they used to have men loading the cane cars. People used to pile the cane, arrange 'em up, bundle 'em up little bit. The men used to come in and grab it, carry 'em on their shoulders, go up the ladder and put 'em into this cane car. There used to be all kinds of accidents, including falling from the ladder. When you fall from a ladder, what would happen [is] you either have a strain, or broken back, broken leg and arm.

[Women] who came from the Philippines were not used to having prenatal examinations. They would go [instead] for manipulation on the stomach. They called it hilot. They just massage your abdomen, and then convince you that they are turning the baby so it will be normal when it comes to term. We would tell them, "It would be easier for you, and it's cleaner, sanitary [in the hospital]. And if there's anything hard or [a] complication, the doctor would be there right away." But occasionally, we would find that even if they came in for prenatal clinics, pretty soon the midwife would come in and register the baby. Delivery at home!

THE REAL THING

I was at home [on December 7, 1941]. We thought they were practice shooting because we heard that all the time. But, actually, we saw the plane passing on this side was different from ours. And then, the superintendent of the factory came out rushing, and he said, "Faustino, you go tell the people it's real thing!" So I told the next-door neighbor it's war. But people were not so convinced that it was real until they finally heard shooting here and there. And then, of course, the radio was blazing [with the news].

Whenever we went to the [Japanese] camps, some look and say, "This people, I wonder if I can trust them. . . ."

I say to 'em, "If he's your friend, well, why should you change now?"

Most of my friends working together, with whom we eat at work, were Japanese. There used to be [a] Japanese girl who took care of the dispensary. The language we used had to be either pidgin English or broken English. And when we don't understand each other, we had to add some other words that would help to explain ourselves. That's how this pidgin English comes out beautiful.

ROADBLOCKS AND RATIONING

We were supposed to stay home after it gets dark. [There were] limitations on going around after curfew hours. Very few were given a pass, and I was one of those who had a night pass. If I was called for work at night, then I would carry my pass. But with the new boys [soldiers] from the Mainland, we had complications at the roadblocks. They halt you, and they look at you. They

Faustino Baysa with X-ray machine (photo reproduced by courtesy of Dole Food Company, Inc.).

didn't know the difference between Chinese, Japanese, Hawaiians. I was never called a Filipino until I showed my pass. Everyone who was not white was Japanese as far as they were concerned. They get you scared because they have their gun pointed at you.

They used to allow only ten gallons [of gasoline] a month that time, and you were supposed to economize. But people who were working used to have extra [ration] coupons. Whenever we talked about going out to see people who were sick, the coupon came in very handy. The problem came when someone swipe the gasoline from your tank. [One time] I got stuck on the way and [I] say, "Gee. What happened?" No more gas in the tank. Then the idea of locking the cap came up. But we never thought of those things before. We trusted everybody.

HOME GUARD

During the war, how many times I wanted to go into the service. And we couldn't get [in] just because they thought what we were doing was more important than going to the war. Agricultural work was supposed to be frozen. [During World War II, sugar plantation work was deemed "essential" to the war effort. Several full-time workers were restricted from leaving the plantation for other work.] [So] they gave us home guard [duty]. We were not shipped out, [but] they gave us commission, rank, training. We were attached to the Twenty-First Infantry. They used to come and pick us up for training at night, about nine o'clock. They furnished us guns. We practiced at the shooting range, with all the ammunition we could get. They even taught us to read the map and [plan] strategies.

We used to train people for home guard and tell them that whenever someone was approaching, they have to challenge them three times before one can do any action. One of the boys was on guard on one of the cane field roads here. Just happened that one old Japanese man was approaching.

This guard say, "Halt!" Then he say, "Halt!" again.

[The old man said,] "I halt already."

"Halt!"

"Why you say two, three time? I first stop already."

"I have to say 'halt' three times so I can shoot you."

The following day, camping [at] night at ʻŌpaeʻula, one of the boys tried to repeat what the guard on duty said: "Halt. Advance to be recognized."

So he [the learner] tried, "Halt, who goes there?"

"Friend."

"You advance. You are very nice."

These were actually happening when they practice up like that.

FOUND, THEN LOST

The good part during the war was [seeing] my younger brother whom I have not seen since I left the Philippines. I was sending him to school, and then [he] went to the [U.S.] Mainland. [When] the war broke out, I didn't know where he was. First thing I knew, one telephone call came in, and here he was. He say, "I'm here at Pearl Harbor." He was a submarine officer. United States Navy. The USS *Scamp* was the submarine he was on. While they were waiting for repairs, he stayed with us here. Stayed a whole month.

[Later] they were on the mission to intercept the Japanese Navy between Japan and the Philippines. [On November 14, 1944] their submarine was lost. We don't know what happened after that. They were just presumed lost and no trace of it. The officer in charge, usually a chaplain, came around. It was real bad news, but the way he came in and relate [it] was so smooth. Storytelling first, then eulogizing. But my brother was lost. So that ends my story of the war.

A NEUTRAL SIDE

[After the war] the union [International Longshoremen's and Warehousemen's Union] came in; they started bargaining. They tried to canvass everybody. So one of them came in and asked me if I wanted to join in on that thing. I just tell 'em I was not eligible for joining in because we were supposed to be a neutral side. My boss, he say, "Management and labor on [either] side and you're in the middle. You going to help both ways, so don't get active on certain sides only."

I had members of my families on two sides so I just had to keep quiet regardless of what all they were going to do. The union is on strike, all right, the hospital was open. So what we used to say is, "If you need help, come."

Well, in the end, one of my friends who was doing all the organizing tried to blame me because they were unable to organize the whole crew at the hospital. It must have been just a manufactured word [i.e., lie] because as far as I knew, I didn't work against it. But I didn't work for it, either.

NO COMPLAINTS

When I went for vacation [to the Philippines], nothing was said about going to get married. My wife and [my] brother-in-law were relatives. She used to work with missionaries in the Philippines. On their way back and forth moving from one town to another, our house in the Philippines was their stopover section. We met one time, but we never thought anything would happen. I don't know how it [the marriage] actually happened.

No more that carefree stuff already. I felt that the responsibility is much more recognized when you have your own family. That happens to me. I have to think twice before I do it. There's something with having a family who is understanding [that] you always want to come home and do your best as possible.

We have our six children, and no complaints. With three children in college, you would imagine what you would pinch. Actually we are pinching all the time. We raise our own vegetables. We try not to buy things that we cannot afford. But we manage. And I tell them often, "You have to be better than Daddy, regardless of how hard we struggle to put you through. Otherwise, pohō."

GLOSSARY

bayaw	brother-in-law, a term of address
haole	Caucasian
luna	overseer
pau hana	end of work
pohō	wasted effort

ABIGAIL BURGESS AND LILLIAN CAMERON

A FAMILY TRADITION

We moved down in Damon Tract, I'm not sure, but it could have been around when I was about thirteen, fourteen years old then. You could always tell a lei seller by the flowers that was growing in their yards. We had crown flowers, we had plumerias, we had 'ilima, pīkake, baldheads, and candle flowers that we use all for making leis.

Abigail Burgess and Lillian Cameron, of Hawaiian-Chinese-Spanish ancestry, are the daughters of Mary Ann Opulauoho and Robert Hew Len. The fifth child and oldest daughter of twelve children, Burgess was born in Kohala in 1922. Cameron, the seventh child, was born in 1926, after the family had moved to Honolulu.

As a youngster, Burgess sold lei with her aunt at the Honolulu Harbor waterfront on boat days, when passenger ships would dock or embark. With their family, the sisters also sold lei in Waikīkī and Downtown Honolulu. In the late 1940s, the Hew Lens opened their Lagoon Drive lei stand, a converted station wagon or truck, also called a "banana wagon." In 1952, the Hew Lens, along with other Lagoon Drive lei sellers, were moved into grass huts on airport property by the then territorial government. After their mother retired, a brother, Arthur Hew Len, operated the stand, renaming it Arthur's Lei Stand. When Arthur Hew Len passed away, Cameron took over the business, with the help of Burgess and other family members.

Burgess and Cameron were interviewed in 1985, after COH was approached by members of the Airport Lei Sellers Association to document the history of their twelve lei stands. Recognizing the cultural and historical significance of lei making and selling in the Islands, COH undertook *Ka Poʻe Kau Lei: An Oral History of Hawaiʻi's Lei Sellers.* While the project focused on the lei sellers at Honolulu International Airport, it also chronicles lei making and selling as practiced elsewhere on Oʻahu.

At her first meeting with the sisters, interviewer P. ʻIwalani Hodges remembers sitting and talking at their aunt's dining-room table for six-and-a-half hours, while Hodges took notes and gathered biographical information. Tape-recorded interview sessions began a week later. Burgess's and Cameron's accounts are juxtaposed in the following narrative.

* * * * *

BURGESS: Well, we lived different places, like Queen Street and close to the fire station. You know, different places around Kakaʻako. And that was, I think, the best place, Kakaʻako. Because we could go down the beach, fish for our own food. All the fish, all the squid, all the ʻōpaes you wanted, limu— oh, there were tons of limu. If you got too much, you just gave it to the neighbors. So those days was really nice, everybody sharing.

[Kakaʻako had] just a few stores here and there, and a church. So, there was mostly neighborhood, where they had Pordagee [Portuguese] camp, Japanese camp, kanaka camp. That meant that people who were Hawaiians usually would try to live in that area. Chinese, they had, but not too many. Not down that area. They had a few around here and there, but they didn't have their own camp.

Japanese were famous [for that], though. When Japanese had their camp or areas, Japanese would always go in that area and live only. They would not mix with the other nationalities. See, Portuguese, Hawaiians would mix. Filipinos would mix. But not the Japanese.

People, lot of 'em really got along. But then, like kids, we all used to fight with one another, with the different groups. Get smart, like calling them names. You know, calling Pordagees "codfish," and all that. We called the Japanese then, "You Buddhaheads." The Hawaiians, they would call, "You kanakas" (chuckles).

We always had more [at home] than our own family. You know, immediate one, which is my brothers and sisters, and my mother and father.

We always had my mother's father, my mother's sisters and brothers. During those times, during the depression time, they would stay with her. Well, we only had about two bedrooms. We hardly had any furnitures in it. So, lot of us slept on the floor. Just throw some mats, throw some blankets down, and everybody slept on the floor, whoever.

You know, this welfare thing, there was no such thing. The only one that would help would be mostly the churches, what little they had. They would make Christmas bags to give the families who really needed it. We thought then it was something like begging and we didn't figure too much that we could accept that. But then, we figured, well, if we didn't, then we wouldn't have anything for the holidays, right? So we did, which was only once. So I was really happy then when I went home [with the Christmas bag] and my mother was, too, because that would help for all the family and the kids, who-ever was living there, her brother, sisters, like that, too, see. So I didn't feel too bad afterwards.

Like my mother was working at the [pineapple] cannery. She had to help out because there was no money, anything, then. And my father, well, he was making very little money. She used to bring [pineapple cores] home when she could. She brought it in a plastic bag and, boy, we thought that was the greatest thing we have. The little we got then during those years, we really thought it was a treat.

We used to even go to sell papers then. That was [my] four brothers. Then when I got little older, I wanted to go sell papers, too. 'Cause maybe I was about eight years old that time. So I begged my mother to let me go be-cause she says, "No, you cannot go because you're a girl." I kept begging her during the months [that] went by till at last she says, "Oh, okay. But as long as your brothers watch you." So I made myself look like a boy. Put [up] my hair, put the sailor cap on below my ears like that. And I had a boy shirt, boy pants.

We had to buy papers. Those days the papers was two for five cents. That was the wholesale price for papers when you buy from the *[Honolulu] Star-Bulletin.* If you sold the two papers, you made a nickel [profit]. So we really used to try like hard to sell every one. And then, if we sold all of it, then we came home smiling. Gave my mother the money. And she would decide the next day how much we would need to buy again.

We used to sell at the old post office in town and all around Fort Street. So we would be yelling, "Paper! Paper! Mister, paper, paper! How about buy-ing my last paper!" He would buy it. (Chuckles.) Then we'd go and get an-other one that we had put on the side. "Paper! Paper! How about buying my last paper." Oh, today, I think of it. Oh, that's not nice. (Laughs.)

But either you do or you die. Even though you hardly had anything, you still were happier then. Today I say, I'm glad, I'm thankful then because I know how it is to live without hardly anything. So if it comes to pass again, I would still know how to.

During the depression, anyway, that's when we used to make paper leis. My Aunt Lizzie—Lizzie Silva—she started going to sell leis. And then she liked it, so she took me. I was, could be, about eleven. If I make my own leis, then we could sell it and I could earn my own money. So that's how I got involved in that. I think most of these people went like that. They thought, well, that was an honest way to make a living by using your own hands and try to go get your own flowers, whatever, or make your own paper and seed leis.

Those seed and bead leis, some of those seeds came from the mountain. You know, different trees. And they got washed down towards closer to the ocean areas by the rain. There was a store, a place that had all these different seeds. We either bought them or tried to pick 'em up here and there from different trees. And then try to drill holes in them, so we could string 'em on this wire or this cord and make into leis. Then you use your own initiative on how you wanted the style of the looks of it by putting different seeds or different beads in between to bring out the beads. See, you put glass beads so that it gives it a different look or brings out the seed [so] they don't look so dull.

Mostly I used to have paper leis. This crepe [paper] that they use and made into different styles of leis. You know, sewed [crepe paper strips lengthwise down] the middle and then made different leis like that. There's certain way to twist it to look like a different style of paper leis. And they all had different names then. You know, like the 'ilima, the mamo.

You could make it all the same color, but then people have different tastes. If it was a Filipino ship coming in, Filipinos like the nice [colors], bright and wild. That's what they got. If it was the Japanee [Japanese] boat coming in, then, well, it's toned down to give their style or tastes. Well, haoles will not go for wild colors. They wanted nice colors but not wild ones. (Chuckles.) So we made it for them. We had to figure how, using your own head in figuring what each kind of people liked and make those leis according to them. So in the papers, seeds, and leis, that's how we had to do the colors.

The seeds and these paper leis, the crepe paper leis, they were good sellers then. That's the thing that was made mostly for these boats that came and the ships that came. These [American] President [Line] ships or the Dollar Line, like that. They [i.e., seed and paper lei] were all made for those people because they used it as souvenirs. See, when they bought it, they took it back with them to whatever country they were going to. That, we did quite a bit, although the work that was involved in it was quite a bit of work. But then, those days, money had a lot of value. So even if the leis were supposed to be sold as twenty-five cents, if you couldn't sell it at twenty-five cents, you went down to two for twenty-five cents just so you made some money. So whatever few money, if you even made a dollar, oh, that would feed your whole family for almost a week.

Well, my auntie and this [other] lady lived not too far away. We would —all three of us—would walk down to Pier 8, Pier 9, wherever the boat was during that times. That was nice during the boat days. Because the President boats, they used to have people come down, pushing their carts of fruits, vegetables. They had papayas, pineapples, and things like that. The tourists or the people who was going away on the boat on the President Line, [or] if it was the Japan Line or whatever, they would all buy things and they would put it in a package and take it right on board.

When they [the lei sellers] started selling leis, when the boat came in and the customers started coming in, there was no such thing as courtesy. It was sell or take it home and eat it. So it was rough and tumble. [If] they didn't sell it then for the boat, that would all have to be thrown away. So that's why they sold it cheap. They would yell their head off. Just imagine, "Here, ten for dollar." Ten cents a lei. You might just as well throw it away.

Lot of times, I would stay on the outskirts. I couldn't get near them [the customers] because I was small and these people [the lei sellers], lot of 'em was so big. And their leis were all [draped] on their arms. When they lift their arms up, nobody else could see anybody else. And I'm here, underneath all those flowers. I just eventually gave up. I would just stay on the outside, figuring, well, maybe there's another customer coming around. If the customer didn't like being shoved and pushed like that, they would tell them, "No, no, no, no. I'm going to buy it from her. Would you mind all moving?" Oh, I felt good when they said that.

[But] after the boat leaves and they [the lei sellers] all resting around, sitting on their mats on the grass like that, they're all friendly, happy, and laughing. (Laughs.) I used to tell my auntie, "Auntie, I thought you was mad at that lady." She says, "Yeah, I was, because she cut in front of me and she shove her leis right in my face and the customer's face. And that's why I wanted to give 'em one punch when that sassy old thing put her leis in my face." But like I said, afterwards, they're friends. But surprising, with the Hawaiians, they didn't hold, you know, getting mad for long time.

I was there maybe only about a couple of years—two, three years. And then, my mother got involved. She wanted to go and sell leis. So, I had to stay home and take care of the house, take care of the kids. I had to be the mother.

We moved down in Damon Tract, I'm not sure, but it could have been around when I was about thirteen, fourteen years old then. The lots were pretty big. Most of the people who had moved there eventually got into selling leis. So you could always tell a lei seller by the flowers that was growing in their yards. We had crown flowers, we had plumerias, we had 'ilima, pīkake, baldheads, and candle flowers that we use all for making leis.

It took lots of time to pick, lots of time to string them. If it was going to be used the next day, all of it had to be picked up and strung during that day and night before my mother left in the morning to go to the pier [or] wherever she went to sell leis.

Early in the morning, the flowers are crisp. 'Ilima was picked up when it was [still] dark. Right after the 'ilima, I would pick up the candle [flowers]. The crown flowers took so much time to pick and you had to have an art to picking up crown. Those crowns usually are picked by the tubful, not by (chuckles) buckets. And plumerias, well, not too bad. Only, the taller the tree, the harder to pick. Then you pick with a bamboo hook. But if it was low, then you can go right around the tree and pick the flowers, which was saving a lot of time.

I had my brothers string so many. If he was about six, seven years old, he had five leis to string. And if the other one was eight years old or nine years old, [he] had five. If you was nine, ten, then you have ten leis. And [at night] you don't go sleep until you finish it. But most of those leis, I stayed up day and night and morning, stringing, so that my mother would have most of the flowers strung before she left. As long as my mother don't go sleep, I won't go sleep either. She tell me, "You go sleep." I say, "No. That's okay."

Once in a while I used to go with her and help her on weekend like that, on a Friday or Saturday like that, if there was somebody to help with the kids [at] home. We sold flowers up along Hotel Street. We went to sell during the war [World War II]. We went paydays and Saturdays. We went to the different bars. Going into places like that, we asked them if they wanted leis. [But] we didn't have too many leis. It was mostly flowers, like little rose for their coats or buttonhole, like that.

And then, we did go [to] Waikīkī areas. The Beachwalk [Park]. We went there just about after the [start of the] war, I think. They had all these station wagons here and there parked along Kalākaua [Avenue]. They would hang their leis and their flowers, whatever they had. They would play music, then sell leis there with their lanterns [at night]. And the big park was nice because some of the people lived in the back in those apartment homes like that. They sitting out in the evening like that, listening to the music, dancing, singing, and laughing.

Sitting, left to right, Mary Ann Hew Len, Lillian Hew Len, and Elizabeth "Lizzie" Silva, string and sell lei at Beachwalk Park in Waikīkī, ca. 1940s (photo courtesy of Lillian Hew Len Cameron).

CAMERON: Yeah, we had a station wagon on the corner of Kalākaua and Beachwalk [Avenues]. That was around '42, '43, '44. My mother would be there in the daytime. And then, towards evening time, then myself, my brother, we'd all go down there with my auntie and my sister, whoever, the family. We go down there after school and all to string flowers, string leis over there, and sell leis.

And in the evening time, my brother plays music—Arthur. He have his group come over there in the evening time to play music. Pretty soon, we get a whole pile of people. Like maybe over 50, 100 people in the whole park. And my brother Arthur and Joe Kahaulelio and them, [they] teach all the tourists to dance the hula. Well, of course, then we tell, "Oh, but you gotta wear a lei. All the dancers have to wear a lei." So, they go to our little corner wagon we had there. And they buy the (chuckles) plumeria lei, put on the lei, just so they could dance over there in the park.

During all those war years, I worked, chee, as an usherette at the old Princess Theater. I [also] worked at the Waikīkī Bowling Alley. I worked there, besides going in all the bars and selling flowers. And going to school and working there. Chee, I must have had about three, four, five different jobs all at once during those years. 'Cause I also worked Downtown [Honolulu] right on King and Bethel Street. Well, they had this USO [United Service Organizations] Victory Club, they called it, that they put up during the war. I'd work at the desk and do all these paperwork to call up all these young girls from the different schools if they could come down on a weekend or something like that to dance with all the military people.

A lot of these young guys, they're far away from home. And they kind of lonesome, come around Thanksgiving, Christmas time. So I used to (chuckles) invite 'em all home, you know. During those days, [in] the old army command car, I'd bring about five, six, seven of 'em. Sometime, ten or twelve. They'd follow me up the hill to Papakōlea 'cause we just moved up there about two months before the war.

And she'd [Burgess] be cooking for the whole family. In I come with about twelve, fifteen of (chuckles) military. And she used to get mad at me. "Well, who the heck is all that?" My mother didn't care. She said, "Oh, yes. Come on, come." She call 'em all inside and we sit down. Whatever we had, we fed all of them.

And then, I'd give 'em leis. My sister was the one got mad. "Well, here we trying to fix all these leis for Mama to go [and take] down the boat, and you giving 'em all away to these guys." I was always one to give, give, give.

BURGESS: Then, they opened the airport [after the war]. So there were three different type of people who were selling [lei]. The boats were one. The town people was another bunch. And then, the airport was another bunch of people. My mother was one of them that had moved there. There was only few trucks out there then. It was decided then to move them from the trucks into the other area because they were going to build the huts, the lei huts. She used her last name, Hew Len's Lei Stand. But then, eventually, my brother is the one took the stand. My mother had him [there] 'cause he was interested in selling leis and all. It was put under his name, Arthur's Lei Stand.

Mary Ann Hew Len, center, and customers at her Lagoon Drive lei stand, ca. 1949 (photo courtesy Lillian Hew Len Cameron).

CAMERON: You remember those days, those old "banana wagons" wasn't made like the kind of parts they get today out of metal and stuff. It was half wooden on each side. They're real solid. You know, this station wagon, you open the back down and you flip the top. We bang a board up, tie rope each side, and put nails in 'em. That's to hang the leis in the back. It looked kind of nice at that time.

Sometimes we don't go home. And we could sleep in the car. You know, small kids, we go sleep (chuckles) in the wagon with blankets, pillow in it. We sleep there to get up early in the morning before we go to school like that. I don't quite remember how many of them [lei stands] were there at that time because I was still going to school. But because she [Burgess] was older, so she was the one that went there with my mother. Then my brother Arthur started to go with my mother over there where the old "banana wagons" [were] just before we moved into the old grass shacks we had over there.

My cousin Peter Mendiola and Joe Kahaulelio, all my brother's friends when he went to entertain, they all came over to help him at the [grass shack] lei stand. Then we got all my family, relatives, and friends. Everybody came. My brother and them would play music. You know, because when they have the rehearsal, when they have to do a show or something, they go in the back and practice with all the instruments. So, that'll get all the tourists. You know, they hear the music. From in the front, when the [tour] buses used to stop, [they] take pictures, they all go in the back. Pretty soon, everybody's dancing. (Laughs.)

He [Arthur Hew Len] and I got so close because he'd be there in the day-time; at night he has to go out and play music, travel here and there. So, I was going there [at night]. [Ever] since my brother died, I was going to that lei stand day and night. I'd go four o'clock in the morning and I leave late at night, seven days a week.

I think the kids today, they don't like that kind of business we doing 'cause the hours we put in. I know the only one that want the lei stand, that still want to keep it over there, is myself and my sister. My sister always did love this business. See, she worked so hard all her life that she couldn't finish school. Lucky she went past sixth grade, being that she was the oldest girl. So, she had to really help my mother with the flowers, and kids, and house, and cooking, and stuff like that.

BURGESS: All that, take care children, and the house. But today, I don't really regret it. Only one thing I regret is not being able to be more happy and freer. I mean, it's embedded in me in one way, how it used to be, [making a] living [with] flowers and all that. I can't change to be anything else. I am what I am.

CAMERON: You know, sometimes I'm at the lei stand and, well, maybe it's getting late. I think nobody's going to buy this lei, well, I'll cut [it down from the display board] and give. Oh, she [Burgess] get mad at me. "Don't give the leis free. You know we have to pay for that." Yeah, I know, but the people look so sad, just walking. So might as well give it to them. (Chuckles.) She get mad at me all the time.

Well, she used to work across the street at the terminal, Department of Transportation. When she gets through working over there, she comes right to the lei stand. She's all business. She don't know what it is to relax, you know. She doesn't know what it is 'cause she's worked so hard all her life that to her, if you don't work, you don't get nothing. She said, "Nobody give you nothing on a silver platter."

[Business has] gotten worse through the years. The [wholesale] prices go up higher. Competition, too, is really hard. That's why, the [flower] growers' [prices] go up higher and higher, and the lei sellers' [prices] are still the same. We not making that kind of money.

Sometimes when you get so depressed, you want to give it up, but then you don't. It's been in the family for so long that you don't want to. Well, it's a family thing. Tradition, and it's the family thing.

GLOSSARY

chee	mild exclamation
haole	Caucasian
ʻilima	native shrub with yellow or orange flowers
limu	edible seaweed
kanaka	Hawaiian
mamo	Hawaiian honeycreeper whose feathers were used to make lei
ʻōpae	shrimp
pīkake	Arabian jasmine

AGNES EUN SOON RHO CHUN

PĀLAMA TO PEARL HARBOR

In looking back, I really didn't know what would have happened to me and our family [had it not been for World War II]. At that time, it would have been just my mother and myself. I would have gone to school, and probably looked for a part-time job, and then probably got employment someplace [instead of entering the federal civil service]. But I know the war just turned everything upside down for everybody.

Agnes Chun was born in Honolulu in 1925. Her parents, Hee Chang Rho and Young Hee Chi Rho, were originally from Korea. Chun lived in the multiethnic Pālama neighborhood with her parents, two brothers, and two sisters.

Her mother worked in the pineapple cannery and took in sewing to support the family. Her father, who was in poor health, died in 1935 when Chun was a third-grader at Kaʻiulani School. As a teenager, Chun worked summers as a trimmer and packer in the pineapple cannery. She went to Kalākaua Intermediate School, then to McKinley High School, but her education was interrupted by World War II.

In the days that followed December 7, 1941, Chun helped with wartime registration and fingerprinting. With school temporarily closed, Chun worked as a messenger and, later, a timekeeper at Ford Island naval station in 1942. Following what would have been her senior year, she spent a half day working at Ford Island and a half day in school, which enabled her to graduate in 1944.

In her career in government service, Chun held various supervisory accounting positions, including that of comptroller in the Pacific Third Fleet. She worked in Korea as financial manager with the army before retiring in 1980 with thirty-eight years of service.

She was married in 1949 to Soon Ho Chun, a teacher. They had three children. Agnes Chun was widowed in 1989.

Chun was interviewed in 1992 by Michi Kodama-Nishimoto for a project entitled *An Era of Change: Oral Histories of Civilians in World War II Hawai'i*. One of thirty-three interviewees of the project, which documented life on the Hawai'i home front, Chun recalled how employment opportunities for women and students increased dramaticaly as a result of war. Although a larger percentage of the total population was working in the Islands than in most other parts of the United States, jobs were still plentiful. There were openings for not only domestic and laundry workers, waitresses, clerical workers, teachers, nurses, and other occupations traditionally held by women, but for traditionally men-held jobs such as chauffeurs, mechanics, and storekeepers. Chun's federal civil service employment record during and after World War II epitomizes this trend. By 1942, 1,400 women held federal civil service jobs normally held by men.

FATHER AND MOTHER

My parents came from Ong Jin in Hwanghae-do, Korea. My dad and mother were married there and they had three children. Their children all died when they were infants. My mother said they suffered from kygŏngki—seizure or stomach disorder.

I don't know whether they had a very difficult time in Korea concerning livelihood. My dad came out here, worked in the plantations, someplace in Kaua'i. My mother just said he upped and decided that he'd come with his friend. My mother found out from friends that he had left. My mother was living close to her sister, and so she stayed with her sister. Eventually after a ten-year separation, when he came to Honolulu, he asked my mother to join him. She arrived here in 1912. Therefore, she never had the experiences that many of the Korean women had, like working in the plantation camp, cooking for the men, and doing their laundry.

They lived in the Pālama area, close to Akepo Lane. I think the neighborhood was a mix of Chinese and Japanese and Koreans. My mother mentioned that she had young lady friends whose children she delivered. And in fact, there was one boy, I remember, Ernest Pai, who was delivered by my mother and, lo and behold, Ernest has wavy hair like my mother. So she always says, "The boy was delivered by me, so he has my hair."

Before his [i.e., father's] illness, he was working at the pineapple cannery and was in charge of a group of men on contract stacking cans of pineapple, and he was also a watchman. As the lead person of the men, he would divide the pay amongst the workers, including himself. For example, if he had three pennies left for six of them he would not keep the pennies but would buy box matches, two for a penny, or whatever, and he would just divide it evenly. My mother said she thought it was so ridiculous for him to feel like that, but that character shows up later on in his other ventures.

My father had very good hands, able to repair things and do things. He made a Korean chess set which were little wooden blocks with the Chinese characters on it. Mother remembers the raves he received from his friends. He was so good at repairing of things that this friend of his one day told him, "Let's go into a secondhand business. I'll be the one going around with my cart to pick up things and you fix them."

My mother tells about the used charcoal stove his partner bought for fifty cents. My father did such a good refurbishing job his partner said, "Let's sell it for $4.50." But my father would not go along with it saying, "How can you do that? You're selling it way over the price you paid." So eventually they broke up because the partner insisted on marking up the goods way over what my father thought was fair.

PĀLAMA NEIGHBORHOOD

I was born in Honolulu [in] 1925. I am number five of the living, but my mother, when she came out here, had six children, so I'm actually number six. The eldest is a boy, and then another boy, and then two sisters. Then there was this one boy that passed away, just above myself, and then myself.

My mother used to tell me that we were living across from Likelike School. She says, if she remembers correctly, I must have been just about little over a year when I would walk to the store, and I would buy butter, and come home. We all say, "Oh, can't be." But she said that's what she thought, that I was very smart at that time.

When we lived in Akepo Lane, I remember living in a house painted green. Then right behind these Akepo Lane houses, where Dillingham Boulevard is now situated, that area was just covered with elephant grass. I remember seeing my brother and my sister catch grasshoppers, and they'd toast [them], and then eat the grasshoppers. There was a walking bridge over that area. You'd go over the bridge to go to the CPC [California Packing Corporation] pineapple cannery. And then there was a ramp going up to the Dole pineapple cannery [Hawaiian Pineapple Company, Ltd.].

The next time I remember vividly is when we were at Lopez Lane and going to Robello [Lane] School. My parents were busy and my father wasn't [in] good [health]. My mother, I think she went to work at the cannery while we were there, also. I also remember she was taking in sewing from the tailors at that time that were located on the base at Fort Shafter. I think they had many ready-mades for the soldiers, but many of them would go to the tailor and they would be fitted. Then the tailors would cut these trousers, and my mother would sew.

I think it was Harry Auld who owned that [Pua Lane] property we were living on [next]. There were six homes in this little courtyard. Our neighbors were so close that if you opened your back door you'd be about ten feet apart. There was only one Japanese family, the Fukudas. The other families were Koreans. There were six units, which included one duplex and four cottages. We started in the back, which was a duplex, and then we moved up to the bigger house. After the war, we moved up to the front home, my mother and I.

He [i.e., father] passed away when we were in the center home. I could remember my mother desperately trying to cure my father. He refused to have an operation, that's the reason she tried so many home remedies. In 1935 the surgical successes were few, so he said he would rather die than go through an operation. Even after he died, I could hear his moaning from the pain. I remember his funeral, too. It was held at our church located in a lane off School Street. I remember he had a lavender casket, velveteen-looking. At nine years old, that's what my recollection is.

In that Pua Lane area, right next to the Chinese store, they had a little dirt road that ran from Vineyard Street up until that Chinese store. There were Filipinos living there. And then in that lane right next to the store, which was running parallel to the homes that we lived in, they had another group of Filipinos living in there, too. They would play music. That's why I'm so familiar with the Filipino music and I like it.

In that lane, in the corner or someplace, there was a Japanese temple or some kind of religious group that met in there. And you had Japanese in there, too.

There was one man that sold fish, right by the corner of Pua Lane and King Street. At that corner about two houses away, there was a saimin wagon in a garage. They had a table and some benches for the customers. It was the best saimin and udon.

[There was] a good stretch of empty lot that ended up by that dirt road that is parallel to Pua Lane. There was a lady at the end of the pathway through [those] bushes. Her husband was dealing in junks. He would push a cart and he would go around and collect junk, rags mostly. She would be washing the rags, cleaning it, drying it, and then he would sell the rags, that was his living.

When I was [young], she would always take that aluminum rice pail, the bentō container with the two layers. She would take the bottom one, she'd take it to the saimin place and she'd buy me udon. [She] bought me the udon when I was ill. She knew I liked udon.

And then there was this one man. He had that vending truck. He was coming around when we were living in Lopez Lane. My mother would buy papayas by the bushel, like. My mother had so much faith in papaya, she says it was a very good fruit. Even up until the time when we moved to Pua Lane, the guy would come and then we would buy vegetables from him.

I remember still this Japanese man would come around with something that looked like a big bag and you would give him maybe twenty-five cents and a bowl of rice, and he would puff the rice. Then my mother would make those [puffed] rice balls, melting the sugar.

This Pua Lane area, Kanoa Street up to Dillingham [Boulevard], there were [Korean] stores. There was a laundry run by Koreans; a furniture store operated by two sets of people, the Whangs and the Parks. Next door was Adam Lee's dry cleaning shop. Then across the street was the Moon family living there, running a grocery store. Then there was another, Kwon grocery store. Isaiah Shon's mother was running a grocery store. Ken Kwak's grandmother had a grocery store.

Between Vineyard and Liliha, there was a drugstore, Korean drugstore. Across the street, on Liliha Street, there was this Teuk Soon Lyum family. Jennie Lyum's father-in-law had a grocery store over there. Coming up this way we had a Liliha Theater at the corner of School and Liliha. All along Liliha Street, they had Koreans living. I guess they settled around a Korean church and in the vicinity.

I always attended the Korean Christian Church, which is now located on Liliha Street. It was founded by Dr. Syngman Rhee. Our church on Liliha was built around '37, a brand-new church right above Kuakini Street. Prior to that time, we had a church where the Korean Care Home is now located, diagonally across McDonald's on Liliha Street. The old church complex contained an apartment building two stories high for four families and a low-rise for bachelors. The church was a long wooden building with a small space downstairs, which they used for the Korean-language school and Sunday school.

They called that [language school], if I recall correctly, Shin Hyung Korean School. Most of our contact in Korean language would be with our parents, and that was just household language. We were there to learn how to read and write and speak, and then also we had history classes. The teacher [Mrs. Ki Moon Sur] who taught me is still living. When we were having history, she would talk about Silla, Koguryŏ, and Paekche kingdoms. At least as far as the writing is concerned, I learned, but if you look at the writing that I do now, it's very, very basic. We were always very inattentive at school. So I really didn't pick up too much in the way of speaking.

KOREANS AND JAPANESE

There was a bathhouse on King Street, you know, close to that [Machida] Drugstore there. In those days, my mother was very anti-Japanese. The other ladies and the other girls were going to go bathe. So I told my mother, "Let's go." But she never wanted me to go more than necessary, I guess. They had the bathhouse divided in two—ladies, one side on the right; the men on the left. And then the pipe on one side, and ours [on] one side, but you cannot see the other side. Against the wall, as you enter, there's this big cement tub. So everybody would get an aluminum basin. You pick up the basin and then you wash yourself outside and rinse. After this pre-wash, you can go into the hot tub.

When my mother was in Korea, the Japanese had taken over. [Korea was subject to Japanese rule and administration, 1910–1945.] When I think about it, she never did say it, but she resented the Japanese coming over. I believe that was one of the reasons why it triggered her to come to Hawai'i. She says around 1910, "We had a lot of this disturbance with the Japanese coming through." What happened was that when she came out here, this anti-Japanese thinking carried over, so she mentioned this feeling to me several times as I was growing up. Even my sister Flora was telling me that my mother used to get so upset when they would come home with Japanese friends.

When I was a teenager we had Japanese neighbors, the Fukudas, and I always wanted to buy a Japanese rice bowl. One day I bought one, to carry in my hand and eat, something that Koreans do not do. My mother raised heck with me and said, "Why? What's so good about that?"

So it carried on, my mother was very much against my sisters and brothers above me associating with Japanese. And even after I grew up and was working, she was not too very keen about my association with Japanese. However, her attitude changed. When I was working at Ford Island, my Chinese girlfriend married a navy chief who was a Caucasian. We also had a very close Korean friend who married a Caucasian chief in the navy. They were so nice. As my mother got to know them, she told me, "You know, I guess it really doesn't matter what nationality you are because you can have a rotten Korean."

CHILDHOOD PLAY

At Pua Lane all the families that were living there had children. We played five-hole marble, and my sister or my mother would call me to pick up the laundry from the line or send me to the stores down on King Street for an errand. I used to get so upset when they would interrupt. We would also play hopscotch. We would put all these safety pins together to make that kini, right?

And then another time what we would do is play what they call [stilts]. You get your empty cream cans. And then we would go into the bushes someplace down by Kanoa Street, and then they have this plant. When you pick the bean, you peel it, and there's this glue-like thing, and then you would put it on the can. And then we'd make holes. We'd tie with the string—poke it in [the holes]—and then we'd make a long handle. We'd hold onto it, with our two feet [glued] on the cans, and walk.

As far as Pālama Settlement was concerned, they had the swimming pool and the kids would go Saturday morning. Early in the morning, they'd have just very little water, then kids would learn how to swim there. At one time, Pālama Settlement, I remember, had a big gym. We would have tap dancing, hula dancing, and things like that. I think once a year, they would have a sort of carnival. They would have clowns. Everybody would perform. I took a little tap dancing, I remember, but I never performed.

We would walk from Pua Lane to the main library. And as we go along, we would come to this place called Yuen Chong [Company]. Well, it was on [North] King Street, this Chinese grocery store that sold sundry items. There were all kinds of crack seed, including whole plums and football seeds. The seeds were put into those small little brown bags, and we would buy those for five cents.

And then once in a while, this was when I was at Pua Lane, I think, the Pālama Theater, right after school, sometimes they would have free movies for the kids. On Saturday they would have movies featuring Flash Gordon, or Buck Rogers. Those series.

SCHOOLING

I remember Na Lei Kindergarten's location. It's right next to the Ka'iulani Elementary School on North King Street in Pālama and in the rear of the fire station. I remember through a picture I still have of us as a group. It was May Day celebration photo and I had a Korean costume on. I remember making paper hats that look like army caps [and] everybody wearing it with one end at the tip of your forehead to the back of the head. I wanted it to look nicer so I wore mine with the ends right above my two ears. The children were mostly Orientals and you had Filipinos and maybe Portuguese, and that's just about it. I don't remember seeing any haole kids.

Just for kindergarten at Na Lei, and then from there on we went to Ka'iulani [School]. We had rows of seats attached together that had tops with compartments. I remember we would sleep on straw mats in between the rows of desks.

We had a monitor system and had to stay after school to sweep the floor. We sprinkled sawdust on floors, which were all oiled. We swept the sawdust, and used foxtail brushes to sweep under the seats. We had to take out the erasers and clap the chalk dust.

At the cafeteria, the teacher sat at the head of the table and we all sat on the benches on both sides. She periodically comes down and looks to see whether we're eating. One day, the teacher came and said to this boy, "Why aren't you eating the meat?" She said, "That's good for you, you know." He had a funny grin on his face because he liked the meat, chunks of meat. He was leaving it for the very end. And here she thought he was sorting them out because he didn't want it.

We had milk in bottles. The milk always had this thick cream, about two inches on the top. What we would do is put the straw in, drink up most all the white part on the bottom and then when it came down to almost about a half, we would shake the bottle which was covered with those milk caps. A curd is formed on the top of the bottle. It sticks on the bottle cap. So we would take off the bottle cap and rub it on the graham cracker like butter.

I went to Ka'iulani School, first grade; second grade, at Robello [Lane School]. Robello School was two stories, and there was a water fountain up front. I remember the teacher I had there. In her class, we used to bring empty cereal boxes, empty cans with the labels on, and we'd play store.

Every day we would have this pint-sized medicine bottle. It was 100 percent cod-liver oil. I remember we would all come downstairs and we would have to take cod-liver oil. I think we were underweight that's why. Maybe you call that malnutrition, I don't know. We'd go outside by the water fountain, stand in line, and she'd pour this into our spoons. We'd hold our noses, we'd take the cod-liver oil. Most of us had something like see mui or orange we brought from home to eat right away after that to take the taste away.

I went back to third grade at Ka'iulani until sixth grade. And then went on to Kalākaua [Intermediate School]. I would catch the streetcar. We rode that, and then later on the trolley came along. I think it must have been five-cents fare. We would try to save money and use that carfare for goodies. So from Pua Lane, I used to walk to Kalākaua on Kalihi Street, and come back. At Kalākaua, they sold cookies. They had this beautiful oatmeal and chocolate cookies. They were big, about the size of your palm. It must have been a nickel, or three for a quarter, or something like that. I never had enough of those.

I decided I wanted to go to McKinley [High School]. Because Farrington [High School] had just opened not too many years [earlier], I used my brother's address. On Vineyard Street right across Central [Intermediate School], there was this Leilani Court, a group of homes and apartments that my sister-in-law's mother owned. That's where the YMCA [Young Men's Christian Association] and playground is now.

I had, for sophomore [year]—most of it was required—core studies, which is English and social studies. Then I took algebra and I took biology. I got into that algebra class and had a good teacher. We go to the board to do one problem assigned as homework. I stand there because I don't know how to work the problem. She comes to me and asks, "Oh, Agnes, are you having problem?" Then she'd help me. But this is how I went through that class.

I was always tall for one thing, and I always was underweight. They put me in P.E. [physical education] for a few weeks, and then they catch up with me again, and then they'd pull me out of P.E. and into the rest class. We spent one period sleeping on the cots at McKinley. I applied for that NYA, [or] National Youth Administration job. It's a government-subsidized program and you got paid. You worked the one period instead of going to the rest room. I went there to help in the library. I got paid and I didn't have to go to P.E. (Laughs.)

And then I signed up for geometry and French in my junior year. I just felt so dumb in that class, that French class, so I dropped French and I also dropped geometry. But they wouldn't drop it for me, they made me go to see Dr. Miles Cary, the principal. Can you believe? So I had a nice chat with him. He was so nice to me. I told him, "I'm having a hard time in those classes and if I really put my mind to it, I think I'd probably be able to [pass], but I'm going to have to, after graduation, help the family and not think about university." Can you believe that's what I thought? So then, he said, "Okay." I had typing in, I think was ninth grade, at Kalākaua. So I just took advanced typing and then shorthand for the first time, I think.

PINEAPPLE CANNERY WORK

When I was fourteen, fifteen, and sixteen, I worked at the cannery. And I had two girlfriends whose sisters were going to summer school, and they had previously worked. So they told me that they were going to work for the cannery at Hawaiian Pine. So I found that this lady, Sara Lee, was not working and was going to have a baby. So I got her card. Then three of us went to the cannery and worked. The first year I went, I went in as a trimmer. And I trimmed pineapple.

As a beginner, you're trying to learn how to hold the pineapple and having a hard time with the juice running down your gloves, and you can hardly wield the knife the right way. The ladies would do extra work and cut the pine for you. But later on, when you didn't pick up your pine and they knew that you were doing all right, they'd just slam it in front of you. You learn real quick that you better wake up.

One experience I had was that while I was trimming I heard this voice, somebody calling, "Sara, Sara!" And this woman or whoever Sara was would not answer, and finally the calling stopped, and then pretty soon I felt this hand on my shoulder. The forelady said, "Sara, I've been calling you," and then it dawned on me, I was Sara.

The following year, I requested a change to go to packing [pineapple in cans]. I got in as a packer. I traveled with those two girls and learned how to pack. So three of us would go from one table to another. And we would have a lot of fun. You know, we were really rascals. But it was really an experience for three years. And then, 1941, June, July, August, that was the last year that I worked. And then '41, December [7], the war broke out.

WORLD WAR II

I was in bed when we heard planes flying over and then the radio was on. I heard some commotion outside, and I got up. When I went out, they said, "Oh, the war. There's a war." There's planes flying around and when I looked up, we saw a plane flying, and it was [marked] with the round red circle.

So we ran inside and as we were listening to the radio, about 9:00, 9:30 [a.m.], we heard this thud-like sound. We all rushed out. There was a little store in the front, and there was a lane next to it, and then our cottages, six of them were in that vicinity. Right next to the lane, there was this duplex. And lo and behold, right under the veranda, there was a huge hole. While we were standing over there, some uniformed people came running. They told us to evacuate. So the whole neighborhood had to evacuate.

My brother had married and gone out of the house. His mother-in-law had just bought a home. So we all spent the night there. From there, we looked towards Pearl Harbor and saw the smoke coming up. We were all scared, and especially at night when they told us all the lights had to be out. At this great big home, we were literally in the dark, because we couldn't do anything to the windowpanes or anything. We went home the next day.

Eventually, they made announcements to let us know—that was maybe a few weeks later—that they wanted us to help with the identification process. [On December 27, an order was issued to fingerprint and register all civilians.] The business [students] were asked to come over to help. Those of us assigned to Central Intermediate went there every morning. Each one of us had to have a [territory] ID, and we were fingerprinted, so this was the process we had to go through. And that was the first time I found out who entertainers were. (Chuckles.) When people came, you have to ask them what they were doing, their occupation. Many of them were entertainers, and so I just kind of naively said, "Oh, what kind of entertainer?" And then, I was kind of hushed. Later on we found out that they were prostitutes, right? (Laughs.)

During the war, my sisters and my brothers were all out of the house, they were married. I was living with my mother. During that time, she wanted to learn to write. She had already learned to read, because she was subscribing to this Korean newspaper, *The Pacific Weekly*. She also had these little Korean storybooks and she read those. I never knew that she was practicing so hard. One day I came home and she had this letter written in Korean characters, called hangŭl. She wrote she had gone down to the "Su Tow Wah." And I said, "Su Tow Wah? What is Su Tow Wah?"

Very indignantly she said, "Why, Su Tow Wah is 'store.'" "Why didn't you write the Korean word for store?" Then it dawned on her that she was using an English word. She gave me a sheepish smile. Although she was not speaking English, she had picked up these little words in English.

In '42, my brother-in-law was working at Pearl Harbor, on Ford Island. He had my sister work there, too. He got a job for her. And then in February, they asked me if I wanted to join them. I told my mother I was going to work, and she said okay. We had no income, really. So I went in as a messenger. I earned ninety dollars a month. So just going to work and coming back, and it's blackout, there's nothing you can do. We were just eating and sleeping already.

We were responsible for picking up the mail and sending out the mail. At this time, the admin[istration] office took care of mail that came in for the whole supply department. The supply department did the procurement for all of the other departments in the station. So they would have aircraft parts that came in bundles, shipped through the postal service. So we would have to have a big [handcart], like a pushcart, the flatbed.

I stayed there just about, what, until June. Then they promoted me to a CAF-1, and I became a clerk for the time section, payroll section. I left that admin office and became a timekeeper. And then I became a [CAF]-2, I think, a year later.

Later on, my mother had a job with the air force, at Hickam Field. I don't know when it was, but maybe after 1942, when the air force and all of the services were recruiting more people from the Mainland. They were being housed at navy cantonment at Pearl Harbor area. Hickam Field had their own cantonment, too. So they were hiring these ladies to do cleaning. So my mother, her contemporaries were going to work, they asked her if she wanted to work. A whole bunch of Korean ladies went to work.

My mother had worked with this lady, Helen Choy's mother. They were cleaning with this disinfectant, I think, and they got toxic poisoning of their hands. Their hands got swollen. St. Louis School was the military hospital. So they put my mother and this lady in the hospital over there, and they were taken care of, and they got well after all the toxins were removed. After she was well, she went back to work. But they were told to be careful about the usage of that.

My senior year, I still worked full-time, and we earned annual leave and sick leave. So the following year after my senior year, around October, they announced that kids who had gone to work, if they want to come back to school, may do so on a half-a-day basis. The Department of Defense worked with them to have us come back to work part-time. So the deal was, you go to school from eight o'clock in the morning to about 11:00 or 11:30 [a.m.]. And we had four courses. And after the fourth course, you go to work.

The Pearl Harbor Drivers' Association had a bus that went all the way into the landing area, way inside of Pearl Harbor, by the dry-dock area. Then from there, they had a launch that connected to Ford Island. Because we worked on Ford Island, we had to catch the ferry or the launch. So what we did was, as soon as class was over, catch the bus—and at that time, it was those trolley buses—we'd catch the bus and get off at the Black Cat Cafe. Across the Army-Navy Y[MCA], they had the Black Cat Cafe. And then, get a hamburger and milkshake, or whatever, and run across the street for the Pearl Harbor bus. We'd catch that bus and go to work, and we'd get there just in time to catch the launch. So that's why we had to rush because if we missed that bus, we'd be late. And then, we'd get to work around 1:00, 1:30 [p.m.]. See, they had two shifts on Ford Island. So we'd work until five, six o'clock, when the day was long, and to seven o'clock sometimes.

GOVERNMENT SERVICE

That was in '44 I graduated. In 1947, September, I transferred from Ford Island. We had Mr. Jong Chock who had a sister working on the Pearl Harbor, on this side. He told me, "Oh, you know, my sister Ethel is looking for someone that can run this payroll check-writing department, as a supervisor." So I went on to that new job, and then I stayed there doing the supervising of the check writing. This was the Fourteenth Naval District Disbursing Office I had transferred to.

Then, shortly thereafter, the check writing was taken over by the Naval Supply Center, so at that time, the bureau decided that they were going to give us new duties in accounting. The name of the office is going to be changed from Fourteenth Naval District Disbursing Office to the Navy Central Disbursing Office. And they put me in charge of that accounting department.

Subsequently, this is now in '51, my first son, Marcus, came along. So I was on maternity leave when they moved from the Pearl Harbor main complex area into the Supply Center. So our disbursing office became a tenant of the Supply Center at Pearl Harbor.

In fact, before we moved from the Pearl Harbor, and before I got pregnant, I had this IBM [International Business Machines Corporation] experience, not knowing what IBM machines were. Our department was in charge of doing the mechanical work of accounting, and so they had the shipyard department—and I guess you would call that the IBM room—take over. So they plugged all the boards for us and they had [these] big electrical accounting machines, predecessor of the computers. And then, so what this assistant of mine and myself would do is, we'd go to the shipyard office with all of the keypunching that was done in our office, and he'll tell us how to put the cards in. That's how I learned.

I was in accounting, and then I stayed there until 1953. Then from 1953, they put me down into the military pay [division]. The commander wanted me to go down there for one reason, that the military pay division had about twenty-five military personnel, and about ten civilians, with a military chief doing the operational supervision. His tour is only two years. Then the payroll master's tour was also two years. The disbursing officer had two years, and the cashier was a warrant officer. He was also military. They wanted somebody there that could keep continuity. I told him, "I don't even know what a pay [record] looks like." But he said, "No, I know you can do it."

Eventually, I looked around the operation and I noticed that there were some things that could really be standardized, like writing letters. Then I also did some changes in the way they entered the items in the pay record. Instead of having each one typewritten, I had rubber stamps made so that everybody had a set of rubber stamps. And all they do is pick up the rubber stamp and just rubber stamp it in, put the date, et cetera. So it became sort of a uniform system.

After I stayed in that payroll office, there was an announcement, the fellow that took my job in the accounting department was going to Hong Kong. So I put in for the job, and I got it. While I was at the accounting office, the job for a budget and accounting officer opened up at Ford Island at the Commander Anti-Submarine Warfare Force Command. I was interviewed by the officer who was leaving, and he left it open so that the incoming officer taking his place would interview me. So after that second interview, I was selected. In the meantime, the civil service terminology changed from CAF [clerical administrative fiscal] to GS, meaning general services. And so I went there as a Budget and Accounting Officer, GS-11.

I was very active with the Korean community. So I, one day, casually told my secretary, "Gee, if I had a job in Korea, I sure would like to go there." When I was there in 1975 for a visit, it was a three-week visit, but I really didn't see much because I had been sick for one week at the hotel. And so, one day, about two weeks later, she saw this Federal [Jobs] Digest or federal newspaper. And she said, "Jobs in Korea!" The army has the overseas employment office, located in the [Prince Kūhiō] Federal Building. So I called over there and the lady says, "You can just put in an application, and if you don't get selected for a job within a year, then we'll just deep six that file." So I came home and I told my husband, while he's reading the paper, and he said, "Up to you."

Just about the ending of June or early part of July, I got a call one afternoon from the Eighth Army in Korea. The comptroller's office called and the secretary says if I was still interested in the job. It was the same position title that I had and it would be at the GS-12, step ten, which is the highest I'm having now. I was selected and that's how I made up my mind to go. And the job is obligated two years, which means my job here, I can come back to, after my contract.

But he [i.e., husband] didn't want to go because he's a schoolteacher, and he's nearing his end of the twenty years or twenty-five years he put in. So I went on my own, and he stayed back. I left here in September '78; June of 1979, he came and stayed with me until August, then came back.

And then, December 11, I came back here for my vacation, and I didn't go back until January 15, 1980. When I was leaving, my husband's voice started to get hoarse. So I said, "Gee, you better check with your doctor." Subsequently he lost fifteen pounds in about two months and couldn't talk. So when I told some people I had already put in thirty-eight years, they told me, "Well, why don't you retire so you can leave?"

So I went to personnel and she said, "If you can convince your commanding officer, you may retire in June and go home, don't finish up your contract, and you don't have to reimburse the government for the transportation cost."

So I showed the commander the picture of my husband. He was so skinny. And he looked like a Korean refugee. So he said, "Who's this?" He had met my

husband and could not recognize the photo. I said, "Oh, that's Soon Ho."
He said, "Oh, I can't believe it."

They let me go. So I retired in June. I came back and stayed for five
months and decided to look for a job. Can't find one because I'm too highly
qualified. I went to an employment agency and I got a job with this House
of Adler. I worked in accounts receivable. Then, about a month later, they
had an opening at the navy for the non-appropriated fund, so I put in for it
and I got that job, as a GS-7. I put in eight years, and then my husband got
sick. He passed away [in 1989].

LOOKING BACK

I know the war just turned everything upside down for everybody, and for
some people who lost their family members. In looking back, I really don't
know what would have happened to me and our family. At that time, it
would have been just my mother and myself. I would have gone to school,
and probably looked for a part-time job, and then probably got employment
someplace.

Sometimes I think I probably could have had a higher [pay] grade, but
one, I'm an Oriental, and I'm a woman. You understand. In those days, in
the [19]70s, it's not what it is today. Had I been a male, I probably would
have gotten a little higher, but what can I say. I was well treated and I really
enjoyed it.

GLOSSARY

bentō	lunch
crack seed	Chinese preserved seeds
football seed	football-shaped crack seed
hangŭl	Korean script
haole	Caucasian
kini	object used as a marker in hopscotch
kyŏngki	seizure, stomach disorder
saimin	soup made with thin noodles
see mui	type of crack seed
udon	soup made with thick noodles

SEVERO DINSON

KONA IS THE BEST

You get your own land, better. Because nobody boss you. If you go to work to somebody, you got to follow what he order to you. Pau pick coffee, then my boss, "Shigeru-san! Hoy. Ah, mo' betta coffee hāpai, no?" They no call me Severo. "Shigeru-san!" Japanese name. If you own land, you go hire somebody, you the one boss.

Of Spanish and Filipino ancestry, Severo Dinson was born on the island of Cebu, Philippines in 1904. His parents were subsistence farmers.

Dinson came to Hawai'i in 1922 to work on Hawai'i Island's sugar plantations. In 1924–1925, Filipino workers conducted a territory-wide sugar plantation strike. On Hawai'i Island, strike camps were set up in Hilo for strikers and their families. In January 1925, strikers marched towards 'Ola'a Plantation in a bid to recruit nonstrikers, but were turned away by police. Dinson, then single, was one of the strikers.

In 1927, Dinson left the plantation to pick coffee for several farmers in Kona. He later boxed professionally on Hawai'i Island and Maui. During World War II, Dinson and his wife, Candelaria Enanoria Dinson, lived on the Honoka'a Plantation. After returning to Kona in 1948, the Dinsons leased coffee lands, ran a pool hall, and then purchased their own coffee land in Keālia. The Dinsons were parents of ten children.

Warren Nishimoto interviewed Severo Dinson at Dinson's South Kona home in 1980 for COH's *A Social History of Kona* (1981). Dinson died in 1996.

Unlike other communities, Kona is the largest single area to remain outside the sugar plantation system that so dominated the history of modern Hawai'i. In the late nineteenth century, Kona gained a reputation as a haven for immigrants who broke or ended their labor contracts with the plantations. Seeking a more independent lifestyle for themselves and their families, these immigrants came to grow, pick, or mill coffee in the area's rocky farmlands. They, and others who joined them later, helped Kona acquire the distinction of being the only area in the United States to grow coffee commercially for over one hundred years.

GOING TO HAWAI'I

I stay Cebu place. Carcar, Cebu. [In a] bamboo house. I work on my father's land. Take care the plant. Ten acre, because we get the rice field. We clean the land. And planting, too. Corn. Get some banana. We no sell that one. Only for eat, you know.

We near the ocean. No more one mile. We get boat—small boat. You got to go over there. The one they call Bohol. The other island, that one. And then, you go fishing in the middle. (Chuckles.)

[The family had] five boys and two girls. You know, like me, as the youngest of my family, if I tell my father I no go school, they no push. My schoolteacher, he told me, "Severo, how come you no come school?" "I no like." Me, number one kolohe I go (chuckles) anyplace. My father, he no lick me, nothing. That time I reach in Honolulu, I cry, because I remember, my house, I no work hard.

I get cousin, he come [back] from Hawai'i. He said, "Hawai'i good." He said, "If you going Hawai'i, you go in the [sugar] cane field. You go cut cane, hāpai." If you go day work, they give you dollar a day. But if you make contract, how many pound [of cane], they count, eh? That's why, sometimes, [based on the poundage] you make dollar, dollar half [$1.50], like that, one day. You get one dollar over here, you get [equivalent of] two pesos in the Philippines. I thought was good already, because double, huh?

Before, plantation pay [your boat fare]—free. In fact, you got contract, you work three year in the plantation, you get free to go back in the Philippines. But now, I come, 1922. How many year now I stay Hawai'i? (Chuckles.) Forget already, the Philippines.

American boat is strong, you know. From Manila, to come Hawai'i, one month. But Japan boat, ah, little more three month, two month. Lucky thing, the *President Lincoln* strong, fast.

Time for kaukau, everybody, they give kaukau. Pākē cookman over there. You can eat any kind. But sometime, you vomit too much. You know, the boat, it go like this [rocks hand]. Even all you ate, it come out, and you hungry again.

Three [passengers died]. One small boy. But me, I no feel dizzy, because every time, I go on boat, eh? That's why, used to, already, for ride boat, like that.

I stay in immigration [station in Honolulu]. I remember, [before] they bring us out, we play indoor ball over there. After that, I think, two weeks, we stay over there. And then, they bring us to [Onomea] Plantation.

SUGAR PLANTATION WORK

I work day work, I think, about two months. After that, I go contract. Cut cane, hāpai. Ninety-five pounds, you must carry to bring [to] the flume. But if day work, all right, because it's easy, only. But contract, you must work hard so you can make money.

I think, no more one year, I think. I moved Pāpa'aloa.

Onomea, I cooked my own. Pāpa'aloa, the Japanese cook. Ishizu, the name. Eat over there. Pay by month, eh? That's why, before, she call me [to] kaukau. (Raises pitch of voice.) "Severo-san, gohan tabenasai" ["Mr. Severo, please eat your meal"]. Now Japanese talk, I understand. You no can talk kolohe to me. (Chuckles.)

That time I come new one in Hawai'i—new man—I no understand what they stay talking about. They told me "daun bilo" ["down below"], but I don't know what is "daun bilo." I understand little bit Spanish. He [the overseer] told me "abajo," all right, go down. "Arriba," go up.

Before, 1924, strike, eh, the plantation. I stay Hilo about three months, I think—no, two months. Because they [the strike organizers] bring Hilo, the strikemen, before. That's why, that time, kinda hard. If single [like me], all right. But if you get wife, get kid, hard time. I pity the kid. No 'nough kaukau. He ate only sweet guava. Cry like hell.

The time we like go inside the 'Ola'a Plantation, they use (chuckles) this red cloth [i.e., armband], over here. So, if trouble already, he know each other. The one no more mark, ah, lick 'em. The strikers, everybody like go inside there, go huki the one no go strike. They like make 'em strike. [But] you no can pass over there. Yeah, the policemen stay watching over there. That's why, the strikers, they go back to town.

From that time, that's the time I think to go back to Pāpa'aloa. I come back Pāpa'aloa, I lived homestead. Before the strike no pau. I no work plantation yet. Because somebody [a striker], he know that you work plantation, he kill you, you know. That's why, you gotta watch out. The time it pau, I go back work.

Somebody told me mo' betta go Kona, because over there, get job picking coffee. That's the time I come in Kona.

KONA COFFEE WORK

If you picker, you look if plenty ripe coffee, all right, you go over there. You find job, you go Japanese place. "Papa, you get hanahana, ka?" [Papa, do you have work for me?] "Ah, hanahana, nanbo demo aru, but zeni nai do, nai do." [Ah, there's as much work as you want, but there's no money, you know, no money, you know.]

When you stay Kona, if you single like, you got to stay [at] the Japanese house—the owner of the coffee land. You will stay until you finish his place. Sometime, five month, two month. If that one pau, no more coffee already, you got to find someplace [else]. Because no more camp [workers' housing], you know. That's why, you got to go here and there.

For three-acre farm, two men is enough. But you get ten acre, like that, five acre, you got to hire about five men. When ripe time, oh, boy.

They pay by [hundred-pound] bag. Sometimes, I pick five bags [a day]. Sometime, I make ten bag. Two dollars, one bag, before. But after that, the other year, he come down [to] dollar quarter. And then, 1931, he hit forty cents a bag. That's the time I was thinking for go [back to the] plantation.

But one thing, Kona, that's the best, because nobody grumble you if you no go hanahana. Like plantation, morning time, (knocking), "Hoy, hanahana!" See, even though you tired, you got to go, because they kick the door, you know.

Man in Kona field with coffee-laden donkey, also called the "Kona nightingale," 1934 (Ray Jerome Baker, 1934, Bishop Museum).

Kona, good only for season time. But no more season, hard time, because no more job. Only hō hana, no 'nough for eat in Kona. Because that place you work, he tell you if you like contract that one, hō hana, like that. By acre, not by hour. We work, because bumbai, you no more rice—kaukau.

Pau season—pau coffee, well, that's the time, hard time already, because no more steady job, you see? After that, I go train up the boxing. "Cyclone" Dinson. (Chuckles.) Good name, eh?

PROFESSIONAL BOXING

That time I come Hawai'i, I know already [boxing]. That's why (chuckles), I no scared. In fact, that time, we come this side, the boat I ride, get one boxer. So, I practice to him. He no like I come Hawai'i. Said, "Mo' betta you go Mainland." If I no married, I sure I go Mainland. One haole like bring me, you know, the time I stay Lahaina.

That time I stay Lahaina, boy, I tell you, that one, hard training, though. I fight this Speedy Garcia. That one, that's the easiest one, that time I fight in Maui. I knock 'em out, number three round. He too sassy, that's why, him.

I fight Red Watai, that time, in Kona. I think '29, I fight already that one. Red Watai from Hilo. Japanese-Puerto Rican. He's number one, Hilo, before. I draw, that one. I no win, I no lose. That's why, we pau fight, somebody told me, "You supposed to take time, [then] you win." Well, no can help. I like get 'em right away, but no can do nothing, eh?

The time I no married yet—I was boxing yet, that time—I go church every time. Because I pray to God that he give me power so that I win the fight.

You fight about six rounds, seven rounds, like that. But one thing, small money. Only 10 percent [of gate receipts]. My [future] wife, she no like. She said, "This boxing, no 'nough kaukau." No can eat. Because cheap, eh? That's why, mo' betta I work. Yeah, went plantation, Honoka'a.

Yeah, we got married '35. You know, my wife, she was single that time she come Hawai'i [in 1926]. Because the brother, he order from the Philippines. The brother stay working plantation, Waialua Plantation. Oh, I see her because I know him [the brother]. I go holoholo over there.

RETURN TO KONA

After the war, that's the time come back in Kona. I like Kona because easy job. Not like plantation, you hoe the grass. We stay Hōnaunau. And then I buy coffee land over there. I buy $1,100, the five acre. Not buy the land, only lease.

1955, I sell the coffee land and I make the pool hall. I bin sell $5,500. I buy only $1,100. That's why I bin bought the pool hall [purchased its lease], because I thought more easy job, eh? We buy the [pool] table, the time we leased that place.

Ah, no can make money. Because during busy time, coffee, nobody go play. That's why, I bin tell my wife, "Ah, quit that kind."

That place over there, my Hōnaunau mauka, I buy [purchase the lease of] eleven acre, that one over there. Oh, they get big coffee place, you know, for grind [coffee beans]. Get big house, too.

That one belong Bishop [Estate]. But before, Japanese, he lease from Bishop. But that time, the Japanese, he like sell. When he wen tell me, "Dinson, you like buy my coffee land?" "Why? You like sell?" "Yeah, I like sell." "How much?" "Oh, the Hawaiian, he like buy $1,000, but one thing, they no pay cash." "All right. I give you $2,000. I pay you cash."

You get your own land, better. Because nobody boss you. If you go to work to somebody, you got to follow what he order to you. Pau pick coffee, then my boss, "Shigeru-san! Hoy. Ah, mo' betta coffee hāpai, no?" "All right." They no call me Severo. "Shigeru-san!" Japanese name. (Laughs.) Got to hāpai the bag, put inside the jackass. If you own land, you go hire somebody, you the one boss (chuckles).

Three people, I hire. Because, before, I get plenty friend, eh? Boxing [friends]. They stay my house. They help pick coffee. Got to pay by bag. Dollar quarter [$1.25], I think, that time, 1948.

Only me and my wife, no can. Plenty ripe. As long can see [the ripe coffee], ah, you got to keep up, pick. Because if fall down, and you go pick up from the ground, ah, (chuckles) this hard, you know.

Me, I tell you, morning time, about five o'clock, I stay in the coffee land already. Especially plenty ripe, oh, I stay the coffee land already, pick the coffee. And then, when my wife, she come down, that's the time we make ten bag, eight bag.

I sold 'em [Hōnaunau coffee land]. Only [for] $3,000. I buy this [Keālia] land. But this one, $9,000. This my own land already. That's why, mo' betta, we sell that [Hōnaunau] one and then we pay all this one, one time.

That time [Sam] Liau, he come, he told me that they like sell this place. So I tell my wife, "Ah, how we can buy? Us, no more money." Oh, I think over, I think over, bumbai, ah mo' betta we mortgage to the credit. And then, I pay Liau by year. Thousand dollar, a year. Ho, we work hard for pick coffee so I can make thousand dollar, one year. But the gods, they help me, so we get 'em, this one.

That's why, now, lucky. I get my own place. Like me, now, old already, hard, you know. I get sick, what? I go welfare? No, no, no. I no like. (Chuckles.)

Ikeda coffee farm, near the present site of Konawaena School, ca. 1930s (photo reproduced by courtesy of the Kona Historical Society).

Kona is the best. Because, you know, any kind, no more trouble. Over here, all the good men. And plenty fruit, any kind. If you no more money for buy the fruit, just only holoholo [and find] your kaukau (laughs). You get free.

You must think that I stay plantation—[Onomea], Pāpaʻaloa, Honokaʻa. . . . Three plantation, eh? But this one the best. I like Kona. Just like in the Philippines, already. Better than Philippines. (Laughs.) As long you got rice, no worry.

GLOSSARY

bin	past tense indicator
bumbai	later
hanahana	work
haole	Caucasian
hāpai	to carry
hō hana	weeding
holoholo	go out; visit
huki	to pull
kaukau	food

HENRY K. DUVAUCHELLE

HARD WORK AND PLEASURES, TOO

In the evenings we used to come into the living room. We had a piano there that my sister, Zelie, played. My three half brothers and the whole family would get up and they're all good singers, good musicians. I was the only one that didn't sing. I was more interested in fishing.

Of Hawaiian, English, French, and Irish extraction, Henry Duvauchelle was born in 1903 in Honolulu, the third of Edward and Annie Duvauchelle's thirteen children. In 1904, the family moved to Pūkoʻo, Molokaʻi, where Edward Duvauchelle worked as a self-educated lawyer, county road overseer, deputy sheriff, postmaster, rancher, and commercial fisherman.

Henry Duvauchelle attended Kaluaʻaha and Kamalō Schools on Molokaʻi; and Kalihi Waena on Oʻahu, where he lived with his maternal grandmother. He graduated from Honolulu Military Academy and studied for a short time at the University of Hawaiʻi. During school vacations, he would return home to Molokaʻi.

Duvauchelle worked for the City and County of Honolulu water and sewers division, various contractors, and beginning in 1930, the Board of Water Supply. He retired in 1961.

Warren Nishimoto interviewed him in 1989 and 1990 for COH's *ʻUalapuʻe, Molokaʻi: Oral Histories from the East End* (1991). Duvauchelle was one of thirteen individuals who were interviewed for their knowledge of ʻUalapuʻe Fishpond, one of several ancient Hawaiian ponds on the island of Molokaʻi. The eighteen-acre fishpond is valued for its cultural and historical significance. In 1966, it was declared a National Historic Site. In the interviews, Duvauchelle spoke of his love of the ocean and shared his deep knowledge of Molokaʻi's rural East End.

The interviews were conducted at Duvauchelle's home in Kuliʻouʻou, Oʻahu, where he lived with his wife, Margaret Wong Leong Duvauchelle. He died in 2000.

The following narrative focuses on his childhood in Pūkoʻo.

EARLY DAYS IN PŪKOʻO

Now my father was first married to ʻAlapaʻi [Kapiʻiwi], another woman, Hawaiian, and he had three boys with her. Later on, he married my mother [Annie K. Wood Duvauchelle] and they had twelve children [the thirteenth died in infancy].

I was born in Honolulu, 1903, in the district that they call Kakaʻako, right near where the *[Honolulu] Advertiser* is today.

Well, my father was born there [on Molokaʻi] and he had quite a lot of property up there. He had accumulated some money so he wanted to buy some cattle, which he did, and went up there intending to do some farming, fishing, and whatever he could do.

Right in Pūkoʻo itself, there were people that were working for—maybe doing odd jobs off and on—working for maybe [rancher Rex] Hitchcock. When he had to drive cattle, they'd go and help. They were cowboys. And when there was road work they'd be working on the road.

Hawaiians. They worked hard. And they made a living the same way as we did, fishing, and jobs every now and then to keep them supplied with some of the better things. Like for instance, they can buy bread, they can buy crackers, they can buy food from the stores. Maybe sugar, rice, and things that they cannot grow themselves.

And then little further up were mostly Japanese people that were doing farming. They'd have watermelon, corn, or other vegetables that they'd grow. The vegetables were just for their home use. But watermelon and corn is what they raised to sell.

Whatever property we had, they'd lease it and they'd be working on that property. Sakanashi was one of them, Ikeda was another, and Seigi. And every time we wanted help we always asked them, they always came. When they wanted something, we always went to help them. We got along better with the Japanese and the Chinese than we did with our own Hawaiians. (Laughs.)

And then little further away from us, maybe about another 100 feet away, was the poi factory, Aipa. They'd usually pound poi by the old Hawaiian way [with poi pounders and boards]. Then they changed, tried to find another way to pound the poi. They had mallets just like the Japanese do with the rice, mochi. Well, that didn't work too well.

They finally got a Model-T Ford and they backed it up right close to the factory. They'd take the tire off and put a belt on the rim and run it through the grinder. Run the Ford and mix poi. That was much better. (Chuckles.)

Then little above that was Ah Soon, a Chinese. He was our baker. He made pies, bread, and in fact, cook a meal for you if you wanted to have a meal cooked at a certain price.

Right in Pūko'o we had two stores. Afterwards there were three stores, right close to each other. So this Ah Sing was one, before him was Akeo, and then across the street was Ah Pun [Chock Pun]. He was with Ah Sing first and he moved across the street. And then Apaiona, [also known as] Lin Kee, he had a store. And later he leased that store out to Chow Kwan. So that was their job.

Now, little further up, Kūpeke section, that's, oh, about half a mile or three-quarters of a mile from Pūko'o, the Buchanans lived there. They had a fishpond [Kūpeke Fishpond] and that was their job to take care of the fishpond and things like that. And that's about the size of it.

We had three houses right in Pūko'o. One house is where my brothers, half brothers rather, lived. Two of them, anyway, lived in the house on the east end of the lot.

And the middle section is where our regular home was. That's where my father and mother lived and all of us children with my father's second wife.

Duvauchelle family, ca. 1930s (photo courtesy of Laura Duvauchelle Smith).

It was this old-style house, somewhat like those that you see today in New Orleans and places like that. A home with the veranda practically half around the house. Then we had quite a big-sized living room and a big bedroom with a big pūne'e from one end of the room to the other. That's where we all slept. My father and mother [were] on the west side of the beds. And all every one of us were on the same big pūne'e.

And the third house was my grandmother's. My grandmother [Mary Lynch Duvauchelle] lived there with one of my other half brothers.

She was a very strict woman. And my sister was her pet, just like my other half brother was her pet, too. So whatever I did was wrong because it contradicted the other two and she didn't like me. She used to tell me, she says, "Ke make au, lapu ana wau." In other words, "When I pass away, I'm gonna come haunt you." (Laughs.)

So anyway, I told my father about [what Grandmother said]. I was really afraid of it, see, and he told me, "Well, next time she tells you that," he says [to tell her], "Hele naonao e ki'o ulu ko po'o ke make 'oe." In other words, "When you die when you get buried I'm going to have my ants going right on top of your head." (Chuckles.) And that was a bad thing for the Hawaiians. And I did tell her that.

Ho, she was mad. But after that, she and I got along pretty well.

I spoke to her in broken Hawaiian. At that time I was living at home and my father didn't want us to speak Hawaiian. But English, you have to learn and get well educated so that you could get along when it's your time to work and so forth.

Now, my maternal grandmother [Pua'ala Wood Williams], she also couldn't speak English. And when we came to Honolulu to go to school, my sister and I had to learn Hawaiian. She used to take that nī'au broom and every time we spoke English she'd hit us on the legs, see, so we had to speak Hawaiian.

Everybody ate in the middle house. We had a kitchen on the west end of it, of that house, and then we had a big dining room. My father expected a big family so he always had a very big dining room. (Chuckles.) To make sure that they have enough room for everybody to sit and eat. All on the same table. We had a long bench on one side of the table and on the other side we had chairs. So the younger children sat on the bench and the old folks— older brothers and sisters—sat on their chair. When we graduated from this [bench] here we went to the chair. (Laughs.)

My dad made sure that everybody had something to do. My older [half] brothers first took care of the cattle. The milking, the chasing—rounding up—of the cattle, branding, and everything else like that. That was their job.

In the home my mother and sisters took care of everything. They had the regular chores of the house like, for instance, cooking, fixing of the beds, and things like that. They'd all work together. And maybe once a week they'll bake bread, the sourdough bread. Oh, was a big pan [in which] she'd make the dough. Took her almost all day to get it ready to bake. And every one of us would give a hand, come in and mix, work the dough.

The younger children, well, maybe we took care of the garden, like I used to take care of the potato patch and take care of the garden with my dad. If you wanted vegetables, you have to raise your own. And if you had a friend that had vegetables that you didn't have and you had something he didn't have, you made exchanges.

In Pūko'o we had a well of our own. We had a tank up by the windmill that used to pump the water up. The water was a little brackish, I think about 250 parts per million or so, salt. We used to use it for our drinking purpose, watering the garden, and so forth.

We were one of the few people that had indoor plumbing. Most of them still had outdoor plumbing. Although we had outdoor plumbing also. So in case anything went wrong, like for instance, if there's no wind for several days. There'd be no water. Then we had to go and use the outdoor plumbing.

[Later] we were one of the first people that had electricity on Moloka'i. We'll buy a whole bunch of batteries, and our lights were thirty-two volts. And that used to run our lights and also the washing machine.

If he [my father] wanted something, he had to work for it. Like when he wanted the Delco [electrical] system, he had to go out fishing to make sure he had enough money to buy the Delco system.

When my [half] brothers left home, then I was in charge of the ranch. Taking care of the cattle, taking care of the milking. In fact, when I was going to school, I had to milk eight cows before I went to school. (Chuckles.)

My sister and I, we went to Kamalō School at that time. She had one horse that she rode all the time. We called that horse "Boy." And the horse that I rode was "Dandy."

Until Dr. [Homer] Hayes, [Sr.] married his Ka'ū girl in Hawai'i and she came to Moloka'i. And she brought her sister there. Well, her sister had a donkey and she couldn't ride the donkey. They lived about little over two miles away from us. And the school was about five miles away from our home. So when we got to her place, we changed. I gave her my horse and I rode the donkey.

One day we were going to school, and I was plugging along behind, you know, quite a ways back of them. [Another] jack made a howl and he started chasing this jack. [This] jack stopped short and turned around and took off.

Duvauchelle children sit on Pūko'o Wharf, Moloka'i, ca. 1920s (photo courtesy of Laura Duvauchelle Smith).

And there was nothing I could do to stop 'em. I was trying to pull on the reins, my saddle moved practically on his neck.

And it just happened that one of the other boys lived up at Manawainui, which is just a little before then. He lived up in the mountains, Charlie Rodrigues. He came down and he had a lasso on his saddle. Took the lasso off and as I was running by him, he chased after me and he threw his lasso and he caught me instead of the jack. So I had to take that lasso off and put it on the donkey's neck and stop the donkey. And he finally had to lead the donkey all the way to school. (Laughs.)

When I was young I used to love fishing. I used to go out on the pier that they had there, on the [Pūko'o] Wharf. And I used to fish with the little bamboo and hook and line and catch quite a number of small fish. Oh, even some of these stick fish and other fish. Awa, for instance, is quite a good-sized fish.

We at least had some of the meals supplied by my fishing. Most of our food was seafood. Either clams, and fish, and lobsters, and crabs, and things like that. And those days, the fish were plentiful.

And I used to go out squidding with my dad, too. He'd be on a flatbottom boat, usually about a sixteen-footer and quite wide, so that the boat wouldn't displace too much water. And the water could be anywhere from, oh, maybe two feet to about eight feet deep. They'd go with poles, see.

And they could spot the squid right from the boat. And right from the boat also, they'd spear them and bring it on the boat. They didn't have to get their feet wet, (chuckles) even. I'd help him kill the squid when he'd bring it in the boat and I'd hit it with a club, see. When my dad went squidding, in one day's time sometimes he picked up forty squid.

And then if he wanted kūmū or other fish like that, he had special places. He'd go, stop the boat and anchor it, and dive with the spear and spear kūmū. And if he wanted 'o'io, we have a little 'o'io spot.

In 'Ualapu'e [Fishpond] there was mullet; awa, awa kalamoho, awa 'aua; and kūpala, or barracuda. He tried to stock the pond [which he leased from the territory] and tried to get the thing so that he could have perpetual fish when he wanted it. In fact, that's the old Hawaiian way of doing it.

I used to catch quite a lot of ulua right on the [Pūko'o] Wharf. We used to do chumming. Even mullet used to come around over there. We used to go with the throw net, and when they come close to the pier we'd throw our net and catch mullet that way, too.

My friend and I, Sakanashi, used to go fishing quite a lot. He says, "Heneri, we go fishing." He doesn't want to go on the boat, he wanted to go on the pier.

"Okay, what you want?"

Then he says, "Oh, weke."

So weke is not too far out from on the pier. We'd chum again, weke would come, and then we'd hook 'em. Every time I used to come home from school, he says, "Heneri come, tako come; Heneri come, sakana come." (Laughs.)

Of course, we had quite a lot of banana trees, mango trees. Mango trees was up in the valley mostly, and guavas up in the valley. Make jam and even for eating fresh like that.

This Kiha Ah Leong. She had quite a grove at Ka'ulu'ulu. Ka'ulu'ulu means "a breadfruit grove." She had some breadfruit up there, she had mountain apple, mangos, few pomelos, few other fruits. And we were always welcome to come over there to get any type of fruit that we wanted.

So one day I climbed up this white mountain-apple tree. Oh, it was quite a tall tree. I was about thirty, forty feet [up]. I was near the top and just above my head was a stump about six inches in diameter. Someone had cut it off years ago. And I was picking mountain apples and stuffing it in my shirt. All of a sudden I heard the branch that I was on cracking. It cracked and it just fell. I just reached up and got hold of that stump up there and saved my life.

Oh, when we were young we used to play marbles, we used to have kites, we had pio. You have a group of people in one goal, a group of people in another goal, all children. And then when you go out, somebody from this end can go out and touch you, pio. See, pio is you put your fire out. So then you're out of the game. Then whoever has anybody left, why, they'd win the game.

In the evenings we used to come into the living room. We had a piano there that my sister, Zelie, played. My three half brothers and the whole family would get up and they're all good singers, good musicians. I was the only one that didn't sing. I was more interested in fishing. (Chuckles.)

Christmas, the family all got together. In fact, even when I was in school, Christmas vacation, Easter vacation, and summer vacation, we always went home. We sometimes bring friends from school that we made while we were in school. And they'd stay with us.

We'd have, oh, a wonderful Christmas. We always had kālua pig and almost like a lū'au, the whole family, Christmas and New Year's. The whole family would get together and close friends. That's how we spent our Christmas.

So we used to have a good life. We enjoyed it. We did our chores and we had our hard work and we had our pleasures, too.

GLOSSARY

awa	milkfish
awa 'aua	medium-sized milkfish
awa kalamoho	large milkfish
kālua	bake in a ground oven
kūmū	red goatfish
kūpala	barracuda
lū'au	feast
mochi	pounded rice cake
nī'au	coconut-leaf midrib
'o'io	bonefish
pio	to extinguish a fire; tag game
poi	food staple made from cooked taro corm
pūne'e	moveable couch
tako	octopus
sakana	fish
ulua	jackfish
weke	goatfish

MARTINA KEKUEWA FUENTEVILLA

HĀNAI GRANDDAUGHTER

*I lived with my grandparents in the
pili grass house. I was born inside that
house, that's where my mother gave
birth. It was only one room. The place
where we slept was all mats, only mats.
The area where you slept was separate
from where you ate, and you cooked outside. That was the oldest pili grass house
in this area.*

Hōnaunau, noted as an ancient puʻuhonua or place of refuge, was the birth-
place of Martina Kekuewa Fuentevilla. Born in 1908, she lived with ʻAna
Loʻe Maʻinui and Mākia Maʻinui as their hānai granddaughter. Hānai, which
means "to raise, feed, nourish, sustain," also refers to the Hawaiian guardian-
ship system in which a child is raised from birth by a foster parent or grand-
parent. Fuentevilla's early life centered around traditional farming and fishing.
She found her first job as a tobacco farm worker and married coworker Leon
Fuentevilla in 1927. Martina Fuentevilla was also an entertainer, song compos-
er, and hat weaver. When she died in 1983 at age seventy-four, Fuentevilla left
six children, twenty-one grandchildren, and one great-grandchild.

Martina Fuentevilla was interviewed on three occasions in 1980 and 1981
by Hawaiian-language scholar Larry L. Kimura. Conducted entirely in Hawaiian and translated into English by Kimura, the interviews were part of
COH's *A Social History of Kona* project and reflect a lifestyle rapidly disap-
pearing amidst resort development and changing values in the West Hawaiʻi
Island area.

A LOT OF ALOHA

When you think about those days, you really feel a lot of aloha. You know, the
way I was kept as a little girl and grew up, you feel a lot of aloha.

My kahu hānai were the ones who raised me when I was small. 'Ana Lo'e is the wife and Mākia Ma'inui is the husband. Commonly, the two were referred to as Lo'e and Ma'inui. They didn't have children of their own, they only raised [adopted] grandchildren. My grandmother had a lot of hānai, about eight or ten, and I was the last one.

Lo'e was from Hōnaunau here, and I think Ma'inui was from Keālia. [When] my grandmother would get mad at my grandfather, she would say, "Oh, you makawela." I asked my grandmother what is a makawela, and she said someone who has no royal blood, a commoner. (Laughs.) My grandmother could talk because she was a kaukauali'i.

I lived with my grandparents in the pili grass house. I was born inside that house, that's where my mother gave birth. It was only one room. The place where we slept was all mats, only mats. The area where you slept was separate from where you ate, and you cooked outside.

That was the oldest pili grass house in this area. Oh, the tourists, it [the house] was always full of them, every day. The cars would come, the tourists would get off. [They] would take pictures of the house and say, "Here, here, come." Me and my grandparents would stand up in front and they would take a picture. (Laughs.)

Thatching a grass house (photo courtesy of the Martina Fuentevilla collection).

And then my grandfather made another house that was [constructed of] sugarcane leaves. You cut down the sugar cane, and cut off the upper part, and dry it. You go out and get bamboo. You're supposed to tie the bamboo together with cord, and then put on the sugarcane leaves. He [grandfather] made it with a hammer [and nails], but you are actually supposed to make it with cord.

We lived up mauka all week from Monday to Saturday. We'd go up mauka to farm. [We] used to get up very early in the morning. We would be finished drinking our coffee and eating our sweet potato by the time the first light of dawn came.

Work was done early in the morning hours because it wasn't hot then. We would go out into our potato patch or sugarcane patch and start weeding there. As it got warmer, well, most of the work would be done. When it got hot, then we came back to the house and ate, and then took a nap or rested in the cool of the house. Later on in the afternoon, toward the evening time when it wasn't too hot, then they would go out again and do more work.

There weren't that many varieties of edible fruits and vegetables then. There were the papaya, pear, mountain apple, banana, pumpkin, and sweet potato. Of course, we also had our lū'au leaves that we cooked and ate with our poi. When we pulled our taro, we used the corms for poi and the tops for greens. If we didn't have the taro, then we used pumpkin to make our poi, as well as 'ulu poi. We also made sweet potato poi.

Martina Fuentevilla and aunt pounding 'ulu poi, ca. 1934 (photo courtesy of the Martina Fuentevilla collection).

You know, before, there were many Hawaiians living there in Hōnaunau. When it was time for planting taro, everybody got together to help to plant taro. When it was time to pull, [they] pull the whole works up except for the offshoots that would be used for replanting.

Sometimes there would be one or two big, huge imu to cook all this taro in. All the people would get together to peel the taro and pound it. Five big poi boards [were used] to pound the taro. These would be men that did the pounding. Everybody divided and shared the food, the poi.

That's how we used to live before in my young days. We grew our own taro and things to make our own poi, and then, of course, [caught] the fish from down in the ocean.

We would go down to the beach on the weekend. My grandfather would say to me, "Grandchild, let's go down to the beach." We would go down on our donkeys. And then, we would get hēʻī. That's what was used to braid into fish traps. [The trap is] like a basket. It's round, but there are openings on either side of the trap. This ʻina, you get that and you crush it up, then you put it into this fish trap. That would serve as the bait for the fish to go in after it. When that was completed, we would go down to the beach.

My grandfather would dive in a certain area where he knew the fish would be. He would put one rock inside of this trap to hold it down in the water. And all you had to do is just wait a few hours. When my grandfather would think that it was enough time waiting, then he would go down and get the trap. And there would be all this hīnālea fish, all inside of the trap. Then he would bring the trap up and shake all the fish out. My grandfather would say, "This is enough fish, let's go home."

When we went ʻupena kuʻu we did it all the way from Kiʻilae till the bay at Hōnaunau. Before, all ages went, from the young to the old. We would go from channel to channel—you know, all these different channels where the fish could be caught with this way of fishing. Some people would go with a stick. They used the stick to splash the water and to move the rocks to scare whatever fish were hiding under these rocks so they would swim into the nets. Then [we] bring the fish up to shore and divide it all among the people who participated in this fishing.

The ʻōhua, it is gotten in April and May [although] the season seems to be changing now. You can tell when it's the ʻōhua season because you can see on the horizon these black streaks, just like rain in the sky over the ocean. The whale, when it comes here during this time, it blows this mucus out from its head, and in this mucus bag is found this ʻōhua. I have never seen that, but my older relatives have seen that and they have told me that [ʻōhua] comes from the mucus of the whale. Of course, when it hits something hard, then the bag breaks open and all this ʻōhua comes out. That's when you have to go and catch them in all these little ponds all along the shore. This 'ōhua is transparent. And so when you go down and put your net in the water, you really can't see them. You have something in your other hand to scare them in, like some kind of leaf or stick. Then when you pull your net up, they are all in the net. As the sun comes up, they get darker and darker until they take the color of small manini.

[Sometimes] we would all go out to catch the 'ōpelu. Maybe I would go with my net and you would go with yours. Then all you did was pull your nets up and bring all the fish in. Sometimes they would go out to feed the 'ōpelu. That was only to feed it, not to fish it. That would be for about three months at a time, just to feed the 'ōpelu. All the canoes would go out—maybe five or six canoes, whatever there were.

Of course, if you disobeyed an order not to fish, you would be hearing it, you know. They were very strict in those days. Nowadays you could be the one feeding the 'ōpelu, and then somebody else can come along and catch all the 'ōpelu. In those days, no, if you did that, you would get into trouble. You'd get a beating with the paddle.

You know, before, when you go down early in the morning to clean and rinse your 'ōpelu, you had all this brackish water coming up along the beach. That's where you would wash and rinse your 'ōpelu fish that had been salted

Tidal pool in Hōnaunau (undated, Hawai'i State Archives).

overnight. [Then] we dried them right on top of the pāhoehoe lava. If the sun is good, then [in] one day the ʻōpelu would dry. I would do that right there where all the kids swim now, that's called Kapuaʻi.

Nowadays, the kids are just small and they know what shame is; they are ashamed to go swimming without clothes. But when we were small, we didn't know what that was all about. We just were accustomed to swimming that way. The pāhoehoe lava would be heated from the sun so it was nice and warm. We would lie on there and dry off, and then we would jump back in and swim again.

Young kids today, no matter how small they are, they pick up these swear words. If we were to say one swear word, our grandparents would hit us with the coconut mid-rib broom. It stung. Boy, did I run when I saw that. [But] my grandmother just had to yell once, and I stopped right where I was. Then she would come and hit me. That's how my grandparents used to punish me.

When I was six years old, I started to go to school. There were not too many of us children in one room. One row [of seats] would be third grade; and one row would be the fourth-graders; and then another row, the fifth-graders. We would be called by classes to stand up and read about Captain [James] Cook, what year he arrived, and about [English explorer George] Vancouver, et cetera.

Of course, in school, we could only speak English. There were some of us who knew the Hawaiian language. We were brought up with our grandparents or we were familiar with the language. But we were not allowed to speak Hawaiian in school.

Most of the children were Hawaiian back then, and Japanese. We Hawaiian kids ate on our own during lunch. Of course, we had a few Japanese kids who were good friends with us and they ate with us. The Japanese would bring rice and whatever kind of fish or meat they had to eat with their rice. Hawaiian kids living up in the mauka region, we'd take just poi. The Hawaiian kids down at the beach, they would bring the fish. And then we would eat together.

When I was small, every time I came home from school I would go and get about three stalks of sugar cane to eat. My grandparents had about, gee, at least an acre or more planted in sugar cane. You would look for the sugar cane lying down, that's the sugar cane that was ready, not the ones that were standing upright. Sometimes there would be two to four of us children and we would divide it all amongst us. You just used your teeth to strip the bark off, and then you would chew on the sugar cane inside.

My grandparents didn't use that to make ʻōkolehao, but some people made their own [sugarcane] ʻōkolehao. My grandparents used to make the

sweet potato sour. They made swipe, and the sweet potato was used as alcohol. You would have to smash up the sweet potato and leave it for several
days until it got sour and fermented. This sweet potato swipe was made in the
gourd calabash. We would get the leaf of the banana and lay it down on the
ground as a mat. We would get these gourds filled with this fermented sweet
potato and place them right in the middle of the banana leaf. Then what they
would do is just sit down and dip out this fermented sweet potato liquor and
drink it. You couldn't stand up once you got drunk. So all you did was sit
there and keep drinking until all that was gone. That was the kind of alcohol
or liquor that was drunk in those days.

We kids used to go and sneak and try a cup of this fermented sweet potato
liquor. Boy, did it taste funny. [It] wasn't to our liking, but, of course, to the
older people, they were accustomed to this. We would see them drink this,
then pretty soon, they would start chanting [in] the old style. My grandfather
would chant, and then later on, my grandmother would chant.

You know, those people of the olden times, they would get up about two
o'clock in the morning to do their work. My grandfather would be sitting
there with my grandmother and what he'd be doing is chanting. My grandmother would weave her mats; or if they were hats she was weaving, then she
would do that and chant, too, until dawn. And I just listened and enjoyed it,
it was very pretty to hear.

We were all living together till my grandparents both passed away. My
grandmother died first, and one year later my grandfather died. My grandfather died in that sugarcane leaf house. [Then] I lived with my uncle and aunty
and their hānai children. My uncle [Mākia Ka'ana'ana] was also an adopted
child of my grandparents. So I stayed with my uncle until I got married.

STRINGING TOBACCO

The first job I did was to be a tobacco stringer. The men folk did the planting of the tobacco, and they planted tobacco all over this area here. The men
folk would go in and pick the leaves. They would fill up these big bags with
the leaves of the tobacco. He [Leon Fuentevilla] was one that worked outside
in the fields.

We would all be women working inside the barn. Most of the women
were Hawaiian. Sometimes there would be fifteen, twenty women at one time
working in the barn. We would string the tobacco leaves. Each lady would get
a bag of tobacco. They would weigh the bag. We got paid by the bag.

You know the long, steel kind of needles that lei makers use? Well, we
would use that to string the tobacco leaves. We had to string the tobacco
leaves back to back and front to front. Then at one end of this stick we would

tie this string. We would tie the other end of the string to the opposite end of the stick. Then we would carry the stick upstairs to dry the tobacco up there. We had to again sort of separate the leaves that we strung onto the string because that way it would allow the air to get between the leaves equally. And then they would be hung there to dry for maybe about two weeks.

Once the tobacco leaves were dried, then we had some more work to do. We had to go ahead and remove all of these dried tobacco leaves from the string and pile it up. Then we would steam these leaves. We had to later remove the back midrib of the leaf, and then the leaf itself was used to make cigars. We rolled the cigar. We used the machine to measure the length of the cigar so that they would be all even and we would cut it. Of course, we had to put some sticky thing on it to hold the whole cigar together. Then [we] put it in the box, [and] the boxes were sent out. You know, that was a lot of work we did with the tobacco.

THE KELEKOLIO ORCHESTRA

Before I was married, when I was sixteen, that's when I used to go with my aunty and [other] uncle to entertain. She was known as the "Songbird of Kohala," that was my Aunty Elizabeth Kelekolio. Then she got married to my uncle [Benjamin Kelekolio]. They both came back here to Kona to live. She instructed [students] in Hawaiian music and Hawaiian dancing. I was the first that she taught how to dance. [And] I played the 'ukulele, as well as guitar.

We were known as the Kelekolio Orchestra. We entertained at all those hotels in Kailua. Of course, the number one hotel back in those days was the Kona Inn. That's where we would go to perform our show.

We used to go all over the place, especially during election time. When it was time for elections, she [my aunt] would go and take her troupe to campaign for various candidates. That was for both the primary and general elections that we went around campaigning. Whether it would be the Republicans or the Democrats, we went. We'd go to Ka'ū and Hilo and to Kohala, all over—Waimea, too.

Those people who were adept in composing [Hawaiian-language] songs, well, they would make songs for the political candidates. They observed the characteristics of this candidate, his ways, and they would try to incorporate that into the lyrics of their song. They would teach us to sing his song. Then we would have a song to sing for him wherever he went. When it was his turn to stand up and give his speech, then we would have a song to sing for him at that time. Sometimes there would be two or three candidates that had their own songs that were composed just for them. And for those who didn't have any songs composed for them, we would sing just any song as backup music for them.

There was [County Attorney, and later, Judge] Martin Pence. His campaign chairman would give us the song to sing for him, [but] I don't know whether Martin Pence understood what we sang about, the meaning of his song. Another one was Sheriff [Henry] Martin. A song was composed for him, his deeds, and places he went to. These things were written into the song, and also names of his friends were included in the song.

You have to understand something about this kind of activity because a lot of people have said this: that if you are not careful about the kind of words you use in your song, then you will get into trouble because some words are not good, they don't have good meanings. If you see that there is something that's not good in it, then you should adjust it to make it better. So when you compose, you have to understand the story and the meaning that you want to use.

I still have my guitar, but I don't play anymore. Before, when people used to ask me to come and play at a party, then I would go. They'd ask me to dance and I would dance. People that knew I used to play music before, they would ask me if I still play music and I tell them, "No, I'm all finished now." I'm getting too old for that.

[But] I sing in the church every Sunday. We were taught to sing in Latin. I've forgotten all of that Latin singing; we don't do that now. Just recently, we have English, and Hawaiian, too, in our hymn singing. The way we do it at our church is, one Sunday we do it in English, and then the other Sunday we sing it in Hawaiian. So, all I do is sing for the church now.

GLOSSARY

hānai	foster, adopt
hē'ī	a vine-like plant that grows down towards the beach
hīnālea	wrasse
imu	underground oven
'ina	young sea urchin
kahu hānai	foster guardian
kaukauali'i	nobility of less than chiefly rank
lū'au leaves	young taro leaves
makawela	commoner
manini	surgeonfish
mauka	inland

ʻōhua	young surgeonfish
ʻōkolehao	liquor
ʻōpelu	mackerel scad
pāhoehoe	smooth, unbroken lava
pili	grass used for thatching
poi	food staple made from cooked taro corm
ʻulu poi	food staple made from cooked breadfruit
ʻupena kuʻu	gill netting

ERNEST GOLDEN

LIKE GOING TO HEAVEN

We picked up a magazine that says, "Civil service jobs in Bermuda." And the jobs were paying seventy-five cents an hour. They said, "Well, there's no more jobs in Bermuda, but you can go to Pearl Harbor." We had no idea where Pearl Harbor was. But seventy-five cents an hour, we would have gone to west hell and back.

It was 1943, and Ernest Golden, a newly hired civilian defense worker, had been at sea on a crowded troop ship for eleven days since his departure from San Francisco. As the ship cruised into Pearl Harbor, Golden suddenly noticed the changing colors of the ocean. "It was," he remembers, "like going to heaven."

Except for a short time spent with his grandparents, Mississippi sharecroppers, Golden grew up in Athens, Georgia, where he was born in 1923. From a very young age, he was driven to leave Athens and the South, to escape segregation and discrimination.

After the war, Golden stayed in Hawai'i and became part-owner of Honolulu Airport Porter Services and at the time of the interview, owner of another airport porter business, Versatile Services, Inc.

He married Evangeline Silva in 1951 and they settled in Lā'ie. He was active in the Afro-American Association, an organization instrumental in establishing a Martin Luther King, Jr. holiday in Hawai'i.

Kathryn Waddell Takara interviewed Ernest Golden in 1988 for *Oral Histories of African Americans* (1990). Golden was one of nine residents of Hawai'i who shared their life experiences with Takara, an instructor and researcher in African American history at the University of Hawai'i. The project was undertaken to address the relative lack of first-person data on African Americans in Hawai'i.

ATHENS, GEORGIA

When I left Athens, the population was approximately 27,000. And about one-fifth of the population was black. Athens was unique because it was and is a university town. I think Athenians considered themselves a cut above people of other parts of Georgia. Nevertheless we were in the South.

Let's say you want to get a sandwich or something to eat. There was no such thing as going to sit down at a table or counter. You stood at the end of the counter and you very humbly placed yourself in position. The service to you was take-out. You hoped you didn't become too conspicuous [whereby] they would say, "Well, look, I'm not going to serve you."

I went to East Athens School. We walked five miles to get to elementary school. Here is a park and you have all these white people in the park. And they would stone you, or they would chase you, and you'd try to find a different way to get to school.

In elementary school I was quite a good student. When I reached the seventh grade, my reputation preceded me, and this teacher decided, "Hey look, Ernest knows everything so I don't have to call on him." So for the seventh grade, I coasted. When I reached eighth grade, that year of coasting had not prepared me to enter high school. I dropped out for about a couple of years.

But it was during the two years that I was out that this incident happened. I was working in a market as a trucker's helper. We were delivering meats all around northeast Georgia. The [Caucasian] man that I was working for was named Collins.

One morning I walked to the market and [the butcher] Tom Gibson said, "Hey, little nigger, go into that cooler and bring me some hot dogs."

When he called me "little nigger," I blew my top. There's a butcher block that had a bunch of knives on it, and I picked up one of the knives and threw it at him. It came, shooop, right past his head. He started after me. This guy was about six feet one, six feet two, and possibly weighed about two [hundred] plus. I was about five eight and weighed about one hundred thirty-seven.

Now, there were two or three blacks in there and they just turned and looked, but there was no way they would come to my aid. But Collins, the man I worked for, he turns and says, "No, Tom, you leave him alone." This was unusual. [This is] the sort of thing that shaped my life and caused me to be void of prejudice.

There was a close friend of mine, a man named Milton Jordan. When we got out of high school, he and I left. We went to Atlantic City and stayed for three months. If you went to work in a restaurant, the first thing you did was eat, okay. We would go to work at a restaurant.

Atlantic City was a boomtown from June through September, and then in September, the place closed up. We left in September and went back to Athens and from Athens, we went to New Orleans for a couple of weeks.

Actually, we were leaving New Orleans, going back to Athens on the bus. We picked up a magazine that says, "Civil service jobs in Bermuda." And the jobs were paying seventy-five cents an hour. Seventy-five cents an hour at that time was a lot of money. So we applied. They said, "Well, there's no more jobs in Bermuda, but you can go to Pearl Harbor." We had no idea where Pearl Harbor was. But seventy-five cents an hour, we would have gone to west hell and back. We signed up for it.

We were civil service employees at that time and you traveled almost as if you were military. We went to Vallejo, California, and somewhere around Mare Island, there's a shipyard there in California. We worked there, waiting for transportation to come to Hawai'i. We had to go to San Francisco in order to get a ship out.

From San Francisco, it took us eleven days. I think I got seasick the minute I walked down to the docks. Actually I exaggerate, but I think for about three days after we were on the ocean, I was sick. I don't know how many men were on that ship, but it was very well packed.

And all of a sudden you start coming to the Hawaiian waters, and I started seeing a difference in colors in the ocean. Something just came over me and, "Hey, this is what I want. This is for me." As we were cruising into Pearl Harbor, it was like going to heaven.

WARTIME HONOLULU

I arrived on O'ahu February 1, 1943. Broke. The war was still on. It was like a frontier. All Hawai'i was under martial law.

We went to CHA3. CHA3 is Civilian Housing Area 3, and it was the housing area for civil service workers. I think the majority were from Pearl Harbor. There was a mess hall, and there were apartment-like buildings that had been erected. There was a bachelors' dormitory, about four stories. I think this was erected later. CHA3, I suppose it went from Main Street toward the ocean, that must have been about four blocks. The two blocks closest to the ocean were set aside for the Negro.

It was sort of a weird setup, really. The mess halls were integrated. The barbershop was segregated. The theater was integrated. I think at that time, the majority of us, both white and black, were from the South. There was tension because you had a mix of blacks and whites from the Southern states and they'd never been mixed before.

Ernest Golden (left) and Milton Jordan in Downtown Honolulu, 1943 (photo courtesy of Ernest Golden).

We would all go into town periodically. There was a ten o'clock curfew. We all tried to rush back from town to beat the curfew and the buses were very heavily loaded. You'd be on the bus, there would be a fight between some black and some white, usually newly arrived whites from the Mainland.

It pulled apart in the [19]60s, but at this time, there was what you would call an empathy from the local people as to what the blacks had endured. And the bus driver would hold the doors as long as the blacks were winning. When everything was over, he'd open the doors and let the blacks disappear.

There were [four] main things that were very much in demand during the war. One was prostitution, the other was the taxi dance halls, the [movie] theater was another, and booze.

You would get in a line. The houses of prostitution were segregated. The taxi dance halls were segregated. Theaters weren't segregated. From Nuʻuanu [Avenue] back to ʻAʻala Park, there were a lot of bars. All of these places were packed. I mean, wall-to-wall people. They were all pretty much segregated, also.

There was a club across from the Swing Club, and I cannot for the life of me recall the name. It was noted for its blatant segregation. I recall that a man picketed the place. His last name was Johnson. And I made some signs for Johnson to picket the place.

The bachelors as such didn't have the social outlet, and I mentioned there were very few women. Ten of us got together and created what was called the Ten Bachelors' Club. All of us were single guys, and by giving affairs that were well done, well promoted, we sort of gathered around ourselves enough female interests in order for us to get dates.

It was invitational. Seldom did we give pay affairs. Funny thing, at that time, everybody had some money. You could walk over and say, "Let me have twenty, thirty dollars. " A total stranger, he let you have some money. But don't ask him for his bottle or something like that because whiskey was rationed and you couldn't get any booze.

One of the highlights of our affairs, we hosted the Nat King Cole trio on their first concert here in Hawai'i. We gave him a reception at a Chinese club called Lau Yee Chai's at the time in Waikīkī. Interestingly enough, the major hotels and things at Waikīkī were not [segregated]. We gave other functions that were very well attended, but eventually, we broke up. I guess once we got married, there was no need to be having the club.

HOME IN LĀ'IE

I met my wife [Evangeline Silva Golden] through a friend. Rev. Collins was one of the first blacks to start a church here. His daughter was a friend of mine. She and the girl that I eventually married worked together and she introduced me. My wife was about nineteen, I think at that time.

My wife's Portuguese, and a black man dating a Portuguese girl in those days, it wasn't the most accepted thing. You could walk up and down the streets together and you were going to get some remarks, you definitely were going to get some stares. Usually from the haole.

Funny thing about my wife, [it] just sort of rolled off her back and never touched her. She's an unusual person when it comes to that. She was never prejudiced against blacks.

Her father was an unusual man [too]. I had reservations about meeting him, [but] the first time I was introduced to him, he was such an outgoing man and he welcomed me with open arms. They all gathered around and the youngest child just sort of fell in love with me and adopted me, and then her family sort of took me over. These were her immediate sisters and brothers.

Now, my family didn't take to it too well. We visited with them [once]. My mother had all the [family's] wedding pictures and everything around, but she didn't have ours. I don't know what Mama did with our wedding pictures.

We lived on Miller Street. My first child was born there. After he was born, we decided that we should move out from this apartment. Renting houses in those days was a son of a gun. People didn't want to rent to the blacks.

She'd go out and find a place and it would be for rent until I came along, you know. After about two or three times, I knew what was happening. So, I would get on the phone and the first thing I'd say is, "Now, look, I'm of Negro ancestry, and if you have any feelings whatsoever about renting to a Negro, you let me know right now so you don't waste my time, and I don't waste yours, okay."

I did this to a man that I got to know quite well. Edward Caminos. He said, "Wait, I don't care what color you are, as long as you pay my rent." So, we rented from him, just two blocks from Waikīkī.

I was looking for some land for an organization I was with, to build a clubhouse. This must have been in early [19]50s. I saw this ad in the paper and I drove around the island, and I came out here to Lāʻie and saw this beautiful place. And I went back and told the group that I was representing, and they said, "Naw, it's too far."

I decided, hey, I'll take it myself. Number one, it was a beautiful spot; number two, it was to get the heck away from prejudice. I had my own thing so that I wouldn't have to worry about my neighbors or worry about somebody denying me the right to rent.

My brother-in-law, he is a stonemason and a carpenter. He says, "Listen, why don't we build a stone house out here?" So, we come out here every weekend. On a Saturday we'd come out and lay a row of stone and then come back Sunday and lay a row of stone. And finally, we got it to the point where we got one section completed. Equivalent of two bedrooms, and we moved in.

Now, the community was interesting. It's a Mormon community, and at that time, the Mormon church was very anti-black. I don't know whether it still is or not. The Mormon missionaries would come out on the [Lāʻie] Point, and they would go to all of these houses, but they never went to ours. Strange thing.

One of the professors [at the Church College of Hawaiʻi], I've forgotten his name, a very fine fellow. He would come out to my house at times and we'd have friendly conversations. He was telling me that I should join the Mormon church. He said that the Mormon religion, one of the doctrines teaches that all souls at one time were white and that eventually they would all be white again, so therefore, why not come on and join the church.

I told him, "I have no desire to be white." It dawned on me at that time, really a breakthrough. I had never known up until that point that I had (chuckles) no reason to want to be white.

It was a strange community that my children grew up in. My son [Bruce] came home when he was in elementary school. He said, "Dad, what's black vin-ne-gar?" So I sat down and talked with him. I said, "That's not black vin-ne-gar. They're calling you a dirty name. But let's not spend time learning the names, let's get as much education as you can. Because the person who's calling you names, [if] you get all the education, you'll be able to hire this man." And this is what he took back.

I think I sort of fortified my family by this attitude that I have. I have met so many people of varying backgrounds and I've loved people from various backgrounds. Because of that, hate doesn't penetrate me. I suppose we gave a certain amount of dignity to the children, because they started making friends, and most of the children started coming to the house.

Their mother [had] her activities in the community. She was attending Methodist church. She helped build it, she helped work with the PTA [Parent-Teacher Association], she helped in the school, so all of these things sort of established us in the community. [Meanwhile] I was busy at the airport trying to put that big void between poverty and me.

AIRPORT PORTER BUSINESS

[Hampton] Brazell was in San Francisco, and he got on the plane with a cap in his hand and landed in Honolulu and started, overnight, a business that is now sought after by many, many people. Now, here's a black man that started something new in Hawai'i. Brazell started porter services out there. This was the first man who hired me [in 1949]. I became his right-hand man.

And then he lost it [the contract], and the airlines gave it to an ex-policeman named Bill Smith. I became his head man. And [then] he lost it. So, by now, I had gone through being the person who was in charge of everything without the name or compensation. I thought by now, hey, look, I've got it, so why don't I take it?

So, I went to school to study business administration. When I finished, the opportunity presented itself that I could become one of the corporate owners of this [Honolulu Airport Porter Services] because by this time, Bill Smith had lost his contract. So, this was in the late [19]50s and I became vice president and general manager of Honolulu [Airport] Porter Services.

Ernest Golden accepts a certificate of appreciation from Japan Air Lines for outstanding porter services, 1984 (photo courtesy of Ernest Golden).

I would give jobs to blacks because it was kind of difficult for them to get employment elsewhere. At one time, [I] was hiring, I suppose, more blacks than any other business here other than civil service.

BACK TO GEORGIA

I'd always had ideas of going back to Georgia. I'd always tell my wife, if the South ever settles its racial problems, it is going to economically go up, because, I would tell her, everything is there. You've got natural resources, you've got labor forces, you've got good weather, you've got everything, right?

At the time that I left, I retired from Honolulu Airport Porter Services. I left in [19]74. My idea was to start an outdoor recreation place back in Georgia. The small farm I had bought was ten minutes from Downtown Athens. I had a fixed amount of money that I was going to use to put together this project. But the money, by this time, because of inflation, was no longer sufficient to do the job that I wanted to have done. I scrapped the idea and went for another idea. I ran a supper club there for a year and four months.

For a while, I would say, for most of the year, I had created something there that had never been seen in Athens, where the two came together, white and black, and there was never an argument in the whole place. They sat and they'd drink together, and they got to know each other. It was one of the most warmest places you've ever been in.

But the town wasn't ready to support the idea that I had going, and I went broke. I then had to leave and come back [to Hawai'i in 1976] and start all over again.

STARTING OVER

Versatile Services started off as a baggage center. [In 1981] I started a [baggage] pickup and delivery service to and from the airport. Eventually I had to phase out that feature of the business and sort of concentrate on the porter services. And that was the business that I went into, and the one that I'm still in now.

I've reached the point now, where I'm relinquishing more and more of my responsibility to the young team that I have. I'm just about ready to start taking it easy. I would now like to start painting. I've got about thirty years more to go. And those next thirty years, I'd like to be productive in some sort of artistic form.

GLOSSARY

haole   Caucasian

ALICE SAITO GOUVEIA

A BRAVE ONE

*Country stores are different com-
pared to large markets. We know the
people and their lifestyle. Like a [cus-
tomer's] funeral, I was always there,
whether it's a Filipino, or a Hawaiian, or whatever. In sorrow, you're
there, [and it] means a lot. We help
in all ways—worry, cry, and laugh
together.*

Alice Saito Gouveia was born in Kaupakalua, Maui in 1918. The second oldest child, she helped tend the family's pineapple crop and care for her younger
siblings. Her father, an independent pineapple grower in Kaupakalua, died in
a field accident in 1925. At thirteen, Gouveia worked in her uncle's store and
garage in Haʻikū. There she performed kabuki in the garage, which was converted on special occasions to a hall for movies and shows.

She later did housework for several families. After her first marriage in
1937, she worked simultaneously as a school custodian, laundress, and poultry farmer. In 1948 she and her daughter moved to Lower Pāʻia, where Gouveia opened Economy Store. She sold the store to two employees in 1975.
Alice Gouveia died in 2004.

Interviewer Warren Nishimoto recorded Alice Gouveia's life story in 1980
for COH's *Stores and Storekeepers of Pāʻia and Puʻunēnē, Maui,* a study of the
historical role stores played in Hawaiʻi's plantation communities. He remembered her as an articulate, assertive, and well-organized individual whose recollections of her experiences as an independent woman entrepreneur willing
to take risks contributed substantially to the study.

FATHER'S ACCIDENT

[My father] used to work in the sugarcane fields. My mother did the same.
My father got paid seventy-five cents a day for twelve hours, and my mother,

fifty cents a day. Then he decided he better go into pineapple [growing]. He wanted to be on his own. The harder he works, the more money he makes, in other words.

He started to plant [in Kaupakalua]. He got the pineapple growing. Then they hō hana, that means to cut grass [to weed] in the pineapple field. Before the pineapple ripened, he was starting another field. They used dynamite to crack the stones. A different type of dynamite was sold. They say it was an illegal one. That's how he died. His face was all in bad shape, [and] I could see his heart going up and down. It's something that a person, even at the age of seven, cannot forget.

They took the door from the house and carried him home [on it]. There [was] no mortuary those days. My father was laid on the futon on the floor. All the children had to sleep beside him, because we were told, "This is the last night you going to sleep with your father." You know, when you're seven years old, you're sad, but you're scared, too.

FAMILY LIFE

My uncle, my father's younger brother, became our father. He was with the kabuki shows in Honolulu at that time. The family and the friends got together and spoke to him: "Your brother died, and [they] have all that pineapple [to harvest], and [they're] living in a gulch. Aren't you going to worry

Funeral of Alice Gouveia's father, 1925 (photo courtesy of Alice Gouveia).

Saito family, ca. 1925: Alice Gouveia, second child from left (photo courtesy of Alice Gouveia).

about them?" He didn't know what to do. He was in the bedroom two days and two nights to make up his mind. Then he decided.

Well, he feel sorry for us and he have to carry the pineapple business on. I know it was hard for him to pick pineapple and to stand the noisy six of us.

He [father] died April the 14th; the pineapple start coming out in June. So, we were there picking pineapple. The pineapple [plant] was about our height. We'd poke our eyes [on the sharp leaves] and we had something like pink eyes all the time.

[We] really [lived] in a gulch. I don't know why they put a house there. When it rained hard, the water would come from all angles up to our waist. [One time], they [i.e., parents] were in Keāhua. No telephones, so they can't call us at all. The kitchen was all filled with water, but what we had in mind was, "Oh, we mustn't forget the pineapple fertilizer that they have under the house." One bag was about hundred pounds, now. Maybe three or four of us would get it to higher grounds and cover it up. We saved the fertilizer. After struggling—you know, we could have drowned—and still, they say, oh, good girls that we saw to it that the fertilizer (laughs) was saved.

[But] all in all, I think we had so much freedom. You know, away from the neighbors. The Costas lived up on the hill. They were the closest. Maybe one-fourth mile [away]. The Watanabes—that's my uncle and his family— lived on the other side of the gulch. The Watanabes were, I would say, little over a mile. How we got there is, go on the winding road up the hill and keep on walking barefooted.

My grandparents were there, too. She [grandmother] raised a lot of bananas. She had a cave; she kept the [harvested] bananas in there. She was a kind-hearted grandma. She doesn't mind if we go there and pick the ripe bananas and eat it. We were always hungry.

We ate the wild taro that grew on the side of the ditch. We even ate Spanish needle—the young shoots—and even pig grass. So, if you ask me how to survive, I can tell you what kind of grass to eat. (Chuckles.)

We had our own chicken, our duck, so we had our eggs. [But] we had to divide [it]. We cracked that [egg] in a bowl, get a chopstick and mix it up, put some shōyu in. Maybe my sister and I—half for her and half for me. We put it on hot rice, eat it.

We ate aku in all different ways. The first meal was raw fish. The second meal, salted and fried. [It] was [also hung] on the cord from the ceiling down. Today you would call it smoked aku. When it got hard, you can't use a knife to cut it. So, we had to use the [carpenter's] plane. That's where our miso soup seasoning came from. You can put miso in there, water, and the hard aku, which was shaved.

MAUI COUNTY FAIR

When the pineapple was taken to the [Maui Pineapple Company] cannery, minus what we owed [for tools and supplies], we got some money. The first truck I remember they bought was a Federal Scout truck. You pull the cord and make kata kata, kata kata [clattering sounds]. That's the horn.

When we first got our truck, my [step]father wanted to take us to the [Maui County] Fair [in Kahului]. We stopped at Pā'ia Store. We all got a hat, a dress, cotton stocking, and a pair of shoes. We got dressed in Pā'ia Store. From Pā'ia Store we did go straight to the fair. I think he was proud of the truck. You know, the truck and how we were dressed had to go together. (Laughs.)

To think that we were going to the fair, we couldn't sleep all night. It was so exciting for us. My mother would give us just fifty cents. Fifty cents was quite a bit for our days. She would tell us, "Try not to spend all of it. Bring some change back." We took our lunch with us, so we don't need to buy any other food. One bottle of soda at the fair was ten cents—double the [usual] price. That was [about] the only time we had a chance to drink soda. Oh, that ice cream was something that we really craved for. That was ten cents, also. One ride was ten cents. Then, we think about what my mother said and take

Maui County Fair (photo courtesy of Alice Gouveia).

back the twenty cents. Sometimes, it's so tempting that we just have to spend the fifty cents. (Laughs.)

KABUKI IN HAʻIKŪ

After graduating from Kaupakalua School, eighth grade, I was told by my parents that they can't afford to put me through high school. [One of] my uncles, Kohachi Watanabe, and his wife said that they'll put me through school. So, I moved to Haʻikū. That is where I learned to work in [their] store, meet the people. The store was in the middle, on the left was a pool hall, and on the right was the garage. It was called Watanabe General Store and Garage.

When December comes, most people are happy, but I'm not. What happened was, [on] December the 12th, she [aunt] fell out of the truck and hit her neck. They brought her home, but she died right away. Here, my good uncle—I could see—he cried and said, "What am I going to do now? With this four children and that store to run?"

So, I finished the first year [of high school]—at least till June—and [then] I decided to help him in the store, as well as [do] the housework. You know, to think, at the age of thirteen. My cousins keep saying that [despite my] being so young, their house seem to be in pretty good shape.

I had to know about the fuse, all kinds of wires, the tires and the tubes, and car parts. When we fill up gas—the tank was either under the seat or the hood—we check the oil. Most of them [customers] were growers, and we wanted to make sure that their cars are well taken care of.

We had canned goods, mostly like meat, fish, and very little of fruits. Everything was sold like ten cents, fifteen cents. The [fresh] vegetables [sold] were only potatoes and onions. Those days, they used to call it the Irish potatoes—the regular potatoes. Sweet potatoes, they could not sell because everybody raised their own.

Oh, that unbleached muslin was really something. Was ten cents a yard, and they would buy linseed oil and [make] their own raincoat. You keep on putting on [the oil], it'll get so stiff it was waterproof. First, it's yellow, then gradually they get brown. I guess they use it out in the field and don't get wet. Those days, well, they didn't sell no raincoat.

He [uncle] had a stage there. I guess it was a garage first, but he made a stage. In Ha'ikū that was the only one. It was a hall and everything. I would say pretty big, so one, two, three, four, maybe five hundred [people]. But those days, they used to sit on the floor or benches. Because it was a garage, we had to scrub all that oil, so that they could put canvas and sit on the floor.

That place was used for silent movies, which had only the wording [i.e., subtitles]. Japanese shows had that benshi. Then, it was used for politicians, also. Meet the candidates kind of thing. Oh, they even used that place for parties. One time, a wedding (laughs) reception.

Kabuki in Ha'ikū, Maui, ca. 1930s (photo courtesy of Alice Gouveia).

For kabuki shows, how they used to let them know there's a kabuki show was, they dress up, get on the truck in the back. They hit the drum and play the flute or the shamisen and throw leaflets all around Haʻikū.

My mother's uncle, Tomita, he was really good. He can paint the faces, he can put out that kabuki voice, he could use a shamisen and the drums and the stick that goes tak tak tak tak tak. My uncle had three trunks of all kabuki outfits. All the katsura, the wig, plus the fancy skirts and shiny, gold-looking top, and whatnot. Swords, hats, decorations, and all kinds of scenery curtains.

We were in the kabuki show with the katana, that's the sword, [in] that sword dance. When we not sad, it's hard to act and cry. But we were forced to do it. My auntie, all my uncles, and my stepfather used to be in it, too.

It was not set price [for hall rental]. That's how it was with my uncle—whatever they wanted to give him. If small crowd, well, he'll say, "Forget it." He was a well-liked person. In fact, whoever was poor, he helped and paid their debts so that they can have a "clean face." That's what he used to say.

Why I had to leave was, my stepfather lost his job, and I think my sister wasn't working, so I was asked by my mother to go where I could get paid. You see, I stayed with my uncle just for room and board. So, I had to choose between my parents and my uncle. It was really hard. I knew my uncle needed my help because of his four children.

MAID WORK

From there, I did go to Tanizaki Store. It's more like serving saimin and make the noodles by hand, and do the housework for Mrs. Tanizaki. I guess I got lonesome. So I decided to go home. Then Mr. Nashiwa, Dr. Nashiwa's father, came over to ask me if I would work for his son. So I took care of [the son's] two daughters and I did the housework.

[But] I wanted to be more broadminded and go to a bigger place, maybe. There was a friend from Peʻahi that I knew. That's how I got into Hansen's place. He was the field luna. His wife did not work, but she was very, very strict. I think I'm not a good housekeeper now, but at that time, I was. I had to be. Working for people like that, I have learned to be doing things a certain way, save time, and to be neat from corner to corner.

They liked me [so] that when he [Hansen] got a transfer to Kahuku, Oʻahu, I had a chance to go with them. We were in [Waikīkī's] Moana Hotel [at first], which was a treat for me, being a country jack. Did I hear like nine dollars or twelve dollars, around that area, it cost a day? That was big money to us, when you get paid only twelve or fifteen dollars a month. They were in one room, and they gave me a room for myself with a telephone in it and two beds. Boy, I felt like a queen. (Laughs.) I think, those days, there weren't too many Japanese that stayed at Moana Hotel. The usher looked at me as though I did something wrong. So, I told him, "Oh, I came with the Hansens, and I'm their maid." Then, it was okay.

[But] maybe I'm the one-track mind that I like Maui. They [the Hansens] tried all ways and means to keep me there. They even tried to find boyfriends for me. I was, at that time, about nineteen. Maybe I had him [my first husband] in mind, that's why I couldn't stay back in Kahuku.

[I worked at] 'Iao School as a janitor, first [after marrying]. Furthermore, I think I did, while working there, some teachers' laundry. Same time, I had my poultry farm in Wailuku. People used to come and buy eggs. I kept some ducks, too. All the garbage from the school, I carried it home and I [fed] the ducks.

ECONOMY STORE

I left it [the farm]. I took my daughter with me, and I left. So, I had to think, "What am I going to do next?" I think to survive was my main concern.

I thought, well, if I had a store, at least I can eat. I knew the food I have in there would keep me and my daughter alive. Another thing was, then, I would be with my daughter most of the time. I didn't want her on the streets or in someone else's home. This way, she can come home [from school] and sort of give me a hand. And somehow, I wanted to be my own boss for a change, because I went through working from maid to janitor to everything, [and] someone was always above me. I wanted to be independent.

I started my store in February of 1948. That was after the war. I gave free soda and free balloons [on] opening day. I was told when I opened the store that, "Oh, this woman, poor thing. In three months, she'll get out of business or go bankrupt."

So I said, "It better not be that way. I just have to work harder and keep it up."

Economy Store—I think it's a good name with a lot of meaning. The word "economy" means to save. Through my hardship, it meant so much to me—to economize on your food, on your clothing, or whatever. Now, I was wondering whether I should [call] it Economy Market, but I felt that if I used the name "store," I could sell nearly everything.

I knew, more or less, the staple items that people need. Nothing fancy, because I thought the customers would be the ones working for the plantation, or Japanese. I bought from Pā'ia Store because it was close by. They were wholesaling and retailing, both. Mr. Morikawa came to take the order. So, the first thing I told him is, "I need rice." (Laughs.) Then, the salt and sugar.

Economy Store, 1972 (photo courtesy of Alice Gouveia).

I had a vegetable stand there in front. I had some green onions, head cabbage, Chinese cabbage, carrots, potatoes, and onions. Maybe a few items like that. Monday was my vegetable day—Monday and Thursday. I left home at 4:30 in the morning because the [vegetable] market will open at 5:00. I wanted to be there when it opens, so that I could get the best of vegetables, not the leftovers.

In the afternoon, Monday and Thursday, was my delivery day. Lot of them [customers] did not have cars, so I did the delivery. Whoever have a phone, calls in. Those that don't have [a phone], they give me their [grocery] order one week or few days in advance. Some had [homegrown] vegetables that I could [buy and] pick up. So, I pick up their vegetables and take [them] their groceries at the same time.

Today, I think, more people buy with cash because big markets are all cash-and-carry basis. But before, they thought the only way to buy is charge. I might get a call from my wholesaler saying that, "When are you going to pay your bill?" And yet, I'm trying really hard to get [paid by] my charge customers. But they say, "Oh, somebody got sick," or "Wait five more days," and that five days don't seem to come. There were times that I was so desperate that I felt, "Why do I have to live like this?" So I decided, well, [although] I might lose some [customers], go cash-and-carry. It's better to sell it cheaper, get the cash, [and] don't charge.

At that time, I made it on my own. I wasn't [yet] married to my [second] husband. If I don't sell so much a day, it worried me. Oh, those days, the food was so cheap. So, if I sold fifty dollars [worth] a day, I was happy, and maybe twenty five dollars on a Sunday.

Then the [next-door] carpenter shop gave up, so [I] took off the partition and made [my] store bigger. I decided, I have a bigger place, okay, I'm going to sell fish. Some fishermen that goes out and get fish, I used to buy from them. Then, they would buy my groceries in exchange for the fish.

I made sure that I don't waste the fish. Whatever could not be sold [whole], I cut it up and made Hawaiian style—dry it up. Another way was the Japanese style with goma, shōyu, and sugar. [Then] whatever could go into bagoong, went that way. The Filipinos told me I made the best bagoong. (Laughs.)

I had all nationalities in the store. I did get a lot of Filipino and Hawaiian trade. Then I got married to my [second husband], Alfred Gouveia, [and] I started to get the Portuguese trade. The Japanese stuck to the Japanese stores. But, later on, they all came my way.

This is what the Filipinos say: "I go another store. The haole come. They make [i.e., serve] that one first. Me, Filipino, us the last. But you, Alice, you treat everybody all same. Even white or black." How I felt was, everybody's money is the same, and if they worked harder for it, it meant more. If they [Caucasian customers] come [in] last, they supposed to wait in line.

Country stores are different compared to large markets. We know the people and their lifestyle. Like a [customer's] funeral, I was always there,

Alice Gouveia in Economy Store, 1970 (photo courtesy of Alice Gouveia).

whether it's a Filipino, or a Hawaiian, or whatever. In sorrow, you're there, [and it] means a lot. We help in all ways—worry, cry, and laugh together.

The [store's] peak was between 1963 and 1965. One morning the front windows of the store was covered with grasshoppers, so green that you couldn't look in or out. That day, I sold almost $3,000 worth [of goods]. The old Japanese believe my ancestors dropped by and gave me good luck.

Of course, I gave up in 1975. I got tired of picking up things, worrying, working on my books, and I thought twenty-seven years is good enough. My sons didn't want no business for the reason that I used them on Sundays and holidays to give my employees a day off. So [two employees] took over and relieved me of all my (chuckles) hardship.

When things were slowing down, I bought this [house]. I decided to go into something else than only the store. What I wanted most of life was one house of my own that no one could tell me, "Oh, you have to move out because I sold it," or "My relatives going to move in." [People] say, "Alice, you wanted one home. Now you have eight." (Laughs.) So, now what I do is take care our rental homes. I'm the landlady.

As I think back [on] all the things we did to survive, I'm not bitter at all. Maybe it's through struggling, I do think you get to a point where [you] have to make the best of things, whichever way it is. I'm glad that I did. But I was a brave one, I think. (Chuckles.) That's what people keep telling me.

GLOSSARY

aku	bonito
bagoong	fermented fish
benshi	narrator
futon	bedding
goma	sesame seed
haole	Caucasian
hō hana	weeding
kabuki	traditional, stylized Japanese popular drama
katana	sword
katsura	wig
luna	overseer
miso	fermented soybean paste
saimin	soup made with thin noodles
shamisen	Japanese stringed instrument
shōyu	soy sauce

VENICIA DAMASCO GUIALA

FROM CLASSROOM TO PINEAPPLE FIELD

Especially those who don't have any job, they come from foreign places, pineapple is the best because they don't screen you too much. So long you know how to pick pine, you understand the luna, what he tells you. They look at you, they put you in the gang, category, where you can do the job.

Venicia Damasco Guiala, born in 1913, was the eldest daughter of a farming family. She received her teaching degree from St. William College in Laoag, Ilocos Norte, Philippines; and, between 1938 and 1949, taught English, Tagalog, and home economics in rural schools.

In 1947 she married Ruperto Guiala, a pineapple field worker who had returned to the Philippines from Hawai'i. He decided to go back to Hawai'i, and in 1949, she left the teaching profession to join her husband on Lāna'i.

They moved to O'ahu when he was transferred to Dole Corporation's Wahiawā plantation in 1952. Four years later, Venicia Guiala began work in the pineapple fields as a seasonal employee. During the 1968 pineapple strike, she became president of the Dole Whitmore International Longshoremen's and Warehousemen's Union Women's Auxiliary, an organization of women field workers which aided strikers.

Retired in 1976, she lived in Whitmore with her husband. They raised two sons, both university graduates. Venicia Guiala died in 1989.

Warren Nishimoto interviewed Venicia Guiala in 1979 at her Whitmore Village home for COH's *Women Workers in Hawai'i's Pineapple Industry* (1979). This oral history project examined the roles of long-term women workers in pineapple fields and canneries, and the effects this work had on their lives. Begun on a commercial scale in 1903, the industry historically had been one of the largest employers of women in Hawai'i, primarily because of the fruit's summertime ripening cycle. During the summer months, students and homemakers often found temporary employment in the fields as weeders, cultivators, and pickers, and in canneries as trimmers, packers, and warehouse workers. Some women, like Guiala, were year-round employees.

TEACHING THE BARRIO CHILDREN

I was born in Batac, Ilocos Norte, Philippines, in 1913. [My parents] were farmers. We get plenty lands. Rice, corn, garlic, onions, tobacco, tomatoes, any kind of vegetable.

I wanted to be a nurse, but I could not pass the qualification physical. Because I'm short. It must be that the one who is good for nursing should be at least five feet tall. I am below five feet.

I [also] wanted to be a lawyer. Because you know I love to talk, eh? I like to argue. We don't have any brother, so I wanted to take that course so that in case we get some problems on the land, I can defend. But we didn't have enough means.

I took teaching so I could help my younger sisters go to school. My father persuaded me to go to the vocational school of teaching. I graduated there and then after that, I taught [for] ten years before I came to Hawai'i.

[At] one time the Philippines was under the Americans. We were not yet independent that time, so we taught the English language. Mostly I taught the lower grades. You know, the beginners. When the district get a meeting, they found out that my pupils were number one in the district. They can read. They can write. Because I get a certain method of doing it. I use the alphabet. For example, "A" like in "apple." The sound of "A" is *A*. I demonstrate how to write, too. As I teach the alphabet, they know how to write it, and they know how to say it.

You know the parents there in the rural area, they come home late [and] they are tired. They don't have time to teach their children about God. They cannot go to town to hear Mass. They are far. So, I always make a point that when we have this recess time [and] they are willing to stay back for ten or five minutes, I teach them how to pray, to know God. And the parents were, oh, so happy about their children, because they practice that. So, that's how I got cooperation of the barrio folks.

Barrio means "villages"—small villages. They were kind of poor. They had to bring their lunch. I have to eat with them, trade my food with the food they bring. And the people like me very much.

In fact, when I am transferred to another place, they cry. They go to the district supervisor, even to the superintendent, to hold me back in that place.

Because I organize the PTA [Parent-Teacher Association]. That's how I called the parents. I talk to them about the progress of their children, and they reported it to me, too.

I wrote articles in the *Bannawag.* That is the Filipino magazine. I wrote a poem. And then when he [my future husband] read the *Bannawag,* he saw that the writer is from Batac. Because he is from Batac, too. He tried to contact me [from Hawai'i]. Then I answered him. Well, after some exchange of letters, there was love between the lines. (Laughs.)

He came to Hawai'i in 1927. He worked in a sugar [plantation]. And then in 1939, he moved to Lāna'i to live. He started in pineapple. And he came back [to the Philippines] March, 1947. By the time, my sisters, they were about through [school]. The only thing that hold me to get married was them. They told us, "You go ahead." Nineteen forty seven, we get married.

He had been a farmer before. He invested income in the land again. Plus, he fix the house. But when the storm comes, the products are all damaged, so he said, "No more prospect. Better to come back to Hawai'i." So he came back Thanksgiving of 1947. He promised that he will call me to Hawai'i.

Nineteen forty nine, I came here [to Lāna'i]. So I have to quit the teaching job. I asked for a leave of absence, and they granted it for two years. But after two years, I did not like to go back. I wanted to raise my child here. Plus my husband is still here. I want to stay here, too.

The community was divided into blocks, with about 150 people in each block. All mixed up, even Hawaiians. But the haoles, you know, the boss, they get big houses and they get fireplaces. Way in the heights. But us in the camp [workers' housing], we don't have that.

My house was a two-bedroom house. My husband furnished it before I came. He was living with a friend. Single man, too. But when we get one child already, the man move out.

My husband built a small shed there. I carried the hot water there and then take a bath. I did not go bathe in the public place [community bathhouse]. Get big one. But I did not like.

We had the community toilet there in the next block. But after one year I arrived there, they put on toilet in the home. And we get running water.

You know how much [rent] we pay for the two-bedroom house? Twenty-two dollars, including light and water. A month. But after one year I stay there, they put it up, because they put the toilet. It came to $27.50.

At first, I did not know what to do because I [was] used to going out and teach. I am left alone when they go to work. Of course, I get neighbors, but they are not of my capacity.

I adjusted. "If people live here, I can live too," I said.

I thought you don't have to work hard. I mean, just the money to come in. But I found out. He was a carpenter. When I came, [his pay is] only $1.33 an hour. Oh, he show me his paycheck—deductions, so forth and so forth. (Laughs.) Only little bit money left.

[But] we don't spend too much because we raise our vegetable. I raise chicken behind the house. So for food, we get the eggs and the chicken.

The Lāna'i people did not like to go to work unless they [the company] give them their demands [in 1951]. It was a long strike [of seven months]. He [my husband] picket, I think, around two months only. He came to Honolulu. Construction job. Because he said, "I got a family. I don't have any income, so I have to go to work." Twenty percent, I think, from his pay, he give it to the union. But still, I prefer to let him work than to stay there with the striking workers. When the strike is over, I called him. So, he came back.

He get low seniority in Lāna'i. So those who get low seniority, they transfer to Wahiawā [in 1952]. Because they need the men to work. We were eighty families who were transferred to Whitmore [Dole Company plantation village near Wahiawā]. Some of them quit. Some of them went overseas. So we were only few who came here.

It's a bigger place and greater opportunity to find a job. Maybe for me and for the children when they grown up. Lāna'i is only a small town. I want to come to a bigger place. That's why when they told us to come to Wahiawā, we quickly packed our things.

In 1953 they [the company] offered to sell [us] the houses we were in, so we put the down payment and we have to pay monthly. The original cost was $4,780. That was fifteen cents a square foot. (Chuckles.) When we bought the house, we paid $34.50 [a month]. Plus the lights and the water, we pay.

My husband only get that much. Maybe we survive with his own pay, but I like to have a little bit saving for the future of the children, too. Because we like them go to school.

My lady friends were all working. And I see that they can buy anything they like. I can buy what I like with my husband's pay, but I think better if I earn the money I spend.

And I have to send money to my parents, too. To those who need the help in the Philippines [like] my sister and my husband's nephew. If they write, even if they don't ask, if I see that they need the help, I have to send them.

I just went to apply at the Dole office. You have to fill up the form, eh? When they asked me what grade [I completed], I put only seventh grade. I was ashamed to tell the correct one. Because the work I am applying is only farmer job. So they might not take me if I told the truth. I don't know, I was ashamed. Because I see these people [with a college education] that are having nice job. While me, I'm only in the pineapple field. (Laughs.)

Sometimes I get up at 3:30, early in the morning, in order to prepare the lunch, the children to go to school, to bring them to the babysitter, to feed the pets. Sometimes, I wash the clothes early in the morning, hang them.

The truck departed at 6:45 a.m. every day. [I leave home] sometimes forty-five minutes before the truck departs, or sometimes half an hour. Because you have time to put on your clothes and everything. And if you forget something, you get time to go back. Like for example, you forget your hat or your goggles. You cannot work without the goggles.

You have to cover your head with handkerchief, and one [other] handkerchief covering your face. Because the dust. You will cough. No good for [you], the chemicals that they put on the plant.

You had to wear denim cloth [clothing]. First you have your [inner] pants. Then you have the cover pants. You don't like to be poke [by the sharp pineapple leaves]. And then, when it rains, or early in the morning [when] the pineapple leaves are wet, you have to [wear] the rubber pants. I don't like my feet to be wet so I have to use boots.

Even here [i.e., wrist to shoulder], it's all protected. You have to put another armband. You got to sew [i.e., cut and sew from] the old pants. And we wear our own gloves. I used the rubber glove in the morning when there was dew and the plants were wet. Later in the day, I changed to the vinyl glove because it got too hot with the rubber glove.

Venicia Guiala, fourth from right, and gang of pineapple pickers, 1957 (photo courtesy of Venicia Guiala).

Venicia Guiala, center, and coworkers at lunch in a pineapple field, ca. 1960 (photo courtesy of Venicia Guiala).

That's why, when I went to the Philippines [for a visit], they said they didn't believe I work because I was not black [i.e., dark-skinned from sun exposure].

[We did] weeding, picking pineapple, removing of the slips [cuttings used for planting].

[Weeding,] that's easy. You have to see that even the small one [weed], you have to pick out. They have to check also if you really pick up the weeds. There are some who just make the grass fall and the roots would still be there.

At first [picking] was hard. You first pick the pineapple, grab the neck of the pineapple, twist [off] the top [crown], and then put it in the conveyor boom [the arm of the picking machine]. Then it goes up to the truck and then [into] the picking machine [bin].

My friends were good enough to help me. Because the ladies who had been working ahead of me, they are smart. So, I have to stay between them. If I cannot go it fast, one on that side grab, one on this side grab. Sometimes I no more and then I say, "Ho, let me some so that I can practice." But they pity me because I was short [and] the boom was high. But afterwards, I catch up.

We [sometimes] go to contracting [piecework], too. If the luna does not tell you how much your percentage [pay above 100 percent of regular day work], I could ask. I could figure out and I could tell them [coworkers]. But if the field does not have too much pine, they have to make the [picking machine] driver go faster. You can run so that you can cover more acre. The acre and the density of the pineapple goes together when you go contract. And the quality of the fruit you pick. Your load must not be bruised. If the pineapples are small and you get plenty load, there's no better work. Oh, you make money with that.

Removing of the slips for plant again, I like that job. Because I am small. I don't need to bend too much. I was fast in removing. But those who are big, they hate. Because they get sore back. The pineapple is low, they have to bend.

I got my laundry [business], too, that time. I work in the field, I still get six [men's] laundry. I have to wash for the single men. They pay me ten dollars a month. My children, before, they were trained. They could deliver the clean one, and they go take [pick up] the dirty ones Friday afternoon.

My bursitis was operated in 1967, May. That was Mother's Day. So, when I was recuperating from this, I went there [to the experiment station]. When I was transferred to the experiment station, we had to reclassify the pineapple because we had new types. And then we have to deal with this insecticides. And this different kind of chemicals, like fertilizer. To increase [the pineapple yield]. To make it sweet. We make sure the amount for them to use when they have to go spray in the plantation. When the work slacks again in that experiment [station], they close it. I went to the fresh fruit again.

[In the 61-day strike in 1968], the men needed the help from the women. So they suggested that the women should have a group also for the picket line. The chairman of the union wanted us to have a meeting to elect one [president] so that we have this women's group. I accepted the job because there is no other way. Somebody told the chairman that previously, I was the president of an organization, the Filipino Women's Club. And that was a successful club. If I talk, everybody come out.

We have to divide the groups into seven groups because there are seven days in a week. We go to the picket line, we serve juice. We have to go and report to the headquarters to clean the building.

When we get soup kitchen, we have to go there and peel some potatoes, clean the vegetables that they cook. The old ladies, we did not like them to go to work. That's too much for them. But they could sew the apron [made of rice bags] of those who work in the kitchen.

[The union] helped the members have a better working condition, better benefits for medical and dental, and the pension that they receive when they get out of the company. It's enjoyable [work] and the pay is good, the benefit is good, the medical.

Venicia Guiala, 1983.

Especially those who don't have any job, they come from foreign places, pineapple is the best because they don't screen you too much. So long you know how to pick pine, you understand the luna, what he tells you. They look at you, they put you in the gang, category, where you can do the job.

"Oh," [some] said, "the pineapple work is hard." [But] I tell those who just come from the Philippines, "Look at me. I'm small. How come I work so long? It's nice, if you know how."

GLOSSARY

barrio	small village
haole	Caucasian
luna	overseer

ROBERT KIYOSHI HASEGAWA

UNITY OF THE FAMILY

I found out that there were four others in Lāna'i who were interned. And I couldn't understand what damage people on Lāna'i —no matter their influence, whose lives were in Lāna'i, whose children were on Lāna'i—what kind of activities, subversive activities, these people can commit in the war that'll harm the United States.

James Shunzo Hasegawa immigrated to Hawai'i in 1918 to attend Hilo Boarding School. He returned to Japan to marry Fujie Yamamoto. They were parents of five surviving children, including the eldest, Robert Kiyoshi Hasegawa, who was born in Hilo, Hawai'i in 1923.

The Hasegawas lived on Hawai'i Island and Maui before relocating to Lāna'i, where James Shunzo Hasegawa worked for the Hawaiian Pineapple Company [later Dole Corporation] plantation. He was active in the Japanese-language school, Buddhist temple, and Japanese community organizations.

Six months after the start of World War II, James Shunzo Hasegawa was taken into custody by military authorities and later incarcerated as an enemy alien. He was one of approximately 1,400 Hawai'i residents of Japanese ancestry to be sent to camps in Hawai'i and the U.S. Mainland for the duration of the war. Robert Hasegawa, who had begun his freshman year at the University of Hawai'i, returned home. Told to leave Lāna'i, he moved his mother and siblings to Maui and supported them by working as an electrician.

Robert Hasegawa was drafted into the U.S. Army in October 1944. In uniform, in late 1945, he met his father at the Honolulu pier following his father's release.

After the war, Robert Hasegawa began his long career in labor. He was business agent for the International Brotherhood of Electrical Workers, executive secretary of the Honolulu Metal Trades Council and Central Labor Council of Hawai'i, director of the Hawai'i State Committee on Political

Education (AFL-CIO), deputy director and later director of the Hawai'i State Department of Labor and Industrial Relations, and director of the Center for Labor Education and Research, then at the University of Hawai'i at Mānoa. He died in 2008.

COH's Michi Kodama-Nishimoto interviewed Robert Hasegawa in February 1998. This narrative, taken from the interview transcripts, focuses on the Hasegawa family's experiences prior to and during the war.

FAMILY HISTORY

I don't remember or recall any discussion we had about what Grandfather did or what Grandmother did, what my uncles or aunts—if I had any, and I do have both—were doing. We never had a real good family history, their history. So that our genealogy just begins with my father, my mother, and us.

My father came to Hawai'i from Japan in 1918 to attend school when he was fourteen years old. He attended and graduated from Hilo Boarding School in Hilo, Hawai'i. Other than learning English, he also learned how to play the 'ukulele, according to a Samoan classmate of his who I met in Hilo some decades later.

He went back to Japan in late 1921 or early 1922 to get married, then immediately returned to Hawai'i with his bride.

My mother's name is Fujie Yamamoto, and she is from Hiroshima, Japan. I'm pretty sure she had a fairly good education, probably as good as if not better than my father, inasmuch as part of the work she did when she came to Hawai'i and when the family moved to Maui, was teaching Japanese language at the Japanese-language school in Keāhua, Maui.

James Shunzo Hasegawa and Fujie Hasegawa with Robert Kiyoshi Hasegawa on her lap, Hilo, Hawai'i, ca. 1924 (photo courtesy of Robert Hasegawa).

She was nineteen when she had me. I was born in Hilo, Hawai'i in 1923. I am the eldest, firstborn. Then came a brother, then a sister, and a brother, and three sisters. Two of my sisters died in infancy, within months of birth.

I don't know much of whatever work he [father] was doing, except that he was in some kind of [tobacco] sales work. I think he was selling Lucky Strikes at that time. The fact is that I learned more about the nature and kinds of work my father was doing at that time from records relating to his internment by the government of the United States.

We relocated to Maui where my first brother was born. And it wasn't too long after that, maybe about eighteen months later, that my father accepted a job at Hawaiian Pineapple Company of Lāna'i. And that's where we moved to.

I recall being in a house [like that of] everybody else with outdoor toilets. Then as my father's work progressed and he got promoted, we got into a larger house where some of us had our own room. I know I had one. And during the days of Prohibition my father used to make his own wines in my room, in the closet. And so my clothes all smelled of pineapple or figs.

All the families had individual garden plots, a site set aside for garden plots. We used to raise all kinds of vegetables, exchange [with neighbors]. We had chickens, we had rabbits. We did all of the things one might do in a plantation community: share what we had.

Fujie Hasegawa with Dorothy, Margaret, Teruo, Charles, Robert, and James Shunzo Hasegawa, Lāna'i, ca. 1930 (photo courtesy of Robert Hasegawa).

I suppose he did a variety of work including work in the fields. And probably as well, did some clerical work, inasmuch as he spoke English and understood all of this, and the plantation management used him as a communication medium primarily to the Japanese community. Many of the plantation people used to consult him.

Over time he became what I would call a camp boss [overseer], whatever that really means. He was a person of some influence and was given some responsibility over a section of the camp. Japanese Camp, Portuguese Camp, Korean Camp, Filipino Camp, that's how we were organized.

The plantations try to keep these people separate so that they wouldn't be conspiring. The kids fooled them. We kids started to mix together; played together, sometimes against each other; we ate each other's ethnic foods. That's in part how the ILWU [International Longshoremen's and Warehousemen's Union] came into being in Lāna'i—but that's getting way ahead of the story.

It's strange, but those people who were engaged in the kind of work to whom people will generally go [were influential]. You need a haircut, you'll go to the barber. You need to purchase your things, there's only one Japanese store and one Chinese store. Go to church, so the temple priest. Other than that, I recall just simply two other Japanese families who were of influence,

Dorothy, Fujie, and Margaret Hasegawa, taken on a trip to Japan, ca. 1933 (photo courtesy of Robert Hasegawa).

somewhat in the same status as my dad. One was a person who was a real good stone carver. The other was a fellow who was almost alternating [positions in community organizations] with my father.

It was the [Buddhist] church that began organizing or encouraging the formation of many groups, subgroups, or groups like fujinkai or wrestling [club]. All kinds of clubs for the ladies, for the men, for the kids, somewhat similar to the YBA's [Young Buddhist Association of Hawai'i] getting involved in young children up to even old guys as either managers, coaches, or big brothers, big sisters, that type.

Although I know that he was asked to head several of these organizations, he wasn't able to provide all the time necessary in order to get through all these things. But he was active in the formation and in, I suppose, the philosophical thrust of the organization, the projects that were undertaken.

He was involved in the organization of the Japanese-language school on Lāna'i. I'm sure they must have had considerable turmoil there because sometime during that period, in the [19]30s, and even into the late [19]30s, there was change in teaching Japanese. For example we'd go to Japanese school and the principal would say, "Okay, attention," and there's the emperor's picture and everybody would bow. It was more like indoctrination to the Japanese culture than it was in teaching the Japanese language. Later it changed. Everybody [i.e., every classroom] had President [Franklin] Roosevelt's picture.

But the cement that held the community together is not necessarily Japanese school or the Buddhist temple. But rather, they were adjuncts [to them], which, in my opinion, was the tanomoshi because that's the only thing that assured the ability to survive to meet emergencies within the plantation community.

Almost everybody was in a tanomoshi group. And we always knew that there was going to be a large activity of some kind in some person's family by reason of that person bidding for the tanomoshi that month or whatever it was. For example, a medical bill, or some person going to school, or something like that, or getting married. I remember once, twice I think, when my dad got the tanomoshi we had a party for everybody.

In fact, the survival of the old-time plantation people like my parents was in that tanomoshi because they couldn't get money otherwise. Nobody ran away with the money; you can't run away from Lāna'i, anyway. There's no place you're gonna go. Everybody honored their commitment.

We all worked in the pineapple plantation. I recall I was a child laborer working for three cents an hour on a ten-hour workday in the summers. And it was physical labor. What we might call hō hana in the pineapple fields, [or] trimming the planting [material] before we planted them. I did do what we called loading work and harvesting—harvesting the pineapple, put them in boxes and loading it on trucks.

The thought never occurred to me that, "Look, you won't be in the plantation labor all your life."

LIMITLESS "FUTURE"

In any case, I took the [college-]entrance examination and I passed. My parents encouraged me, "Take it at least. Find out!" So the commitment my parents made, that if I pass, I'm going.

And then this is why my father made the arrangements for me to stay with a family of one of the Hawaiian Pineapple Company's personnel in Honolulu while I would work during the summer to earn enough money to pay some of the costs of my college.

And my summer earnings were more than sufficient to carry me through the first semester, which was cut short by the war. So the initial thought of expenses or how expensive it might be and what kind of sacrifices my parents would have to make to ensure my continuation in college, that was, in fact, rendered moot by the war.

I recall in my high school class of approximately twenty-two who graduated, less than half took the college-entrance examinations. And I thought there were about seven of us who were accepted, who passed the examinations, and came to Honolulu to attend University of Hawai'i.

I tell you, it was a total cultural shock for me. When I came to Honolulu, my father brought me over within a week after I graduated from high school, on board the SS *Humu'ula,* which was a cattle boat. We rode overnight and got into Honolulu Harbor and I saw Aloha Tower and I thought, "Well, I'm in Honolulu now."

On the way, I looked at all the tall buildings, you know, on King and Fort Streets. It was a shock simply because I've never seen buildings this tall. And so we went to the Martins' home where I would be living during the summer.

They treated me like a part of the family. They woke me up to be sure that I can go to work. I worked the night shift, oh about eight to ten hours. So I just walked from 16th Avenue, from about 16th and Maunaloa, all the way down to Wai'alae Avenue and get the streetcar and get down to Hawaiian Pine[apple] Cannery's lot. Then when I got through working, I caught the streetcar and came home.

I was, at that time, doing repair work, or building pineapple boxes, loading boxes. The boxes were made in such a way that you could lay a dozen pineapples, at least, in the crate. And they [the crates] used to get wrecked all the time.

During our mealtimes, we used to talk about what the university is like. Especially those of us who were going there as prospective students, discussing things with the guys who were already there, past their freshman year and going into the sophomore year. And some of those folks, their stories were pretty intimidating. You know, "If you don't do well, you're going to get a 'cinch notice.'" And we said, "What the hell is a 'cinch notice?'" "Well, it's a notice that tells you you'd better improve or else." "Or else what?" "Or else you either repeat or you're going to get out."

In going to the university, I had left the Martins and I went to live with the Aults, Kenneth and Mrs. Ault, at Ferdinand Avenue [in Mānoa]. So it was close for me, just walking down to the university from their residence. And I was doing yardwork and whatever household chores that had to be done.

I wanted to be a physician. That was one of the goals, an impractical goal because there was no way I was going to make it because we didn't have that kind of money to do that. Alternatively I thought of becoming a lawyer. Of course, that was impractical, too. So I had harbored those two notions. That's why I pursued the courses that I took at the university, all designed to get me into premedical school.

I had many of the science courses, algebra, zoology. I remember two instructors of mine, one was Shigeo Okubo. My zoology instructor was—I forget his first name, but the last name will never escape me, it's [Jens] Ostergaard. He was a Dutch person, very interesting person. And very inspiring teacher.

Those two I remember very distinctly. Shigeo Okubo for the fact that the first six weeks, he gave me a cinch notice. He says, "You don't seem to understand algebra, the concepts. And yet you're applying these very concepts in your chemistry class where you're scoring about ninety-nine out of a hundred, all the time. But in my class, you can't even understand $a^2 + b^2 = c^2$." And then I said, "Yeah, but if you tell me how many oranges and how many apples, I can figure it out."

Chemistry was really my meat, I really loved it. It was real great to do many of the basic experiments just to understand what the chemical reactions are going to be so later on you can apply all of these principles to do any research that you wanted to do. We just had basic test tubes and Bunsen burners in high school, but come over here and you find everything else. All instrumentation. It was just almost like being in a toy shop.

So it was really mind expanding, the limitless, quote, "future."

THERE WAS MISTRUST

I don't remember very much of where I was on that day [December 7, 1941]. All I know is that I received a call, as did all of the ROTC folks. We were directed to the university armory and by Monday, we were all fixing our rifles, our Springfields, and putting firing pins in there and issued ammunition and all that.

Well, the issuance of all of this stuff happened after the [Hawai'i] Territorial Guard was mobilized. And we were part of it, at least I was part of it. It was in a couple weeks or so, I think, I got into the PFC [Private First Class] promotion. I had a pay voucher anyway, that says that I was promoted to PFC.

Basically, we were to guard the coast, so many of us initially went by the Honolulu Harbor area. Some of us were assigned different beach areas. Later on, I was assigned to the unit that enforced the blackout in town, Downtown. I was based in Sand Island. And it was a time that many American military were just flowing in.

And then there was a lot of concerns that we were armed expressed by people in Merchant Street, the business, the haole community. Within, I think it was a couple months, we were disbanded because we were Japanese. That was really the basis, as far as I'm concerned, on which we were disbanded. That there was mistrust.

I thought, well, if that's the reason, okay, so be it. There's nothing that I can do about it that I can change.

I don't have any grandparents, at least as far as I'm concerned. I don't have them, I didn't know them, didn't need them, didn't talk to them, didn't write to them. They didn't write to me. We were the family unit here. As far as I was concerned, we're all Americans.

After the war broke out, I was conscious, quite conscious, of the fact that I was a dual citizen. I had assumed that I was a dual citizen, that my father had registered me [at the Japanese consulate]. And there was some, I would say, considerable discussion in the press and among the radio personalities about dual citizenship. I think the thought that was conveyed to me by listening to this was that as long as one is a dual citizen, one cannot be a full American.

And so I went to the Swedish consulate because they were the consulate doing business with the Japanese people [during the war]. And I met Shimeji [Ryusaki], who is now Shimeji Kanazawa. And she was the person through whom I did all of my inquiries. I took what was then the family's koseki tōhon that I had from Mother and told her what the nature of my business was, that I wanted to expatriate. And so she looked at this, she says, "According to this, you have already been expatriated."

And so she, oh about couple days later, sent to me the translation of that koseki tōhon, in which I determined then, that I was expatriated from dual citizenship, from Japanese citizenship, back in 1936. And so I was quite surprised about that. That my father had asked his father, according to the document, to initiate the termination of my Japanese citizenship. I was the only one in the family whose birth had been registered at the [Japanese] consulate here. And my father didn't tell me anything about this.

Soon after the war started in December, by the end of '41, I was out of the Aults' and I was living at this dormitory run by the Hongwanji temple at Mō'ili'ili, right on Isenberg and Young [Streets]. Because university closed down and there was no longer any need for me to be with the Aults. And Mrs. Ault was going to be home. Both Mr. and Mrs. Ault were among the kindest and friendliest people I met to date.

I got a job with the American Can Company. We were making cans for Dole, for Hawaiian Pine[apple] Company. Factory was adjoining the Dole plant and I was first one of those mechanics making sure the can machines were operating properly. And I got advanced to inspector's position where I used to grab a few cans as they were running off 600 cans per minute and checked them.

So it was shortly after that, perhaps about six months after I started to work in American Can, that I had a call from the Red Cross, advising me that my father was interned, and that he would be in Sand Island, and that it was urgent that I get back home.

ALREADY GONE

That was in June, late June of 1942. I went to American Can, told them I have to return to Lāna'i because of what occurred and the information from the Red Cross. Went to the dormitory and told Ed Yoshimasu, who was the dormitory head at that time, that I have to vacate. I don't know when I'm going to be back if I'm going to be back at all. And then made arrangements to get back to Lāna'i.

I recall no contact with the family [prior to the Red Cross call]. You couldn't make a telephone call, for example. You know, everything had to be by letter or wire. At that time, I didn't know where my dad was. I pretty much assumed that he was still on Lāna'i. So it was a shock when I went back to Lāna'i to find that he was already gone. And then we found out that he was in Sand Island. But prior to that, he was on Maui someplace.

I suppose like anything else, there is some kind of a formal hearing convened so that there is a record of what happened and why people were interned and perhaps why they were not. In my dad's case, there was a hearing convened in which he was questioned on when he was born, when he came to the territory, and all that.

Now at the hearing also, there was a discussion of my dad's employment situation and community relations with the manager of the Hawaiian

Pineapple Company on Lāna'i, a Dexter Fraser. We all called him "Blue" Fraser primarily because he has blue eyes. In any case, he testified; he was questioned.

He described my dad as someone quite influential in the community. He also indicated that the first and only time that the consul general, the consul of Japan, visited the island of Lāna'i, that my dad took him around to visit various people in the community. Dexter Fraser made much to-do about the fact that my dad was involved in the Japanese societies in the community. That when there was a dispute in the temple versus the organizations, my father used to be in the center of the action to bring about some resolution. He made much ado about the fact that my father's children were going to Japanese school. And that my father's influence in the Japanese school was considerable.

The ultimate shot that Dexter Fraser took was in response to the question, "With what you know about Hasegawa, would you take him?" Meaning "Would you intern him?" And of course, his comment was, "Absolutely."

As I review the documents, I cannot escape the fact that Fraser's primary concern was that all of my dad's kids, all of us, were going to Japanese school and that we were being indoctrinated in Japanese and not American systems. That plus the influence my father had over the—within the Japanese community, not over it—was great enough that with his knowledge and his leadership, he could be very, very destructive should he choose to do so.

Now this testimony, I got years after my father's return and my discharge from the army. And it was astonishing to me that out of this flimsy background, that the United States government would intern my father. And I found out that there were four others in Lāna'i who were interned. And I couldn't understand what damage people on Lāna'i—no matter their influence, whose lives were in Lāna'i, whose children were on Lāna'i—what kind of activities, subversive activities, these people can commit in the war that'll harm the United States. You have to remember that the island was totally owned by the plantation. That all of its citizens, in fact, were economic entities, economic entities belonging to the plantation.

I found out much later that, for example, in my wife's background, she's also from a pineapple [plantation], from Kaua'i. The manager of that plantation took affirmative action to prevent the internment of several people on Kaua'i. His employees. We also found out that the sugar plantation manager in Waialua also was the same type of a person. That he intervened actively, strongly, to prevent the internment of community leaders, such as my dad on Lāna'i. In Lāna'i, it was just the opposite.

My recollection is that, first of all, I think it was a temple priest, the reverend, got taken. Then there was a Mr. [Tokuichi] Okamoto, who owned the

Japanese store there. There was also a Mr. [Kenichi] Takeshita. And Takeshita was, I believe, the chief accountant for Mr. Okamoto. There was a Mr. [Takazo] Arita. I think it was Arita. He was the barber. Okamoto, Takeshita, Arita, my dad, I think those were it. Yeah, there were four and the temple priest makes five.

So, now what does a Japanese store owner have to do with the war effort or whatever it was that gets him interned? The accountant for him? The barber? What sane reason, what justifiable reason was present to influence the United States government, on the say-so and story, presumably, of the manager of the island plantation, to justify the internment, the apprehension, the seizure of a person, and then shipping that person off, outside of the [territory], to some strange location and leaving the family in a lurch to fend for themselves against the very plantation manager whose say-so resulted in the internment? I just can't figure that one out.

[When I returned to Lāna'i] everything, everything was in a jumble. Everybody wanted to talk and so we tried to calm everybody down and say, okay. She [my mother] was in a state of shock. But then after a while, she came to accept what had happened. Didn't like it, but had to accept the fact that he isn't there.

I started to work for the pineapple plantation. I probably worked there about four to six weeks. And then the plantation manager [Dexter Fraser] called me into his office. And he made no bones, it was a very quick execution. He said, "Son, if Uncle Sam can't trust your dad, we cannot trust you either. So I want you to leave the island. Take your family with you." The only recollection I have of having responded to him was, "Don't call me 'son.' When do you want me to leave?" "As soon as you can arrange it." I said, "Okay."

So I went back, told my family exactly what happened, what the discussion was. I think we all were more resigned to our fates [rather] than acting or reacting in anger or anything. You know, it's there, it's happened. So what the hell are we going to do about it, you know? What do Japanese say? Akirametoru? More it was acceptance with some anger beneath. But on the surface not an exhibition of anger or "Why?"

Because the family had been on Maui prior to going to Lāna'i, I decided that the family should go to Maui. I immediately contacted the Red Cross in Honolulu—I think it was by telegram from Lāna'i—and asked them for help in finding a place for us to stay in Wailuku, Maui. You couldn't go to the [Buddhist] church because the church is [closed down]. You couldn't go to any person because if we went to see friends of ours, they would be in trouble now, in view of what's happened to my dad. They were all concerned and scared of the plantation manager.

Some of them were very good. They talked to me, "Too bad what happened." They expressed friendly concern, but you could sense a change—sort of they wanted to keep arm's length. One can sense that very quickly, especially in a plantation town where everybody has skeletons in their closet and nobody is so reserved as not to disturb those skeletons. They bring them out and they rattled them every now and then so that we all disciplined each other. And we had to terminate the tanomoshi. It was the end of the societies that my mother and my dad were in. All went underground or became defunct.

We had a lot of things in the house that my father had. For example, he had the scroll, you know, the artwork. Heirlooms that both my mother and my father kept. Some people volunteered to hold some of the things for us in trust. We never did get back anything. As far as I know, I don't think my mother made any effort to reclaim any of them.

By then, it was really traumatic when I started to see that we were actually packing things to leave this island without knowing where we're going to be at, pending response from the [Red Cross]. And will we be able to get on board that *Na'ia,* the sampan, to take us to Maui? And so, we're packing these things and my mother is crying and I'm telling her, "We can't take these things, we can't take these things." The family treasures that she wanted to keep.

Hasegawa family, Maui, ca. 1944. While incarcerated, James Shunzo Hasegawa requested that this family portrait be taken and sent to him (photo courtesy of Robert Hasegawa).

A SMALL COMMUNITY

So we went to Wailuku. When we got there, among the first things that the family had to do was to register at their different schools. My two sisters went to 'Īao Elementary. My two brothers were just high school age, so they registered at Baldwin High.

Having done that, we had to assess, how much rent can we pay? They [the Red Cross] found a place that the rental was eighty-five dollars and it was a huge house, you know. The rent was so high that I didn't think we could make it. And that's what I told my mother and we started to look for another place and asked the Red Cross to help us, too.

But then at the same time, we were looking and we found a place. And we went to see the lady who owned the place and she didn't want to rent it to us because there were too many kids. My sister remembers very vividly that Mother literally begged that person to let us have the home because we had no other place to stay. And that's where the family stayed right through until my sisters graduated from Baldwin High School.

Of course, the brother right below me thought he'd quit school to help me and so I told him, "No way. Get your high school diploma at least. We'll be able to manage somehow."

Then I found a job as an electrician with CPNAB, which is the Contractors' Pacific Naval Air Bases. They were creating an airport at Pu'unēnē, in the cane fields. And there were barracks and buildings. So I got a job over there and that was in 1942 and early '43.

It was pretty tough for the family because we were not known by the stores and by the merchants, so everything we bought had to be in cash.

And Maui, Wailuku, at that time was a small community, like Lāna'i. News goes fast out among the Japanese community. When people found out about my dad's internment and the reason we were on Maui, there were certain things that my mother could not get out of the market owner. My mother told me this some time ago when we were visiting with her, that there were certain cuts of meat that she couldn't get. No merchant would sell to her, but will sell [to] somebody else. She was even being bypassed in line.

There is a lot of resentment that my mother harbors with certain merchants. And more particularly, the older of my two younger sisters, because she accompanied Mom and she resented a lot of things that were [done] by Nihonjin merchants. It's not only merchants but also even our landlord. There was a real arm's-length kind of relationship, a "Talk to us if you have to, don't talk to us if you don't need to." That type, even aisatsu.

I did get a letter from him [my father]. He was in [Lordsburg, New Mexico]. Now he was so downhearted, he asked the family to go to the coast, to the Mainland. His intent at that time was to take the whole family back to Japan. So that is when I wrote him, I told him, "Look, none of us is going to be there, so don't count on us. But if we have to, if you keep on insisting, maybe Mother will go and the two girls will go. But I can tell you, the three boys will never go."

That was my way of indicating to him that, "Look, if you want to go to Japan, go. I can take care of the family, we'll all stay here." That was a revelation to him, you know. The fact that my letter was so strong to him that we won't go unless we're forced to go. And the force is not coming from him, it's going to be coming from the U.S. government.

And my younger brother, Teru, wrote to my dad to tell him that nobody's going to go to the coast, including Mother. From my brother Teru's standpoint, so long as we don't go, he's going to have one hell of a time to go to Japan. He has to come back here.

So, psychologically, there were a lot of things going on which, on the surface, looking at communications, seemed to be odd—that wouldn't be the family's way of reacting and all of that. But there were subtle reasons for phrasing our letters the way we did, because we knew that all our communications were being censored. So I wanted to be sure that there would be no mistaking, misimpressions, or misunderstandings, or misinterpretations of what we are saying, see?

So I think at that time, when he got the letter, he abandoned all hopes of going back to Japan. That he'll have to make do with the cards that [were] dealt him. Because otherwise, he's all alone.

Probably about the fall or late summer of 1943, we got through with all of the [CPNAB] jobs. At least the electrical part was through. And so now I was faced with another decision. And that was, the job is through there, I'm through, where am I going to work? And so I had a choice, either go to Moloka'i, and there was a job ready, available for me on Moloka'i, or go to O'ahu and take my chances. So I got the family together and told them that I'm going to Honolulu on the blind, but I'm sure I can get work there because it's a big place.

And of course, my brother again said, "I'm going to quit school." He had only one more year, I think. And my younger brother had two or three more years. I said, "No, you finish your school. Because I'll have a job." I was that confident. Because I had union help on Maui, through the union members and contractors who knew me.

And then I found work with USED [U.S. Engineer Department] as an electrician. As soon as I got here, I started to make my contacts and I was referred to USED, and bingo, they were looking for anybody who had the skills.

I made arrangements at that time to stay at Komeya Hotel. The Komeyas readily took me in. Mr. Komeya and my dad were really good friends from way back.

ACTIVE SERVICE

I was already in the Enlisted Reserve Corps of the army. I had my serial number and everything else. But I was doing defense work and all of that, so that was the situation when I volunteered. I was turned down. And I thought at that time, that I was turned down because I had too many dependents. Then sometime in the fall, probably September or October [1944], I was called into active service. In other words, I was drafted into active service, changing my status from Enlisted Reserve Corps to the army of the United States.

When I got called into active service, this is the first time that I thought, "I wonder if my father is going to get released." It was just a passing thought I had, pretty sure that he's going to get released. Subsequently, I found out that yes, he was released, he was paroled. So out of Santa Fe he went. Now where does he go? Of all places, he ended up in Colorado, in Denver. That's what he told me. And he worked at the Brown Derby Hotel.

[In December 1945] I met him at the boat and he did not know at that time that I was in the army. I was already drafted. And I was in uniform. And I was at the gangplank, all these people coming down, all with badges, names. Finally met.

And I took him to Komeya Hotel. And Komeya Hotel had maintained my room even when I was in the army. They just left it alone, they didn't rent it out. Met Mr. Komeya, they were having tea for a while, talking stories. Then because I didn't have too much time and Mr. Komeya knew that, he told my dad we're going to have lunch.

At that time, [Samuel] "Sad Sam" Ichinose's restaurant was right at the corner of Hotel and River Streets and there was a big crab [sign] outside with a smiling Japanese-character face. Took him in there and I lit a cigarette and he looks at me and says, "You smoke?" I said, "Yeah, I smoke." I said, "What kind of drink do you want?" I already knew exactly what he was going to say. "Dewars White Label." That was his drink. So I told the bartender, "Two." He says, "You drink?" I say, "Yeah, I drink." I said, "Dad, I'm in the goddamn army for cripes' sake."

So he told me at that time, some of the things that happened to him. The fact that from Lāna'i, he was taken to Maui. Maui to Sand Island. Sand Island to the Mainland. And you know, several places in the Mainland, and ended up in Santa Fe. Well, I didn't know that he was in Lordsburg, New

Mexico until I looked at some of the documents that we have. There must have been other places also, except that we didn't have time to discuss these.

Sometime on the second day, my father told me that the FBI knew more about the places that he'd visited in [prewar] Japan than he remembered. There was a record of when he left, on what ship, what date, what time, what port. He says it was a real shock of how they got the information or where they got the information or when he was under surveillance, if he was under surveillance. And he doesn't know.

He went to Maui simply because the family was there and my pass was only for three days. So there wasn't much time for him and I to talk. And then I was in the army for three years after that.

My father tried to determine, according to my mother, from Fraser, what the hell had happened. "Why did they kick me out?" I don't think he had a satisfactory answer at all. He did ask for reinstatement to the position. I don't

Fujie and James Shunzo Hasegawa, Maui, Hawai'i, ca. 1946 (photo courtesy of Robert Hasegawa).

think that my father wrote that intending, or with the fullest expectation or desire to return to the island whose manager had thrown his family out. It was more, I think, establishing some kind of a record that he wasn't even considered for reinstatement. And that was clear by Fraser's response. He [said], "Well, we're open to you being reemployed, but not at the job that you held." So that's no reinstatement.

But I really don't know because I wasn't there. I was in the army. So there's a gap in my knowledge as to what the family was going through. All I know is that I assured my mother that whatever job I had, "You'll have all the money that I earn."

Every week I used to send [money home]. I used to keep one paycheck just to pay my expenses, my rental and some food. And this went on for less than a year. Subsequently, I sent every check home. Because I was able to shoot pool. And I used to make some money on the side.

When he [my father] got back, he started work for Von Hamm-Young Company. He was always in sales. And essentially, he became, if I might use the word, "rehabilitated." He was able to buy a piece of property there, build his own house over there in the tract at Kahului, and live there.

He did volunteer work for [Hawai'i] Department of Education, DOE, in teaching citizenship. And my father related his own story, the fact that he wanted to be an American, couldn't be an American because of the law, and then when the law was changed, and it was possible for him to become an American, he did. And so there's a lot of American citizens living in Maui today, many of them senior citizens, and many of them younger people of alien birth, who are American citizens today by reason of my dad's teaching.

In retrospect, I think it was a good thing that it happened when it did, simply because basically, I had some, I suppose, unattainable ambitions and goals. And that I was forced to grow up right away. I was able, really, to get rid of any thought that I might have had—that in fact, I had, when I was going to high school—as to what I wanted to be or to do, when my dad got interned and I was faced with having the family to think about. So there was more a reality check on me than I would have otherwise have experienced.

And as it turned out, while the prospective future looked very, very bleak, the experiences that I've had, in retrospect, are very rich, rewarding, and satisfying [because] of what I've been able to, with the help of many, many others' help, accomplish in my life. I think the greatest satisfaction I have is in the maintenance of unity of the family.

* * * * *

Fujie Hasegawa has written poems throughout her life. She wrote this poem after husband James Shunzo Hasegawa was incarcerated in 1942.

POEM BY FUJIE HASEGAWA

Kankin no mi ni naru
otto no rusuchū wo
haha omou ko ni
kansha no namida.

During the absence
of her interned husband
a mother cries
tears of gratitude
for the child
who thinks of her.

(translation by Lisa Sakamoto)

Fujie Hasegawa (photo courtesy of Robert Hasegawa).

GLOSSARY

aisatsu	greetings
akirametoru	resignation, acceptance
fujinkai	women's society
haole	Caucasian
hō hana	weeding
koseki tōhon	family register
Nihonjin	Japanese
tanomoshi	mutual lending association

LEMON "RUSTY" HOLT

THE RASCAL OF WAIKĪKĪ

When the tourists came, we would take off our tights, dive into the water, and come up with manini, one or two manini, showing the tourists that we were catching the fish with our tights. We'd hold it up, and if the tourists dropped [only] a nickel, we turned around— we didn't have any tights on—and we showed them our ʻōkoles.

Lemon "Rusty" Holt, the third child of seven born to Augusta Helen Lemon Holt and Edward Holt, lived on the Lemon family estate in Waikīkī, from his birth in 1904 until his departure in 1930. Of Caucasian-Hawaiian ancestry, Holt gained recognition for his football prowess at Kamehameha School and the University of Hawaiʻi. Later he became a postmaster, personnel department head, and store and apartment manager.

In 1985, at a robust eighty-two years of age, Holt related his childhood experiences and family history to researcher/interviewer Michi Kodama-Nishimoto for COH's *Waikīkī 1900–1985: Oral Histories.* Kodama-Nishimoto recalled the vintage football and surfing photographs which covered the walls of his home. Also affixed to a wall was a huge surfboard. Holt's narrative largely focuses on growing up in Waikīkī. He fondly recalled spending times "hanging out" in the area of his family home near Kapiʻolani Park and Kūhiō Beach. Lemon "Rusty" Holt died in 1999.

FAMILY HOME

[Grandfather] James Silas Lemon was a businessman who came from Quebec, Canada. He was French-Canadian. He moved to the United States to work. Because his name was too much like a Frenchman's name, he took out the hyphen between Le-Mon and made it strictly a sour Lemon. He married Mary Ann Wond from Kauaʻi.

Silas Lemon owned the whole block bounded by Paoakalani [Avenue], Lemon Road—named after him—down Kapahulu [Avenue] and along Kalākaua [Avenue]. He paid cash for the whole thing. My mother used to say, "Five thousand dollars? Hmm! Much less than that." So I never did know [exactly].

On the property, there was the big house. That big house had six bedrooms; a huge, big living room. Nothing but koa, koa, koa, and more koa in that living room.

[My mother] Augusta Helen Lemon married my father Edward S. Holt. My mother and my father had a house right next to the big house. It was smaller than the other one, the original big house. But it had so many bedrooms, you would get lost going into it because it was built like old homes were built at that time—lattice all around, enclosed porches—and whoever got to a room first, they slept there. And that's where we all grew up in my family.

There were three boys and four girls in my family, my immediate family. They were all delivered by my grandmother, who had been a nurse and administrator of the Kapiʻolani Maternity Hospital.

Many of the families then did outside cooking. They believed in charcoal stoves made of kerosene oil cans. [Sakazo] Tahara cooked for my family. Tahara would not cook on the [gas] stove. He said, "You can't cook good rice on a haole stove. You have to use charcoal." He worked for our family for quite a while until he decided to start his own [restaurant] business.

The property was one acre. There must have been ten mango trees. Also, in the yard, there was a lemon orchard behind and a lemon orchard in the front. Then there were momi apple trees, custard apple trees, and bananas everywhere.

There was a man who was a great friend of the family. His name was John Wise. He was superintendent of the Kapiʻolani Park—the zoo and the park. He gave a lūʻau every month. Now in order to make his haupia, he had to have a hundred dried coconuts. Once a month, my grandmother would say, "You! Get a hundred coconuts down—dried coconuts." There must have been a hundred coconut trees in the yard, and I climbed every one of them.

Well, also, we had chicken, roast chicken, every Sunday. My job was to catch the [chicken] that she pointed out to me, my grandmother did. And I would chase that chicken all over the yard until that poor [chicken] just lay down and said, "Come and take me."

Later on, I thought, "Hey, this is a good opportunity. Take it." So I started to chase the chicken onto the beds of violets and onto her prized maidenhair that she had from one end of the yard to the other. I did not have to chase any more chickens after that.

We [also] had in the backyard in a big, big cage, Sammy the monkey. And this monkey just came there once as a little baby monkey, from where nobody knew. They used to call him Sammy Lemon, the monkey.

As I think I told you, we had bananas growing all over the yard. Also, my grandmother grew a lot of Hawaiian chili peppers. So this cousin of mine, Kainoa McKinney, went and got a banana, a ripe one, made a hole down into it, cut some chili peppers in half, stuck them into the hole, left the skin on because a monkey will take a banana and do his own skinning.

So Sammy took the banana, peeled it off, stuck it in his mouth, and before anybody could say, "What?" he had eaten the whole banana. And then, that chili pepper hit him and that poor monkey went mad.

Somehow, Kainoa leaned over laughing and Sammy stuck his hand through the wire, grabbed a hold of Kainoa's hair on the top, in the middle, and he would not let go. So I had to pick up an old hoe with a long handle, stuck it in. He let Kainoa's hair go and he grabbed the handle of the hoe. Kainoa always had a bald spot in the middle of his head, and it wouldn't grow back.

THE NEIGHBORHOOD

On the corner of Paoakalani and Kalākaua [Avenues] there was a little beer shop. One of my uncles started it as a hobby and a place he could get free beer. Then, later on, that same corner became the first Aoki Store. Next to Aoki Store was Diamond Head Clothes Cleaning Shop. Next to that was a little barbershop, and she [the barber] always gave me a mush bowl haircut by putting a bowl on top and cutting me all around, back of my head, and on the side.

Next to that, it was a linen-cleaning laundry. The owner was an old Chinese man from China. Whereas nobody in Waikīkī liked me because I was such a truant or a rascal, Old Man "Tailor" thought I was number one. He did all of the white laundry from the only hotel at that time, Moana Hotel, and Seaside Avenue little bungalows.

Along Kalākaua [Avenue] from where the Royal Hawaiian [Hotel] is now on the mauka side, it was nothing but duck ponds. We used to go down, collect duck eggs, bring 'em back to where we lived, put them in gallons of water, seal it, and hide those gallons in the sand. Well, after a year or six months, those duck eggs were pretty ripe.

Well, about that time, Mrs. Aoki was giving me a bad time. I wanted crack seed, and no way could I get it. So I got a bunch of those eggs, ripe duck eggs, got on the streetcar and as we went past Aoki's, I started letting them go. Unfortunately, I missed Aoki's. I missed the barbershop, and the eggs went right into my good, good friend's laundry shop. I felt worse than

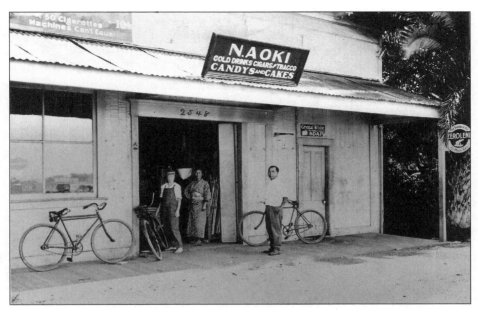

Aoki Store, ca. 1914; one of Lemon Holt's sisters stands in the entrance, left (photo courtesy of Harold Aoki).

anybody, I guess, because I had done something to a person who liked me and I liked him.

After [the laundry], there was the stream that came down from Mānoa and Pālolo, came all the way down to the ocean. The Akana family lived on one side of the stream, and we lived on the other side.

Waikīkī had two streams. Fourth of July, when the ocean acted up, along came the South wind, those streams had plenty of water. It rained, rained heavy. And when it did, chickens, ducks, pigs [from farms upstream] came washing down the rivers. We had fun catching them with throw nets.

ROYALTY IN WAIKĪKĪ

My father was a staunch Royalist. He was a member of Queen Liliʻuokalani's mounted patrol men. And when annexation took place, because somebody was afraid that there would be violence, which there was, my father was given the job of taking the then minister of the republic to hide him in Nuʻuanu Valley. Later on, he [Edward Holt] became a Democrat and was always that way.

My grandmother and Queen Liliʻuokalani were great friends, very close friends. Occasionally, Liliʻuokalani came to visit my grandmother. And when she came, it meant climb a couple of trees, get the haohao coconuts down.

You know what that is? Haohao? Means a coconut with the meat just right that you can eat it with a spoon. Anyway, she liked the coconuts from two trees, and nobody dared touch those two trees. It had to stay there so that when she came there would be coconuts for her. Well, I had to climb those two trees, get the haohao coconuts down, husk the outer wrapping, and give it to her.

Also, I had to go out to the stone wall [at Kūhiō Beach], in the front of the stone wall, dive and catch three or four or five or six manini. She liked manini. She ate them raw. I also had to go out near Queen's Surf and dive for wana, plenty of wana there, bring that home, then go back out to Queen's Surf and dive for līpoa. She liked līpoa! And my grandmother, in the meantime, would be cooking Hawaiian stew. And that's what she had, whenever she came. So that's the story of Lili'uokalani. She was a nice old lady, real courteous, pleasant, nice. [But] I do not recall her saying "thank you" or tipping me with two bits.

Prince Kūhiō was a real nice person. He [was] pure Hawaiian, and he spoke English like a college professor. He always dressed nicely. [Rarely] saw him without a shirt, tie, nice trousers, and his shoes were always polished.

Everyone liked him, Prince Kūhiō, but not very many liked his wife. He had fruit trees in the front of his yard, and the kids used to come along and attempt to help themselves to fruit. She had a couple of spitz dogs. She would let the dogs go, and they would come out there roaring. And so we never liked the dogs, and we didn't quite like her.

The prince had a sixteen- or eighteen-foot solid koa surfboard. I don't think I ever saw him take anybody else out surfing tandem, except me. I always went with him. The other kids would say, "Prince, why you taking that guy?" He would say, "Well, he can swim in if anything happens. He's a good little swimmer!"

So, when we got through we would bring the board to his pier there. The board was so long that he never carried it. He had a couple of pulleys under his pier. All he did was put a hoist in the front and a hoist on the back. He pulled on the rope and up went the board, and it stayed there.

PEDDLERS, PRIESTS, AND TOURISTS

We had one man, old Chinese man, and I can't think of his name. I should remember it because I was his best illegal or legal customer. He carried two baskets on a stick, one basket in the back, one basket in the front, and also a can, a five-gallon or ten-gallon can. In those containers, there was black sugar manapua, pepeiao, [pork] hash, and one or two other items.

Joe [Akana] would talk to him and point to the front basket. While the old man was talking to Joe about the front basket, I would be in the back helping myself and stuffing things, all I could stuff, into my pockets.

The other peddler was the ice cream man that sold ice cream—two cones for a nickel. And those days, it wasn't the type of cones you have nowadays—it was that curly, sweet cone. Fort Ruger, there were soldiers. They bought these bottles of beer, drank them on their way home to Fort Ruger, and the empty ones, they threw into our yard. And then the next morning, I picked them up, and I got an ice cream cone for every two bottles. And when a nickel or dime or twenty-five cents was hard to look at, those two bottles for a cone was pretty good.

Father [H. Franckx] Valentin was the minister [of nearby St. Augustine's Church]. He was a very good friend of all the big family haole ladies. He was a nice man—big, tall man. We all liked him.

He had a car every year or two years. Not a new car, but a car passed down from the big families to him. And this time, this particular time, he had a big limousine that he used.

One day, one of the kids thought of a good idea, a funny idea. They wanted to see if Father Valentin would use a couple of cuss words. Up to then nobody ever heard him say anything like that, but we were wondering, what would a father do if something happened?

We backed [the car] in the corner where you couldn't see it very well. We jacked it up somehow, I don't remember how, and we put on these four-by-fours under each wheel and took the tires off. I don't know how long we had to wait, but we had to wait quite a while before he came out. Anyway, he started the engine, got in, raced the engine, then put it into gear and started off, and he wasn't moving!

When he got out, he looked. He said a couple of words. Mike said to me, "Lemon! Lemon! Lemon! I heard him. I heard him." He said, "Two bad words! I heard him." (Laughs.)

We had tourists those times, but you could count them on your right hand. They were so few. Of course, these Stonewall guys [a group of boys who congregated at the Kūhiō Beach stone wall], me included, would try to get nickels or dimes or two bits from these tourists. We'd be in the water right below the stone wall.

When the tourists came, we would take off our tights [swim trunks], dive into the water, and come up with manini, one or two manini, showing the tourists that we were catching the fish with our tights. We'd hold it up, and if the tourists dropped [only] a nickel, we turned around—we didn't have any tights on—and we showed them our 'ōkoles. When they dropped a quarter, we thanked them and did not show them our 'ōkoles.

Stonewall Gang, Waikīkī, ca. 1928 (photo courtesy of Ethel Valente).

Nightly almost, they [the boys] came to the stone wall and played music. It was really home-style stuff, but we thought it was very good, not knowing too much about it. Tourists, what few there were, would walk down, especially on Sunday nights, and listen to the music.

POLO GAMES AND HORSE RACES

They had polo games out at the [Kapi'olani] Park. Those days, the automobiles that they had, had rumble seats. I remember one time getting into Frank Baldwin's, the Maui man, into his car, two-seater. I remember getting into the rumble seat and keeping my finger on the lock so that the rumble seat could not collapse and lock itself, which could only be opened from the outside. He came and got in his car. Drove it down onto the grounds, parked it, and I got out. That was my way of getting in. Joe had his own way. He jumped the fences.

[The Dillinghams] would come in the family car, a big black car. I think it was a Pierce Arrow. Car stopped in front of this small little grandstand and one of the Dillingham boys got out. He escorted his mother to her seat. Another Dillingham boy escorted one of the Japanese ladies who took care of the boys to her seat—held her arm and took her in. Then Ben Dillingham escorted the other lady to her seat. Here Joe and I were looking at it. He looked at me and he said, "Huh, sissies!" Years later, I couldn't help but think of that time and realize what perfect gentlemen those guys were.

The polo field was in the middle of the race track. The race track, if I'm not mistaken, was a mile long. It started on the Diamond Head side and went all the way down to where the old zoo was.

But only on big holidays were the races [held]. Like February 22nd, which was the big day where they had parades and horse races. July 4th and one other day I don't remember. Anyway, the whole place was jam-packed.

The majority of people attending those horse races were families. Families, because nobody ever thought of driving from any district in Honolulu, unless the sulky or the wagon was filled up. So when a sulky came along, it was usually filled up with people—mother, father, aunties, maybe uncle, and children—all sitting on the floor.

Anybody who had money went underneath [the grandstand] and bet on whatever horse they wanted, shook hands, and that was it. It was either silver dollars, kālā, or five-dollar gold pieces, ten-dollar gold pieces, twenty-dollar gold pieces, fifty-dollar gold pieces, and hundred-dollar gold pieces.

SCHOOLING

The first Waikīkī [Elementary] School was opposite the Moana Hotel—across the street. There were three rooms, first, second, and third [grades]. In one corner of the property there was a graveyard and an old Hawaiian church. And in the graveyard on the mounds, the caretaker had planted watermelons. At night the kids and I used to go there and steal watermelons. Sit on the mounds and eat. And those watermelons were absolutely sweet. They had good fertilizer.

My schedule going to Waikīkī School was three days schooling and the rest of the week, surfing. So that when I finished the third grade, I don't think it was possible for me to add two and two and make it come out four, because it always came out three.

[After several years at St. Louis, a Catholic school] I went to Kamehameha [School] and stayed there until 1927. Being a boarder was nice. We wore uniforms to any function—to school, to work, to the dining hall, always with uniforms. The uniforms had pockets so we could slip in food whenever we wanted.

I want to explain that during my time, there were probably only fifty eligible boys to take part in sports. When I say "take part in sports," there was football, baseball, basketball, shooting—which was a big thing at Kamehameha—track, and swimming. So I managed to play football, baseball, no shooting. I ran track and I swam. My nickname [Rusty] was given me by Ezra Crane

Kamehameha School all-star football player Lemon "Rusty" Holt, 1926 (photo courtesy of Lemon Holt).

who was sports editor of the *Honolulu Advertiser*. I was known by that nickname since Kamehameha time.

Later on, Kamehameha tried an idea of [alternating] two weeks school and two weeks on your chosen subject that you would graduate in. Like carpentry, electricity, machine shop, welding, drafting, and vocational training. I chose vocational agriculture. So they gave me a boar and two sows. I stayed up there in an old shack that leaked water every time it rained.

I remember the first day it [the program] started. I was supposed to have gone up the hill with my pigs. Instead of that, I got on the truck with the carpentry boys because someone had said, "Hey, two bits an hour. Boy, that's good. I'm glad I'm taking carpentry." They were going to the Royal Hawaiian Hotel [construction site]. It started in '26. So I got on their truck and went with them to Waikīkī. My job with a few of the boys was to carry these four-by-four posts, about twenty-four-feet long. We had to carry those into where they were building the Royal Hawaiian.

Well, the next morning, the truck came for the carpentry boys and I started getting on the truck. One of the instructors came along and he said, "You are in vocational agriculture. Up to the farm." I had only one day at Royal Hawaiian, but I can say that I did have a little share in building the place.

LEAVING WAIKĪKĪ

Well, when my grandmother died [in 1919], they had to settle the estate. In the family, no one needed the money so it just dragged on and on and on for a number of years until, finally, someone decided that maybe they ought to settle the estate and give the heirs their shares and all that. My uncle Nani Lemon was the administrator, and he wanted $100,000.

When they couldn't sell it, when nobody wanted to buy it, they leased it through the bank to [the] Mossmans. And [the] Mossmans started the Lalani [Hawaiian] Village, where they had lū'aus, hula dancing, and so forth. Something happened and the Mossmans went out.

So, finally, the Bank of Hawai'i bought it for $86,000. The whole thing, except the parcels that were given out to James Silas's friends. And today, you couldn't buy that for $20 million.

I was the last one [of the family] to live there. I know a few still down there, guys who I surfed with up until I was seventy-five years old. There are some who recognize me as I walk, on account of my participating in athletics. But the rest of the people are all strangers.

My time, or prior to 1919, it was like a big family. Like Aokis, and Tahara, Diamond Head Clothes Cleaning Shop, and then the barbershop, and then Old Man "Tailor." Then the Akanas. Those were good days.

GLOSSARY

crack seed	Chinese-style preserved fruits and seeds
haohao	soft or immature type of coconut
haole	Caucasian
haupia	pudding made from coconut cream
kālā	silver dollar
koa	endemic Hawaiian forest acacia tree
līpoa	brown edible seaweed
lūʻau	feast
manapua	Chinese cake
manini	surgeonfish
mauka	inland
momi	mamee, type of fruit tree
ʻōkole	buttocks
pepeiao	Chinese meat dumpling
wana	sea urchin

JENNIE LEE IN

A BASIC PERSONALITY OF LIKING PEOPLE

One of the reasons why I became so active in the [Church of the] Crossroads was every Sunday—we spent all afternoon till evening—we played volleyball, sometimes we had dances, we cooked there, we had programs, and then one of the guys took us home. As long as we say "church," it was fine. Oh, my father would cut my legs off if he knew we danced.

Born in Kohala, Hawai'i in 1921, Jennie Lee In is the youngest child of Kui Sung Lee, an immigrant from China who came to Hawai'i to work in the sugar cane fields, and Tung Moi Lim Lee, who was born in the Islands.

At the age of six or seven, after In's mother died, the family moved to the Kauluwela/Liliha area of Honolulu. She attended area schools and graduated from McKinley High School in 1938. In then matriculated at the University of Hawai'i, receiving a bachelor's degree in vocational home economics in 1942 and a certificate from the School of Social Work in 1944. That same year she was hired as a caseworker at Pālama Settlement. After eventually earning a master's degree from the New York School of Social Work, she returned to Pālama Settlement for a year.

She married, divorced on the Mainland, and returned to the Islands in the mid-1950s. She was hired as the executive secretary for the Commission on Children and Youth. She subsequently remarried and raised a family, while teaching part-time. From 1970, she developed and taught a program for pregnant teenagers.

Widowed in 1973, In later married Dr. Andrew In, former dean of the University of Hawai'i College of Education. She retired in 1983.

Michi Kodama-Nishimoto interviewed Jennie Lee In in 1997 for *Reflections of Pālama Settlement,* a project which examined the origin, goals, and development of a unique Hawai'i social institution. The project also examined the settlement's relationship to the broader reform movement that inspired the establishment and proliferation of settlement houses throughout the United States between the late 1800s and early 1900s.

EARLY CHILDHOOD

I was born in a little town called Hālawa on the Big Island, North Kohala in 1921. There were three sisters and three brothers and myself.

Mother was third-generation U.S. citizen, and I remembered how hard she worked. She was truly sort of like a pioneer woman, went down when the stream was running to wash clothes, used flour and rice sacks to make underwear, raised everything from turkeys to pigs for the table, and had a going garden.

And at the same time as a child, I remember how at nights, under the kerosene lamp, she would read to me while the other kids were doing homework, and kind of delighted in nurturing me, although she herself was sick most of her life.

My father was a [sugar] plantation worker. We later learned that he came over as an orphan with his older brother, and he must have been only about fifteen and the brother was maybe seventeen, eighteen.

We have a picture of him, which I can't locate right now, getting off the boat. And I guess it's the immigration picture with him—[his hair] in a long queue—wearing shoes that have a crook at the end, which was considered stylish in those days.

And according to my brother, who heard this story much later, he very early was one of the rebels, because they used to have German overseers who used horsewhips on them if they didn't work. So in the cover of dark of night, he ran away with a group of men from Kohala and lived in a village in Ka'ū, which is quite a distance away. And the Hawaiians had these huge hukilau, and they would bring in the fish. My father peddled the fish. So he knew Hawaiian pretty well.

Later on, it was arranged for him to marry my mother. He went back to North Kohala to work for the sugar plantation. I guess by then, the statute of limitations or whatever was over. The last job I can remember him working at was in the mill. His job was to test the acidity or the pH factor in the molasses in order to make sure that they crystallized. I would tail along when my sister would deliver his noon or supper lunch pail, and we would walk that distance to deliver it.

He did not value education like my mother did. He was a stern taskmaster, and didn't put up with idleness; he didn't put up with foolishness. He was much older than my mother, I think seventeen years difference. He drove himself: he worked six days a week in the plantation, and the seventh day, he worked as a gardener for one of the haole plantation doctors who lived in the end of the valley where we lived.

And, of course, for us kids it was great, because there was a stream that we used as our playground a lot, especially when the rainy seasons came and we could float banana logs and go down the stream a distance, like a raft.

We had wonderful Okinawan neighbors, Japanese neighbors, some Puerto Ricans, and some Filipinos who lived scattered in the valley. I vaguely recall that at one time, my mother didn't have enough breast milk to take care of me, and I was sent to one of the oba-chans nearby for supplementary feeding. But that is only things somebody told me. In other words, I'm not sure that it happened. But there was the strong neighborhood kind of exchange and support.

There was the church that my mother insisted we be part of. And there was a very, very wise Chinese Christian minister, in the sense that he never put pressure on my mother or us to commit ourselves to the church to be baptized and so forth. When my mother was sick, we would send somebody to go tell the minister. He would come, and he would just sit with her. And sometimes it was just to take her pulse. Chinese have a tiny little cure-all pill—I guess like aspirin—prescribed for anything. He would give these to her and pray.

Then there was a Chinese society, which still exists in North Kohala, called the Tong Wo Society. The practices were, I guess, more Taoist than anything. I mean, a lot of superstition and lot of ancestral worship and offerings of various kinds for the deceased. And that was part of our social life, 'cause there would be gatherings for Chinese New Year, for full moon, for the Autumn Festival and so forth.

And the school was a very important part of us. I went through the second grade at Hālawa School. It's no longer there. And I apparently, even at that age, was kind of an outgoing kid and very verbal. I guess I was kind of a teacher's pet, because the weekend that my mother had her stroke, I was in Hilo with my second sister as guest of my first-grade teacher in her home for the Easter vacation. They had to call us home, and then we had to take the train back from Hilo to Kohala because my mother was no longer able to speak. [Her mother died when In was six going on seven years old.]

Immediately after she died, which was a matter of three days—no medical rescue at that time—the two oldest sisters were farmed out to work in families. In other words, they were live-in maids.

The older brother, who was then about thirteen, really took my mother's death very badly, because he was the one she relied on a lot. He felt that he was kind of abandoned, because my father sent him to Hilo to stay with, not really a relative, but the man had the last name as we did, Lee. At the same time, my father thought it would be good for him, because the possibility for high school in Hilo and further education was much better than in Kohala.

When Mother died, it was tough, but already I had had all the support and was still getting it through my siblings, who were very generous with helping me out. And the twin brothers and my sister—who's immediately above me [and] is five years older than I am—became mother substitutes, plus my father taking a big hand in it.

Now, as I look back on it, he was—after my mother died—trying to be mother and father, and didn't know how to be mother. So his way of handling it was to prohibit us from doing anything that he thought might contaminate the family name or put us in bad straits.

We moved out of the valley, and I guess he quit his job on Sunday as a yardman and lived in the plantation home. It was more convenient in the plantation community, because there was a store within 200 feet from our house. And the doctor was available; you could go to the clinic. But we missed all of the freedom of climbing guava trees and playing in the stream and catching fish.

MOVE TO MATERNAL GRANDFATHER'S HOUSE IN HONOLULU

We were still intact, the four kids and Pop. And the two sisters came to Honolulu and, again, found homes that they lived in and worked [in] as maids. The older brother continued to live on the Big Island and was never really part of the household until years later.

Grandpa I remember very well. Up till the time when I was maybe twelve, thirteen, he was in and out of the picture a lot. And he was a tailor by trade. The family story is, his father was also very good as a tailor, and they went to California during the gold rush to make jeans for the miners, and sewed whatever kind of denim that they wore in the mines.

After we came to Honolulu, he [my father] didn't have the [appropriate] kinds of skills, because he was a plantation worker, so he worked in restaurants as a dishwasher, vegetable cutter—labor grade-one jobs. And then—I don't remember how many years [later], maybe four—he cashed out on a life insurance policy that he had saved long time ago, and bought us a home and moved away from Grandpa.

He quit working then, and my older sisters and brothers had to go to work to help support us. When we moved into a bigger home with a larger yard, he planted a full vegetable garden. Using a balancing bamboo pole, with one basket on each end, he went to the neighborhood and peddled his vegetables to make cash.

And he raised rabbits and chickens and ducks. One of his specialties was raising capons. And that was the way we survived.

FROM KAULUWELA SCHOOL TO CENTRAL INTERMEDIATE AND MCKINLEY

When I came down from the Big Island, I had just finished second grade, and I was to go to third grade. My aunt took me to an interview with the principal of Kauluwela School [who] said, "But I have no room in the third grade. It's all full." So my aunt said to her, "Well, you talk to her and let her read to you." And she did, and so she put me in the fourth grade.

I probably didn't have as nice a haircut. I didn't have earrings like some other Chinese gals had. But I was enough of a tomboy that I could do jump rope and play hopscotch as good or better than they. And in class, I was fine.

I was forced to go to Chinese-[language] school by this lovely aunt, who made dresses for me now and then, because she thought I needed to have some refinement and some ways of dealing with the [cultural] differences. We were Hakka farmers in Kohala. And you came to Honolulu, you were in Punti society, and you had to be able to not stick out like a sore thumb. I hated Chinese-[language] school, but I went for two years, and I can handle some Punti now, although I prefer not to because I'm proud of being Hakka.

There was never in my life any kind of instilling that we were lesser than others. In fact, my father used to say the two things in life [are]: one, you want to be honest; and two is never let anybody put you down. So in various ways, he was telling us, "You're just as good as anybody else."

And I think it finally found its own solution with the fact that, in high school, I found the Church of the Crossroads, and that meant a lot to me, because that was where more than ever you were told you accept people for what they are and not where they came from.

I never told him but one of the reasons why I became so active in the [Church of the] Crossroads was every Sunday—we spent all afternoon till evening—we played volleyball, sometimes we had dances, we cooked there, we had programs, and then one of the guys took us home.

As long as we say "church," it was fine. Oh, my father would cut my legs off if he knew we danced, because to him, that was as bad as pornography today is to some people. You know, be in a man's arms!

[At McKinley] I did best in science: geology, astronomy, chemistry. Also, I had a leaning toward home economics, partly because of the teachers. But we had also some beautiful social studies teachers. And I became very good friends with the ag [agriculture] teacher, go to visit the garden.

In my senior year, the four officers in our senior classes [were]: Adelino Valentin, a Filipino; Hilda Blackman—I don't know where she came from —was a haole gal. I was the secretary. And Masaru Otaguro was Japanese. And, you know, it never really occurred to us until we had to, one time, put on a forum and go on the radio with a Senator [Guy Mark] Gillette from Iowa. The Senate sent him here to talk to the population to find out whether we were ready for statehood. And it was pointed out, here we are, four students of different ethnic backgrounds.

STUDYING VOCATIONAL HOME ECONOMICS AT UH

You know, nobody went away to college in the Mainland. If they did, they weren't in our circle. You either were going to University of Hawai'i, you were going to work at Pearl Harbor [Naval Shipyard], or you would go to a business school.

My father said to me, "You do what you want." But he says, "I'm not supporting you. I got nothing to support you with." And he said, "Besides, I think any girl who goes on to college is just wasting their money, because they graduate and they become housewives. So what's the use of going to college?"

I wanted to be a teacher like my aunt and my cousins. And of course in those days, all females in our family were moving toward being home ec[onomics] teachers. And with my grandfather's skill in tailoring, we had several in the family who were extremely good seamstresses and very good cooks.

So I knew I was going to college, but you didn't focus on a vocation very early then. But as you went along and you had to choose, that seemed to be the most viable. And I had had all my sciences, which fit into the home ec thing. So that's where I went.

During the first year of college, I think, I lived at home. And I worked for the National Youth Administration in the UH home ec lab feeding rats and cleaning cages. The second year, I got a job as a maid across the street where Atherton House is. And I lived in and earned my keep and got two, three dollars extra. And then one year got better pay and worked down near Lē'ahi Hospital. But that was a problem of commuting.

Then, from then on, there was always [a] student job I could get in the home ec lab. Correct papers, proofread teachers' textbooks or whatever they were putting out, make sandwiches for teachers' meetings and that kind of thing until the war [World War II] broke out.

The first thing you notice was the air raid shelters that you were asked to build prior to December 7th were now being used. So in our home, Father shored up the one that would not cave in, with more lumber and so forth. You learned to carry, always, your gas mask. You immediately notice in class that except for four men, the whole 4,000 population had dwindled so that there were only women in school. And some of my classmates, women, left because the [U.S. Army] Corps of Engineers and other groups wanted them, and they could get good pay for that.

So when we graduated in home ec in 1942, there were only fifteen of us. You became closer. And you were then aware [of] the hardships of your Japanese friends, whom you never really think would ever have problems of discrimination. And you noticed that their parents weren't really allowed to go out to visit each other. And some of your best friends' families were sent somewhere and interned as enemies of the country.

Of course, my best scholastic year was that last year, too. Partly because you didn't have the distraction of playing around (chuckles) with the guys. And partly because I guess you feel like, "Well, this is it. The last year, I gotta do good."

First job I got was a call from Hilo—I don't know how they got my vitae and got my name. But I had to accept and be interviewed on the telephone when this job was opening. I went up as a home supervisor for the federal program called Farm Security Administration, which was then concentrating on helping families to be self-sufficient.

Well, the job was challenging, but the more I worked at it, the more I realized that the home ec skills alone were not going to help people change or make it better. 'Cause the satisfaction of really reaching the depressed and the disenchanted was not going to happen if all I did was set up blueprints that look right and show them how to clean their sewing machine and how to can takenoko and stuff.

Then at that point, I ran into a social worker in Hilo whom I had admired very much and he [Morris Fox] became a mentor and a life-long friend. And he suggested that I might want to go into social work to improve in the human skills area. Well, the University of Hawai'i School of Social Work had this only one-year study program. So I came back, studied social work for that one year at the UH.

So I guess that was a wise move, because even later on when I went back into home ec, that kind of supplemented and expanded the goals I had. And of course, it fitted in with a lot of the church philosophy, too. You know, accepting people as equals, as the right to be different, not knowing all the right answers, because your answer may not be the right one for them, and maybe not even for you. So it was combination of church influence, education, and I think a basic personality of liking people, reaching out.

WITH THE RED CROSS AT ST. LOUIS HIGH SCHOOL'S ARMY HOSPITAL

Here I get stuck in an army hospital, and I gotta go be with all these wounded, and "What am I doing in this kind of place?"

Well, the [American] Red Cross establishment is part of the military social work arm. First thing, I go put on a uniform. I have to go through the wards and meet the new soldiers who have come in, ask them if there's anything we can do. And one of the first ones I met, I walked into an orthopedic ward, and this soldier sees me coming in and he yells at me, "Get the hell out of here, you slant-eyed Jap." And so I turn around and I go out, and I say, "Okay, I can't do anything here."

They assign me the maternity ward because they were now beginning to have [problems of] pregnancies of local girls by servicemen, either they weren't going to be married because they didn't want to get married, or the military had such strict rules about military and local girls getting married. And, you know, sad stories [of] how some of them really loved the guy, and some of them were caught in a situation where they became pregnant. And those days, no birth control, you know. So many of these kids had to have social-work help in the terms of adoptions.

BECOMING A CASEWORKER FOR PĀLAMA SETTLEMENT

Somebody had heard about me working for the Red Cross, local girl, trained social worker. And so [in 1944 Pālama Settlement executive director] Ted Rhea called me up one day and asked me if I'm interested to come down and talk with him about a job with Pālama.

One of the problems was we were in the midst of the war, and we had, [in] particular with the Japanese elderly, those who were kind of stuck in their own homes because of the military regulations that they were not to meet out in groups. And we'd invite them to the settlement house for English classes, music, or home ec courses.

There were the mass athletic programs, like big swimming classes. There were basketball courts that the kids played on. There were some established baseball and things, out in the field. There were art classes of all grades, but mainly elementary kids because by the time they were intermediate and high, many of them were working. There was a game room, which was free play.

One of my jobs was to spot the disruptive ones who would come and just run in the halls or run in the game room and kind of not know what to do. And I would approach them and eventually try to lead them into one of the established classes.

There was a camp down in Waialua called Pālama-by-the-Sea. We took hundreds of kids out there. And the whole idea was to take city kids and give them a chance to get out of the city, out into the open.

And the [public health] nurses or teachers would tell us, "Why don't you have this?" or "Why don't you have that?" and "How come this kid isn't into this or that?" And it would be kind of a talking session when we would then say can we or is there a possibility for our opening other kinds of programs for the kids.

And you know and I know that some of the best contributors to an agency are the people who are ongoing, who know the families, know the kids in and out. One of the custodians had been there for years. And I know sometimes he'd tell me, "No waste time on that family. We had 'em for twenty years that way, you not going change; they going be like that. Go try something else."

The man who was probably one of the greatest contributors in the early days was Nelson Kawakami. He ruled that locker room and all the athletic facilities there. And I know couple of the social workers were not too happy with the way he bribed the kids or disciplined them. But he ran that program for years and developed skills and pride in kids who remembered Nelson for years.

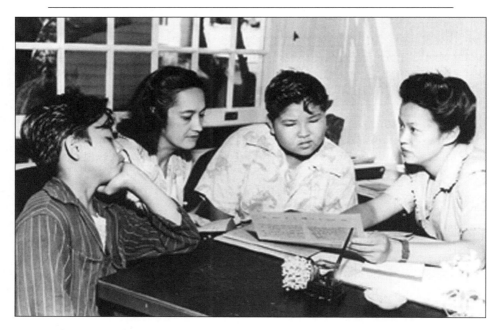

Case worker Jennie Lee In, right, and truant officer Thelma Espinda talk with boys at Pālama Settlement, ca. 1945 (Pālama Settlement Archives, photo reproduced by courtesy of Pālama Settlement).

MSW AT NEW YORK SCHOOL OF SOCIAL WORK

I went away after almost two years at Pālama and went to New York School of Social Work with the settlement helping me find living quarters in New York, and the community scholarship program supporting some of the tuition monies. And the understanding was that I would return to spend at least one year back at the settlement.

I chose to go to New York because I had always thought of it as the center of great activities. So when I got accepted there, I said to Ted that I would want to go and get my degree. And typically of Ted, he went down his list of settlement houses. Helen Hall was then director at Henry Street Settlement in New York. He arranged for me to live there, and work a bit for room and board.

Henry Street Settlement had lots of things to offer. It's in the Lower East Side neighborhood, which was traditionally known as a poor neighborhood where immigrants gathered first, and then worked their way up or out. One of the things which was really eye-opening was their very, very good playhouse. They had a really decent music school.

The children's program I was involved in was mainly the play group, what we called the game room, which was, again, a free-play area where I issued equipment and tried to intervene so there wouldn't be any big fights.

The big thing I remembered in terms of its contribution to me was how Helen Hall attempted to use the staff as an example of how you can come from all places and backgrounds and become a cohesive and caring group. Many of us were students, some from Julliard School of Music, some from school of social work, some from nursing schools.

Dinner was a formal affair; we all had to dress and march into the dining room. Miss Hall would shift us around so we'd get to know each other. And at the end of the dinner hour, we always had some kind of a program. She would use staff members; the music person would lead us in singing, the Episcopalian priest would do a storytelling. The priest was not part of the settlement but he lived in the neighborhood. Some of us would have to tell a little bit about where we came from and what we did.

The other thing I learned was, I used to have to take the bus and the subway to go from Lower East Side to where the school was. And often at nights we wouldn't get through doing library work till midnight. I would come home by subway, and then take the bus over the Bowery, and walk several blocks from the bus stop to the settlement house.

And in those days they had what they called cellar clubs where gangs hung out. I came home, and I saw this group of young guys, maybe teenagers or young adults. And just as I was approaching, I heard one of the fellows yell out, "Henry Street!"

One of the other guys was trying to approach me by walking up the steps. And immediately, the fellow stopped, and I went by. There was silence. I was alert enough to know that the person who approached the steps was probably wanting to intercept me in some way. And just the scream, "Henry Street," stopped the whole thing.

So there was a respect in that neighborhood for the settlement house. And after that, I never really worried too much, even if I came home late at nights.

My field placements were very interesting. The main field placement was in relationship to my thesis, which is using group activities to help the population that was growing older at that time. And the famous center at that time was Hudson Community Center for senior citizens. And I went there twice a week and did field work and also gathered material for my thesis.

In addition, I had to do field work in the public welfare section. It was very depressing. My route was in the lower side of Brooklyn in a place called Williamsburg. And one of my clients was a young man who was on drugs.

I had a number of pregnant teenagers in a section outside of Long Island City, where the only real scare I had in my year in New York was walking the street one day to one of the girls' home. A big black car came along next to me on the sidewalk and went around once and then came back again, and slowly followed my footsteps. At first I pretend I didn't notice. Then finally I stuck my hand in my pocket where I kept a notebook for all of my interviews, took the pencil out and starting putting the car license number. And then the car shot away. So it was kind of scary at that point, but you use whatever wits you have at the moment to be careful.

RETURN TO PĀLAMA

I don't think they had filled that position when I left, because they knew I was coming back. For me, I can honestly say that my skills in group work became sharper. And thereafter they always kidded me, "You're only half caseworker, you're a group worker." I knew [in] what areas I could do group work, and I also became more confident I could run groups.

I think the main thing it did, it gave me little more confidence in what I had been trying to do the two years before. And you weren't hitting in the dark so much. You had known that these things were also being tried other-wheres, and they've had their failures and successes.

At the same time, however, we were being criticized by some folks, in-cluding some of the old-timers, that we were spending too much time and too much money on too few people. Because when you limit yourself to smaller groups, you don't have as much energy or equipment or time to spend on mass activities.

I like to think that Pālama also learned from us that the group offerings can be helpful in many different ways, and the old model is not necessarily the only and the best, but you can change and you can also keep what is good.

MARRIAGE AND MOVE TO THE MAINLAND

I was getting married and going to live in the East, which I did for six years. It was hard, but that's a choice I had to make, because my prospective husband wasn't going to come back to Hawai'i.

I worked in the Jewish community center as a game-room attendant on a part-time basis. I worked as a schoolteacher in Connecticut and taught home ec. I worked in a school system in New Jersey as a visiting teacher, but the kids called me "the hooky cop," because my job was to go search for the kids who didn't come to school and reasons for them, and then work with the families. And sometimes, even take them to court.

RETURN TO HAWAI'I IN 1954

I was being a lobbyist for children's legislation. At that time there was a Commission on Children and Youth, which still exists today, although there's talk about wiping that department out. We didn't run programs those days. There was only me and a secretary.

My main job was to get the main agencies that dealt with children and the court, health, education, social service, and labor departments to talk to each other, to handle particular problems that cross all those lines, but [which] they had never really taken time to sit down and figure out.

Of course, one of the biggest things we did while I was working there, was to provide the first community service for the—today called the mentally challenged, I guess. And that was when the schools were ordered by the legislature to begin to have classes for the educable, and the health department [was required] to set up clinics for diagnosis and treatment. So that was a job that required a lot of meeting times with all the different heads, and then writing up reports that's agreeable to all of them, and then presenting it to the legislature to provide for funds and positions.

That job lasted till I was remarried and was pregnant. I went into retirement, so to speak, for twelve years just raising the family. Then very quickly after that, when the daughter was in the sixth grade and my son was in the second grade, it was time for me to get back into a job. My husband was to retire in about four years, and there would probably not be sufficient funds to send them through college.

I went back and worked first in part-time jobs with the state hospital as a social worker, as a nutritionist lecturer at a senior center, then as a lecturer for Head Start staff with the University [of Hawai'i], then part-time worker with Teacher Corps, which was trying to train teachers to work with disenchanted, unmotivated kids.

Then I finally got a full-time job with the state Department of Education and went into a job that I loved very dearly, because it combined my experience and my training both in home ec and in social work. With another teacher, we started a class for the pregnant teenagers on the Windward side which drew students from Kahuku to Waimānalo.

I enjoyed that job wonderfully for thirteen years and saw it develop from just a few classes to a full-day program. We were able to give them credits in a whole variety of subjects with the help of a couple of part-time teachers.

I see them [former students] on the street, and we talk about their families. Some of them now have children who are old enough to graduate from college. Some of them are out in the work field. In that job I was able to use many, many different skills from all the different kinds of jobs that I've had in the past.

GLOSSARY

haole	Caucasian
hukilau	seine
oba-chan	aunt or older woman
takenoko	bamboo shoots

MAE MORITA ITAMURA

AN INDEPENDENT WOMAN

I feel that I accomplished my aim in my life. To take good care of my own family. At the same time, make some money to take care myself. Because in this life, you have to be independent, you know. Gee, when you come and ask me all these questions, just like dream, you know. (Laughs.) Going into the past, yeah? Good, sometimes, you remember.

Mae Morita Itamura was born in 1905 in Nāhiku, Maui. When her father became ill in 1923, she quit high school and worked as a gasoline pump attendant for Kitagawa Motors in Spreckelsville. The following year, she clerked at Tam Chong Store in Lower Pā'ia.

A few months later, Itamura became a bookkeeper at Maui Dry Goods in Lower Pā'ia. When Maui Dry Goods opened a liquor department, she was placed in charge of it. While at Maui Dry Goods, Itamura took on side jobs in order to support her family. She worked as a touring theater group organizer, an insurance salesperson, and a bookkeeper at another dry goods store.

In 1937, Itamura opened Pā'ia Liquor Store in Lower Pā'ia. She married Masao Itamura in 1953. Her nephew took over the store after Itamura retired in 1972. As a retiree, Itamura enjoyed golfing and traveling. She died in 1991 at age eighty-five.

In 1979 and 1980, Warren Nishimoto interviewed Itamura at her Lower Pā'ia home for *Stores and Storekeepers of Pā'ia and Pu'unēnē, Maui*. This compilation of the recollections of thirty-three individuals who were directly involved with stores serving Pā'ia and Pu'unēnē provides researchers with first-person accounts of the beginnings, maintenance, and decline of that role on the Valley Island. These accounts supplement existing literature on plantation life, add to the history of Maui and Hawai'i, and contribute to the growing body of knowledge on entrepreneurship in America.

FAMILY

I was born in Maui—Nāhiku, under the waterfall, Honomū Waterfall.

Both [parents were] from Hiroshima. My father came first. He came under contract to HC&S [Hawaiian Commercial & Sugar Company]. He supposed to go back under three years' contract, but he met my mother in Kula, you see. She was a widow at that time with two children, so my father married her. And then, I was the first child [of that marriage]. I had ten brothers and sisters, but five died.

We moved to Ka'elekū [Sugar Company], Hāna plantation. I think that's where they moved next. I was about ten or eleven. I was going to school already. But in between, I don't know where they went. I don't think they stayed in that waterfall place for long, you know.

[After being fired from Hāna plantation for labor organizing] he had to leave there and come to Kāheka. Then, while he was there, there was another big strike all over Hawai'i. Before that, nobody believed in striking. They just get kicked around, you know. So, my father joined and helped them. So he got kicked out again (laughs) from Kāheka. Then we went to Lower Pā'ia.

He bought that small hotel in Lower Pā'ia. Upstairs, maybe ten or eleven rooms, that's all. To buy a hotel, he needed the cash. Those days, they had tanomoshi. You bid so much interest, and then, the highest bidder—that month—win that $50, or $60, or $100. If five persons at $20, that amounted to $100. He had [borrowed] $1,000 [from more than one tanomoshi].

He didn't know how to cook or to run a hotel because he was a contractor and sugar planter. He had no experience in business. He took sick, and then the hotel went bankrupt.

So, I had to work from that time, see? I paid all his bills. And my father owed so much money. If I don't pay, it's shame for me, see? I could not just let it go, so I had to pay.

I had to quit high school. I had six months more to go. I used to take business, typewriting, and bookkeeping. But what I really wanted was to be a sugar technologist because that seems to be interesting. That's math, you see? I used to like arithmetic.

I was going to University of Hawai'i. My girlfriend Elsie Kuramoto's father wanted me to continue school. He said, "I can support you." But nobody to support my whole family, so I told him, "I don't want to bother you." My brothers were all small, too.

Oh, yeah, that's the time I worked Kitagawa [Motors]. I lived with them [in Spreckelsville]. You know, pump gasoline. Fix the tires. Tubes, like that. You patch up. You rub the surface of the tube with sandpaper, and then put patch on.

When you need the job, you have to do all kind. Then if something else comes, then you just move. Then I worked Tam Chong [Store]. Sell dresses and coats, like that. Then I went to Maui Dry Goods.

MAUI DRY GOODS

We had about nine or ten workers. The workers were all Portuguese. Mostly. Except me, I think. It started with Joaquin Garcia's mother's store. Then they sold it, and this company was formed, Maui Dry Goods and Grocery Company of Maui. They had one branch in Pā'ia. Quite a big store. Coffins and furniture upstairs, and then groceries and dry goods downstairs.

We had quite a lot of good customers. Few were Japanese, but mostly Portuguese [from] the plantation and in Lower Pā'ia. Because this was Portuguese concern. They all get stocks in there. You know, they own so many percent. And they tell their friends to go to that store.

[Some] charge, you know, [and order takers] collect end of the month. That, the boss had to okay. Sometimes they [the customers] won't pay for one whole month, but somehow, they had to pay. Otherwise, we didn't give credit.

Once in a while we had big sales, and oh, we had to work until twelve o'clock at night. You see, [what] we couldn't sell, we cut down and put on sale. On sale, was all cash-[and-carry] and couldn't bring back.

The Honolulu wholesalers get [goods] from the Mainland, and they distribute all over Hawai'i. They always carry one satchel, and then they took orders; then the goods come. They sent straight from Mainland, some big orders, but small orders come from Honolulu.

Mostly dry goods I used to order. The salesmen brought the samples and says these are coming out and all that. Then if I liked it, I ordered.

Cloth dress goods, that's the main thing. By yards. Like Indian Head cloth. That was a famous white material—thick kind. You sewed dresses, or you made pillowcases, all kinds. Ten cents a yard, we used to sell. Came in all colors, too. But white, we used to sell the most.

And what else? Before Christmas, I order lots of toys and presents—mirror and powder sets, like that. Oh yeah, and we used to carry plates, too. Teapots and teakettles, and all those.

The boss takes care the groceries. Mostly salt salmon, codfish, because we had mostly Portuguese customers. Fifty-gallon barrels, those salt salmon. They come wet, not like codfish. Irish potatoes and flour. They make bread, eh? And canned goods—salmon, tuna, and beans, red beans, and all kinds.

Yeah, that was pretty big store. [But] the plantation store was the biggest. Theirs was entirely different way of business, you know. Because lots of them [i.e., customers] are private growers. They raised and sold the sugar cane to the plantation [a practice called kompang]. They scaled the tonnage and they have credit on same. Once a year, they paid for all those groceries [with] kompang money. All cash, you see.

One of our [store] boys found, I think, $2,200. He say, "I'm lucky. I get $2,200. I found 'em on the road." I say, "Let me see the envelope with the kompang money. You know, they slave long time. The whole family depend on that money. You better give back."

He won't give back. He bought one car, and the car turned over in accident. Then, I think he got fired. All kind of misfortunes because I think he did wrong, yeah? That's why I never do wrong. (Laughs.)

Must be around 1932 or 1933, I think, the liquor opened. They made special room for that because of liquor department, you know. That's when Prohibition pau. I order and sell liquors. Saleswoman for liquor, dry goods, grocery, if they want. But by then, no coffins. By then, there appeared two new mortuaries.

Each wholesaler had franchises of different brands of liquor. American Factors carried Budweiser beer, and so on. Hawaiian Oke had all kinds of

Lower Pā'ia, Maui, ca. 1935 (photo courtesy of Tadayoshi Tamasaka).

Hawaiian stuff. They used to make when the liquor didn't come during the war [World War II]. They made with sugar and molasses, and they sold. And then they call that Hawaiian Sunshine whiskey.

I worked in the liquor [department], so I learned the liquor business from there. I always remember not to forget to be good bookkeeper. If you don't make money, just stop. No use hanging on if you don't make money, yeah?

Yeah, the manager taught me lots of things. To be thrifty. He used to tell me, "Don't waste paper," whenever we throw away all the old paper bags and wrapping paper. He said, "No. You straighten out the used ones and you use." (Laughs.) This was a good lesson for us. I was young, then.

MOONLIGHTING

I used to sell insurance. Moonlighting. My brother used to take me [around]. [I made] 20 percent of the first premium. So if they pay $200 a year, I got $40, eh? So, more I sold, more money I made.

I like to sell. I used my technique. I had a brochure with the pictures. The mother crying for the daughter after they had accident, and so forth. You have to actually let them see the consequences. If you don't have insurance, then you don't have anything. Usually, they would buy. Filipinos, Japanese, all kinds.

And then, I used to take some shows around. Japanese shows. Once a month or twice a month, like that. They came from Honolulu with the [silent] movies and also Japanese live shows. Mr. Matsuo, showman, used to bring. Movies or those singing, dancing, and acting shows, like that, they had. All those old historic moving pictures. *Shijūshichishi no Seppuku Monogatari* [Tale of the Forty-Seven Retainers] picture.

Then I get ready for them—hotel and where to stay. Then we hire the car, and we went to all the camps. Those days we had lots of small places, you know. Keāhua, Pūlehu, Kailua 1, Kailua 2, Camp 10, Camp 4, Camp 2. All no more now, see?

We had one narrating, always. Get the interpreter [the narrator], the boss, and the [camera] operator. And we set up. Outdoor. The movie machine to grind the films. Yeah, with the screen. They had the bench lined up. We borrowed the benches. If the rain come, they refund you the ticket.

But most of the time, they have shows in the theater. And then, I stand by the door and collect tickets for them. Oh, only thirty-five, forty cents. Cheap. Children are all free. Everybody came. Filipinos and all. Sometimes about 100, sometimes 75. It depended on what kind of movie we were showing. So, if they made $500, I made $50. Not bad.

I used to go and help at [Pā'ia] Mercantile, [too]. That was a Japanese big store carrying dry goods and all that. I used to help them whenever I can. Oh, sometimes, bookkeeping, and sometimes, selling.

And then, I got sick, and I went to Kula Sanitarium. I recuperated about four months, I think. I thought I really had TB or something, but no. I was lucky. I didn't go to the TB sanitarium, but they had these restorium, they call that, to have rest. After that, I just took over [selling] insurance mostly, because that's big money and I didn't have to go here and there.

PĀ'IA LIQUOR STORE

Then I opened my own [liquor] shop [in 1937]. I read once in a magazine that the best way to make something of your life is to be self-employed. You can be the highest-paid woman in the whole world. More you sell, you make more money, see? While you work in the store [as an employee], it's same salary. You can't advance more than what they give.

I heard this Maui Dry Goods, that main stockholder didn't want me to get the [liquor] license because I'm young girl and no young single girl in Hawai'i can get that license, those days. He said I shouldn't get the license because I'm not qualified to run a liquor store. Even in Honolulu, they didn't have [unmarried female licensees]. That's what this fellow argued.

At that time, I had $2,000 saved in bank. So, I bought the liquor stock in cash. The liquor was down there. Down the wharf.

This [stockholder] fellow said that against the law. "She get no license, and she bought the liquor." So, the inspector said, "You can buy any amount so long you don't sell it. That's not against the law."

You see, they have seven liquor inspectors. Liquor Commission. [Including] one chief inspector. This chief inspector voted for me. That was how. I was lucky. Four to three. I got the liquor license. After I got the license, I didn't worry because I knew I can run the store.

I got this license because there were my good customers—all rich people. You know, these doctors and some bookkeepers up here. They said, "Mae, you go and open, and we'll buy liquor from you."

They wanted this good whiskeys and drinks, like Canadian Club, and all that. They [Maui Dry Goods] don't carry, see? They won't let me order that high-price stuff.

I rented one small place. Right in Lower Pā'ia. Rent was cheap, those days—thirty-five dollars a month. Then, I had some carpenter [who] made those shelves. I bought one icebox for the beer. Big cooler. And then, I just opened.

WORLD WAR II

Then five years after, all of a sudden, came the war. 1941. During the war, each civilian person had a permit to buy liquor—one quart of hard liquor or one case of beer in one week. We sold all what we had in one day. Then, when new supply came in, we sold all again.

I can't buy all what I want. Because they don't come from Mainland much because the war. But I was lucky because I had the biggest quota on Maui, and everything went by quota. I had fifty cases of beer a month and so many cases whiskey.

They added up the sale slips of the month of April of 1940, and then they based the quota on that. I used to put down everything on sale slips. And then, at the end of the month, I added up and paid gross income tax on that. Lots of people didn't put down because they didn't want to pay the tax. So, it pays to be honest.

You [a retail customer] can't buy without the [ration] card. There's a place to stamp. We put, "February 28, one case beer, Pā'ia Liquor Store." So he can't buy [more] until next week. When the liquor comes in, you see them. That's long [line], boy. And, when that quota is gone, we closed the door, and we go and play golf. Seldom we opened until noontime, I think. No charges, everything cash.

Only thing, you had to be careful. Look twice at the cards, you know, that they were obeying the law. If you make a mistake and you sell two [items to a customer in a week], you had to pay big fine. And they close your store if too much mistakes. But I was lucky, I never got caught once.

Then, across, I rented another place [in 1942 or 1943], and I had two. And then, I put one more here [in the present location], so I had three. That must be around 1948, I think, after the war; 1945, the war ended.

After the war ended, the servicemen could all buy the liquor, too. You should see, they lined up, you know. They bought so much cases of liquor, truck after truck. In one day's time, they cleaned up all our supply.

That [VJ] Day, in September [2, 1945], I think, they allowed them to buy. That night, they [Native American and Caucasian soldiers] shot one another. There's a big gulch in between the other side and this side where they camped. There were two battalions. Six [soldiers] got killed.

Then General Harland Smith came down to my place and he said, "Mae, I'm going to close your store. You're responsible for killing those soldiers. They drank and fought, shot one another, and they got killed."

I said, "No, General, I have the legitimate license. If I don't sell, they go to someplace else. That's how American enterprise is run. If you close me, the civilians going to make lots of money because they will buy and sell to them for double or triple the price. Anyway, they want to drink, and you can't stop them, General." He didn't close me. (Chuckles.)

[When the war ended], I got all that stock from the officers' club of the marines. General Smith sent this lieutenant to see me. He said, "General wants to sell to you all—[lock], stock, barrel—everything to you."

I say, "Sure that's all right, but certain things I don't want to buy. I tell you what you do. You fly around the Hawaiian Islands, and you sell these item." I mark [price] 'em all, you see? Benedictine, all those liqueurs, after dinner kind. For Maui, they are not good sellers. So I took all the whiskey, and rum, or gin, Scotch whiskey. That's how I got all those good things. He sold all the unsellable kind to others.

SECRET OF GOOD BUSINESS

You see, in those days, we had to compete with the big stores, like this plantation stores and all that. In order to get our customers in, I buy so many cases of liquor with only my label. Mine was Gold Eagle whiskey. They bottle that for me in the factory. But you have to buy 100, 250 cases one crack, you see? Then they gave me special price, cash. You sell them little cheaper, and then they [the customers] come.

You have to know the people—what kind of taste they like. I don't drink myself, but I make them try—about ten, fifteen people—and then, I get their opinion.

I have to have all kinds of motivation so that I can make money by pulling our customers to my place. To do that, you have to do something that all the other stores don't do. That's the secret of good business.

You see, we did favors for them, so they'll be all messed up if they don't pay [their liquor bills]. I won't give the service—[like] make tax return for them.

This happened when I just started. I saw this man with one letter, and he said, "Morita, you come and see this letter. What the government say?" "Oh, you don't pay [taxes] for four years. You pay big tax, and then you have to pay penalty." Then, he get surprised and he says, "I don't know what tax is."

You see, those days, they don't send that W2 or anything. Then, I thought I better start get the paper and make for them before they get more debts. Mostly Filipino customers. Maybe around 150, 200. Yeah, lots of them, I made for them. Even now, no charge. They're mostly single, and they work hard. They bought liquor just to relax.

They bring their papers that shows what they earned. Then, I add all that up. Then [they] pay the tax. In those days, was cheap because only you pay

4 or 5 percent. Those days, [they] had to have about two years' tax return receipts before they can leave Hawai'i. I got all those things ready for them, and then they went back to Philippines.

I also write letters for them. English or Japanese, if they want. If they cannot read the letter, I read it for them—explain to them. But, main thing, be kind to them. They don't need much to make them happy and come to you.

MARRIAGE AND RETIREMENT

1972 [I retired]. All that time I was looking for somebody to take over my business, but nobody seemed to care in my family. If I ever wanted to sell, they [real estate agents] offered me big money. But I want some of my family to hold on to it because you can make good living out of this place.

Then I put my nephew—my brother's boy—through college, and he graduated, got married. He was teaching, then he told his father he wants to come back to Maui. So, he runs the store nighttime, and daytime, he works for HSTA [Hawai'i State Teachers Association].

In 1953, I got married, you know. My parents, Japanese style, wanted me to get married so many times. I say, "How am I going to leave this family and go off getting married?" Because I cannot tell my husband to support them.

You see, those days, we were taught to be good to your father and mother. Be grateful for them because they brought us up, and then they fed us and took care of us. We had to pay back all of those things. That was the whole thing in my mind—to pay them back.

Those days, I had no time to think of future. I had to fight for my existence—just to get along. Now, I take it easy. I play golf and go wherever I want—China, Russia. I'm really blessed. I worked hard, but to me, I don't mind so much. That was no burden.

I feel that I accomplished my aim in my life. To take good care of my own family. At the same time, make some money to take care myself. Because in this life, you have to be independent, you know. I think if you take care yourself and know what you do in your life—you know, set one goal—then you'll get it done somehow.

GLOSSARY

| pau | over, finished |
| tanomoshi | mutual lending association |

EMMA KAAWAKAUO

WAIKĪKĪ, IT'S PART OF ME

I took hula lessons from Lalani Hawaiian Village. The hula was considered not a cultural thing that it is today. In fact in some segments of the community, in your church if you will, and some of the schools, the hula was very much frowned upon. So in reflecting back, I thought it was unusual that my parents who were, I would say, maybe a little bit old-fashioned, allowed me to take hula lessons.

Emma Manouaokalani Kaawakauo was born in 1927 in Honolulu, Oʻahu. Her mother, Emma Manouaokalani Kaeo Kaawakauo, was a longtime teacher at Waikīkī Elementary School. Her father, Elias Kahoohuli Kaawakauo, was a printer and news composing room supervisor for the *Honolulu Advertiser* and the *Paradise of the Pacific* magazine.

The Kaawakauos lived in the Hamohamo section of Waikīkī for more than thirty years. Emma Kaawakauo attended Waikīkī Elementary School, St. Andrew's Priory, and Graceland Junior College in Iowa. In 1955, she began her thirty-plus years in state government as a clerical worker.

Michi Kodama-Nishimoto interviewed Emma Kaawakauo for COH's *Waikīkī, 1900–1985: Oral Histories* (1985) and described her as "soft-spoken and thoughtful."

FAMILY BACKGROUND

We always say we are pure Hawaiian. But I learned from my aunt, my father's sister, that we have Spanish from his side of the family.

I guess it shows in some of the members of my family. He [my father] says, "I don't recognize that. I'm pure Hawaiian!" (Laughs.)

My father's name was Elias Kahoohuli Kaawakauo. He was born on Molokaʻi in Wailau Valley. The family originally came from the Big Island on the Kona side. They were part of the Great Mahele of the land that was assigned to the families in the 1840s or so.

He lived in the valley until his parents died about, oh, I guess he must have been about five or six years old. He was sent to live on the east side of the island with an aunt. But I guess because of the occurrences in his life, he lost his speech.

They had a poi factory on Moloka'i. He'd help make the poi and then deliver it. I guess working around animals, in particular the horses or the donkeys, somehow or other, helped bring his speech back.

By the time he was ten or eleven, they sent him to Lahainaluna School, which is where he got interested in the printing trade. But in the meanwhile, this family, they moved to Honolulu. I guess, by the time he was about thirteen or fourteen, because he was also very talented with his hands, carpentry work, he was prevented from going back to school. They felt that he was more useful helping here in Honolulu.

He ran away from the family and went out to look for work. He met this man who happened to see him on the street. That was how he went to work for the *[Honolulu] Advertiser*.

My mother was the oldest child of her family . . . [who], going back, oh, three or four generations prior to hers, were from Waikīkī. She went to Waikīkī School, then to Central Grammar School, which was the only intermediate school at the time. And then, from Central Grammar, she went to McKinley High School, and then to two years at [Territorial] Normal [School] training.

Her first year of teaching was on Moloka'i. Then the next year, she went to 'Aiea Elementary School, and then the third year at Waikīkī [Elementary School] where she remained until she died [in 1962].

HAMOHAMO HOME

After my parents got married in 1924, their first home was in Cunha Apartments. It was right across the street from the park—the [Honolulu] Zoo and the [Kapi'olani] Park.

Before my brother was born in 1925, they decided to purchase a home. I remember my dad saying, "It was an exorbitant price of $5,500!" (Chuckles.) They moved to Hamohamo Road [now Kūhiō Avenue].

Our house was built high. You had to climb about eight stairs to get up to our front porch that faced the mountains, or the mauka side. I think one of the reasons the home was built so high is that we had a spring below, underground.

The front, our hedge, was of various colored hibiscus plants. We had three huge mountain apple trees in the front yard. Under the mountain apple trees, were what we called laua'e. It's a type of fern.

On the side, we had four o'clock blossoms. Somehow or other, the flowers would wilt seemingly at the hour of four, so they were called "four o'clock blossoms." And pīkake plants on the side there.

At the back on the side, there were two mango trees. And in the back, three huge mango trees. So, there was fruit plentiful at some time of the year to eat. My dad planted some papaya and pomegranate trees in the backyard, too.

I had an older brother, and myself, and a younger sister. My father built us swings from the mango tree in the driveway.

[In the neighborhood] there was what we call a tamarind tree. The fruit from it when they were green, it's just like a glue. We'd get the cream cans and the [end] part that wasn't opened, we'd put the tamarind on our feet and put the cans and walk around, see who could stay up the longest without falling down.

There was a little wooden bridge [over a stream] that we could walk over in order to get to the zoo. We used to go and catch fish with a net and put them in a little bottle.

The [zoo's] elephant, whose name was Daisy, and the lion, they're almost like an alarm clock. Certain hours of the day, you know, we'd hear the trumpeting of the elephant or the roar of the lion.

HAMOHAMO NEIGHBORS

Mr. Matsuzawa, had, well, it was a cart on two wheels, wheels with spokes on either side. The top part, it had a little roof. The only thing I remember was shave ice, but I know he had other things like candies. . . . He would go daily, take his cart, you know, on foot, go down to the park.

My recollection of him was that the various flavors that he had for his shave ice, whenever he used a bottle up, he always left some at the bottom. Sometime during the week, he would put all these together and give them to me. (Laughs.) [I would] mix it up with milk. You know, make a milkshake.

[There were also] over the fence conversations with Obā-chan [the elder Mrs. Matsuzawa]. She did the family cooking, and rice was cooked outdoors on her little—it wasn't a stove. She had these huge rocks, not quite boulders. She placed a grill between these two boulders. She would cook the rice in the wooden Japanese container.

If I wasn't there, she always would go, "Ima!" (Laughs.) I guess it was easier for her to say "Ima" instead of "Emma." So, "Ima!" and I would go and sit on the fence and just chat with her while she cooked, even though her English wasn't all that well. But I guess, if you really liked communicating with someone or talking, you'd find a way of either hand motions or broken pidgin.

What I remember about Mr. Kiakahi [another neighbor] was that when [Franklin] Roosevelt, I guess in '32, was running for president, he was the main supporter. All of the families that I knew of, [including] my parents, were very strong Republicans. He was unusual that he was the only Democrat in a sea of Republicans. (Laughs.)

He would stand on the corner of the street up on Kalākaua [Avenue] and sing, "Happy Days Are Here Again," with his huge lau hala hat, and talk about President Roosevelt. I remember that, sitting across the street on the beach and watching him. (Laughs.)

LALANI HAWAIIAN VILLAGE

The Lalani Hawaiian Village was located fronting Kalākaua [Avenue] and on the side of Paoakalani [Avenue]. The village was very interesting. In front of each of the grass huts was someone who was doing poi pounding. I also remember there was a little taro patch by the hut.

People, if they were interested, they would come in for the tours. Either Mr. or Mrs. [George] Mossman conducted these tours, or one of the daughters. They were taken through and cultural things were explained about, again, the poi, and the tapa making, and the kapa quilting, and the making of leis, and what we call today Hawaiiana culture.

Most of them were tourists, people who were visiting Hawai'i either from Mainland or foreign countries. In particular, during the summer, we had the military, especially the navy, sailors, when ships were in at the time.

Most of the time the tours were included with the entertainment, the program, and with the lū'au. The pig was cooked out in an imu in the back, right in the back area where the food was made.

I took hula lessons from Lalani Hawaiian Village. For a period of time, the hula was considered not a cultural thing that it is today. In fact in some segments of the community, in your church if you will, and some of the schools, even if I may mention this, at Kamehameha [Schools], the hula was very much frowned upon. So in reflecting back, I thought it was unusual that my parents who were, I would say, maybe a little bit old-fashioned, allowed me to take hula lessons.

And I think, perhaps the reason was that they cared very much for the Mossmans and were close to them. Mrs. Mossman was a colleague of my mother's. They both taught at Waikīkī School. Mr. Mossman was Scots Hawaiian. But they [the Mossmans] both spoke fluent Hawaiian. It just seems that perhaps Mr. Mossman was trying to bring back the Hawaiian culture at that time.

For the first two months, this is a guess, we had to exercise. They were exercises mostly in limbering up the body. The first thing that we started learning were the ancient hulas. And I understood why it was that we had to go through all of this.

Then from that, we were introduced to what was then known as hapahaole hula which involved our use of the pebbles [as rhythm instruments].

As I learn from the clipping, we graduated actually a year later, you know, in January. Our commencement, which we call 'ūniki, involved various types of costumes. We were taught to make our own ti-leaf skirts. The top part [the bodice] was real tapa that had been handmade.

After we graduated, I entertained with the Hawaiian Village. During the regular year, it was every Saturday night. But there was also once during the weekday night. We would get five dollars for a night.

One night we'd use the holokū and the ti leaf. Another night the ancient hula and the ti leaf or the grass skirt and the ti leaf. The highlight of the program was the finale. What it was, on the ocean side of the stage in the village was a miniature volcano. It was made of lava rock. In the back was a huge stump of a tree. On this stump, their oldest daughter, who was my hula teacher, did a dance for Pele [the volcano goddess], I would say, or to Pele.

A member of this Punohu family, who lived above on Paoakalani [Avenue], worked at the village. He simulated a volcano by being on the back side of it, you know, away from the audience, and putting kerosene in his mouth. There was a torch just below the top of the volcano. He blew that, you know, spit out that kerosene, and that was your flash of fire.

He was very good at it, to some extent that we'd hear, after the dance was over, he'd be reprimanded by the daughter. "You did it too well tonight!" Her skirt would be singed (laughs) in the front.

He was, I think, considered the best coconut tree climber in the Islands. The village had a lot of coconut trees, and they were quite tall. As if he were walking on the flat ground, he would just literally walk, instead of grasping with his legs and arms and then pulling his body up. He could manage, no matter how windy it was. I've never seen anyone else do it quite like how he did it.

NEIGHBORHOOD MERCHANTS

[Also fronting Kalākaua Avenue] there was a grocery store. It was Ibaraki Store. Let's see. Next to it, I remember a beauty shop or a barbershop in that area. There was also a cleaners. And Tahara's Restaurant.

Actually, for my part, the only time I went to eat in Tahara's, or allowed to, given money to eat, was when I went to the beach. It was practically an all-day thing. We'd have money to go across the street, and go to Tahara's, and have lunch.

They made the best pipi kaula. (Laughs.) I mean, all their food was 'ono. But in particular, their Hawaiian food. But of course, they made things like the saimin and your stew. You could either have your stew with poi, rice, or macaroni.

Next to the cleaners, there were several things, but I remember a restaurant being in that area which was right next to the Aokis. Of course, the Aokis I remember perhaps more well because my parents shopped at Aokis.

They had a little freezer where they kept the meat. They had a butcher. He'd let you—well, my mother not me—go in and pick off. "You want this part?" and he'd cut it off and put the rest back in. (Chuckles.)

Oh, this is another memory I remember. It was a little laundry, just above the Aokis. They were owned by Chinese. I shouldn't forget that. That's where my father took his laundry, his shirts. They'd put the water in their mouth and what we ordinarily would sprinkle with our hands, they'd swhitt! [They would spray from their mouths.] While they're ironing, you know.

I also remember after, I guess, their work was done—you know, we'd go by at certain hours of the day—they'd have their little opium pipes. It was about a foot, maybe longer than that. The end part of it, what we call the

Banzai Cleaning Shop and Tahara's (also known as Fujika's Unique Lunch Room), ca. 1935 (photo courtesy of the Harakawa collection).

pipe, curved up. They would have a little container, like a little bottle, with some liquid in it. You would see this liquid almost like coffee perking, you know.

SURFBOARDS AND SURFING

My dad, one of his hobbies was making surfboards. He would give them away. He used to make boards out of redwood. About four to six inches thick. Then he would carve out the board. He experimented with what they called "hollow board." It was a board about fourteen feet in length. There were two pieces. What he did was, he glued them together in the inner part. So, it was like a miniature boat, actually.

I have fond recollections of going surfing with my dad when I was small. He said that I would be at the bottom of the stairway in the front, with my bathing suit on, of course, and a towel, waiting for him to come home from work.

His surfing area was at the foot of 'Ōhua Avenue. He'd prop the board up against the sea wall. He would look around to see where the best waves were. Whatever the direction is, we would either go out towards Diamond Head, directly out, or towards the Royal [Hawaiian Hotel].

What he'd do is, he'd put me on the board. His chin would be right on my 'ōkole, my rump, so that I wouldn't fall off. He'd paddle out.

I guess he knew the ocean. We would catch one wave and we would ride all the way into the beach. Of course, it would have to be high tide because you had a lot of reef out there.

WAIKĪKĪ ELEMENTARY SCHOOL

I went to the Waikīkī Elementary School which was located right across from our home on then Hamohamo Road. The school was actually a large rectangle. The buildings were on Hamohamo Road, or Kūhiō Avenue, and Kāneloa Road.

At the time I started school, we had a principal who loved flowers, so all of the grounds were well landscaped with many varieties of flowers. We had to be careful when we played (laughs) not to get into the flower beds and everything.

Our new principal—I think this was when I was in the fourth grade—was someone who believed in physical education. So all of the flowers went and grass was planted over. She built all of the jungle gyms, the swings, everything that children needed. Actually, as we grew older in upper elementary, that was our playground.

WORLD WAR II

My grandmother went to the [St. Andrew's] Priory. Also, two cousins from my parents' families. They [my parents] asked me if I wanted to go. I must have said yes, because I went.

My eighth-grade teacher was born and raised in England. Because England had been in the war at least a couple of years before we did, we were knitting for Bundles for Britain. So we were knitting balaclava helmets. This is what the men wore underneath their helmets.

The war began in December of '41. All of the school systems closed down. We went back in—it may have been February or March, sometime during then. I think some of the buildings at the Priory were being used for the war effort through the Episcopalian Church, but we went to school through the summer.

My father was a—what do they call them? [Block] wardens. He patrolled the area at night. And my mother, I think, when they set up either a Red Cross unit or whatever, one of them was at Waikīkī School.

So actually, in the first few weeks, maybe even the first two months, my parents were not at home. My grandmother lived in the next block, so we stayed with her in the evenings. Then my parents would come and get us, and then we would go home and go to bed.

Somehow our parents were able to instill in us this deep sense and belief in racial equality. Members of both sides of the family did not all feel this way for there were a few with very strong anti-Japanese feelings. I do not recall that any of us kids ended lifelong friendships or turned down making new friends because of the war.

Other than going to school with many of the children, especially families in the Japanese camps, there was a close tie 'cause most of these parents were issei, or from Japan. Somehow or other, they got along very well with my mother since she was a schoolteacher. Because many of them were issei and consequently non-citizens, she was able to vouch for them, shall I say. Through some commitment on her part, she organized classes to teach them English.

LEAVING WAIKĪKĪ

The background is a bit complicated and there is much I don't know, but I'll try to piece things together. Sometime in the latter 1950s, before 1959, my parents were approached by a couple of people who represented a group who were interested in developing property in Waikīkī.

During this time, I think it was not an unusual occurrence, for many areas within Waikīkī were beginning to or had changed into non-residential areas. Well, it seems that these people obtained, I believe, a five-year option to develop our property and my parents were compensated for this option.

In this five-year interim which included 1959, we moved out to the Niu Iki home on Kalaniana'ole Highway with the understanding that the Waikīkī property would be developed. This did not come about as planned.

[Eventually in the mid-1960s] the property was developed, and not sold, through someone who had casually stopped by our home in Niu Iki. He brought up the subject of developing property and seemingly because my father liked his personality after meeting with this man several times, my father had total confidence in him.

My first full knowledge of what was taking place was when we all met at the savings and loan institution to sign the documents—my father explained a little to me of what had transpired and what we were going to do. I asked to read the documents before signing and when doing so, realized that there was no way we could meet the mortgage payments, stipulated in the documents, once the property was developed into apartments.

I attempted to caution my father and suggested that our family lawyer be brought into this. He became quite angry and refused to even consider this, so I dropped the matter and went along by signing the documents.

Construction began in 1965 and the buildings were completed in the summer of 1966. It was a struggle managing the apartments and keeping them occupied, and we had to sell the apartments, including the property, by 1968. It was a loss both financially and emotionally, but it ended a two-year struggle and worry.

We finally did go to our lawyer, sometime in 1967–68, but it was already too late. All the documents were legal and binding.

But this did not end our dilemma. In filing his income tax returns for 1968 and 1969, even though he went to a reputable tax service, somehow or other, the entire amount he had received for the Waikīkī property was not entered on these tax returns.

So by 1971, he owed an amount in back taxes and penalties for which he had no available cash to pay. And the only means for payment was to sell the Niu Iki home on Kalaniana'ole Highway.

We moved to our present residence in Mō'ili'ili in October 1972 and my father lived there until he died in December 1978. The tragedy for my father was not owning land in the final years of his life, land he had worked for all his life.

WAIKĪKĪ REFLECTIONS

Prior to the time in spring of this year before we started the interviews, I'd occasionally go into Waikīkī. It was usually mostly just to walk along and sit at the beach, or to go to an occasional movie, or go out and eat somewhere in Waikīkī.

I don't remember ever saying that, "Oh, I don't like the way it is now compared to the way it was before." But you know, after we had those interviews, the first time I had to go out to Waikīkī—it was for something—and I got off the bus, and I was walking around. And you know, there was a bit of resentment.

I caught myself. I said, "Now, how come you're feeling this way?" I said, "Oh, Emma, I think it's because you've been going back into your childhood." (Chuckles.)

But, I think, generally speaking, I don't mind the change all that much really. In a sense, it's just like, "Oh, I remember Waikīkī when, and it's part of me. It's too bad that's not a part of you."

GLOSSARY

hapa-haole	in this context, Hawaiian song with English words
holokū	seamed dress with yoke and train
imu	underground oven
issei	Japanese immigrant
kapa	in this context, a quilt
laua'e	a type of fern known for its fragrance
lau hala	pandanus leaf, used in weaving
lū'au	feast
mauka	inland
obā-chan	granny
'ōkole	buttocks
'ono	delicious
pīkake	Arabian jasmine
pipi kaula	broiled jerky
poi	food staple made from cooked taro corm
saimin	soup made with thin noodles
tapa	bark cloth
'ūniki	graduation ceremony

ROBERT KAHELE

THE SHARECROPPER

I wouldn't know how to live outside of Waipi'o. Like in a big city, everything has to be bought. Most of your needs have to be met with money. Whereas, down here, you don't need to have that much. All you have to do, probably, is dig down in the soil and you get what you need.

At the end of a road that runs through Honoka'a and Kukuihaele towns is remote Waipi'o Valley, located on the northwestern coast of the Island of Hawai'i. Taro, cultivated in the valley for subsistence since at least the 1500s, became a cash crop in the nineteenth century. The recollections and observations of Waipi'o Valley residents and workers were recorded in 1978 by Vivien Lee and Yukie Yoshinaga in COH's *Waipi'o: Māno Wai (Source of Life)*.

One of those interviewed was Robert Kahele, who spent most of his life taro farming in and around Waipi'o Valley. Born in 1917, Kahele grew up in an extended family, speaking both Hawaiian and English. When he was very young, his family moved from Waimanu to neighboring Waipi'o, then to Kukuihaele. Kahele left Kukuihaele School after the eighth grade to work for the Honoka'a Sugar Company. Inducted into the army just prior to the outbreak of World War II, he did his basic training on O'ahu before being sent to Hilo. On April 1, 1946, shortly after Kahele's army discharge and return to Waipi'o, a tsunami struck the island, nearly taking his life.

Lee and Yoshinaga interviewed Kahele in Waipi'o Valley at the taro patch that he sharecropped and at his home. Yoshinaga remembers Kahele's willingness to share his knowledge with them and with the Caucasian young people who moved into the valley to farm taro in the 1970s. Largely self-taught, Kahele had a special interest in psychic and spiritual learning. He died in 1984.

A WAIPI'O VALLEY CHILDHOOD

I stayed in Waimanu until I was about four years old, I think, when we came back to Waipi'o. [People] had to move out of Waimanu. There came this manmade famine. The domestic pigs would get into the taro fields and destroy completely the taro. So the people began to suffer because these tame pigs went loose. People had to go up the side of the cliffs, go look for—you know those elephant ears ['ape]? Well, they start using that as food. And when that elephant ear thing sort of ran out, they went to wild bananas. After that, it got so bad that didn't have anything to eat.

After that ordeal over there, people had to move out. And so they came over here, came to Waipi'o, looking around for jobs. Over here [farmers were] still planting rice that time and most of my uncles and my father got into this rice harvesting. The first job I had working down here, I was chasing ricebirds. I wasn't even going to school, yet. I used to go send the birds [flying] with that tin cans rattling.

[Then] the [Honoka'a Sugar Company] plantation have an opening and my father moved up Kukuihaele. My father was working for the plantation as a luna with couple of workingmen under him. That's where I started going to school, in Kukuihaele. The kids were well disciplined those days. The teachers made sure that you came, and when you came to school next day, you brought your homework along. Those that were slow, they had time for the slower ones. And we really learned; they were pretty strict.

One teacher who really inspired me was John Thomas. Like, I figured, he was Hawaiian and I'm Hawaiian. See, I really wanted to get somewheres like him. In fact, he offered me help financing my way to school. The thing was, they wanted to send me to some school in Honolulu. My parents left the decision up to me. [But] my one thought was, I could help my parents by going out to work at an early age.

I think when I was about twelve, he [father] died, and I sort of took it upon myself to be the guy to take my father's place, because all I had was my sisters and my mother living up at the house. [My brother] was living with my uncle. When my father passed away, I sort of became the man of the house, so I attended to the taro field. Like go to school and then come back, I start working on the taro patches. We had patches that could keep us going year around. The taro would be cooked by my mother. My mother cook 'em when I go to school so when I come back, she's got 'em all cooked, peeled. And I pound 'em. We had to make poi.

As soon as I came out of the eighth grade, I start working for the plantation. Pulling that hoe in the [sugar]cane line. Of course, our working hours were shorter than the grown ups'. But still, this was work that had to be done in order to support my family.

That's why I do a lot of this reading and all, to catch up with those days that I was working in the cane fields. When you do your reading, it's almost like you catching up with the education that you lacked when you were

Waip'io Valley, ca. 1946 (photo courtesy of the USAAF).

young. Even [though] I didn't go that much schooling, but by reading, I sort of became like self-taught.

There was this one case, like in World War II, I was in Honolulu. I went to the Honolulu Art Gallery. And on one section of that gallery there was these abstract paintings. And when we got there, me and my friend, he said, "Does this abstract paintings make any sense to you?"

I said, "No, they just like, you know, colors."

He said, "Oh, it makes sense. People paint those things because it makes sense to them. But if doesn't make sense to you, you try do this: bend over and look between your knees."

And with me being, what would be the best [phrase] to use is "country jack," I did just that. And all of a sudden, I felt a pat on my shoulder. He [the art gallery guard] says, "You don't appreciate this abstract paintings in here. How about taking a walk around the block." And that was the most embarrassing moment. I figured my friend, he would have keeled over, laughing.

But quite a while after that, I made up my mind. I would, someday, learn to interpret this abstract. In other words, just trying to grasp the feeling of the person who painted that picture, just what he's going through, his emotions. After going through that, I'm not a critic, you know, on these abstract things, but at least I can just sense the personality that painted that picture.

LEAVING THE VALLEY

When I made eighteen, that's the year they [still] had the depression. I went work for the federal-funded program like Triple C [Civilian Conservation Corps] in Waimea. I worked over there for about a year and a half. Then I quit over there. You got to come back in camp certain hour, and in the morning you had to stand in line for your sandwich and all that. Too regimented, that type of life.

[Just before] the war [World War II] break out, that was my chance. I was figuring if they [army] didn't induct me, I would have volunteered. There wasn't any war then, but I just wanted to get away from here. After my basic [training], which was three months at Schofield [Barracks], I came back to Hilo. That's when the whole thing happened, Pearl Harbor and all, and I spent four-and-a-half years in the army.

THE TIDAL WAVE

After the army, I still had to come back and try to still help my family out. So I stayed over here [Waipi'o] and start working. I stayed down the beach with my uncle. I was working [on Genji Araki's] taro patches at the time. Well, [on] an April Fools' morning [April 1, 1946], I was sitting on the porch. I heard that, just like rocks rolling, just like something drawing that rocks back to go down to the ocean. And all of a sudden, just like the river was sort of swelling up. Then, the water went back, started draining the two side[s] of the river, just left a little bit water in the middle. That [water] went back like tubing, just like a funnel. So I keep watching, and that wave start coming up again, start taking the chicken coop. Then he [my uncle] said, "We better get out of here."

In the meantime, we had one neighbor right below us. He was this Filipino. His house went, part of his kitchen went. His leg was all swollen, and so we had hard time to get him [to] go with us. We had to bring him up to our place, get him on the horse. There was my two nephew[s], my uncle, this Filipino guy. We rode on two horses. The bigger horse took three, that was my two nephew[s] and the Filipino. Me and my uncle was on the smaller horse.

From the river, we went towards the Waimanu side of the valley. We got as far as the pond down there. We were on the sand hill. When we got there, we couldn't go forward because the ocean was cutting through, cutting in front of us, and cutting through the back of us. And we turn around, here was this big wave coming up again. I don't know how big, but pretty sure probably was about twenty feet high, I think, judging from where we sat on the horse. See, tidal wave is quite different from this other type of wave. The bottom is thick and the thing just spill over. So our horses went in that pond. Everybody was all in that pond, swimming.

I got caught in one piece of broken up layers of reeds. The wave just lifted it, almost like a mattress. The wave lifted one end of that and just went over me, just pinned me under. I had the feeling that this probably was going to be the end of me. But you could see a million lifetimes pass before your eyes. You see those beautiful lights when you under there, though—green, yellow, blue, purple, orange. Like Christmas sparklers? That was the beautiful part of that thing. I became calm the last moment, just planning how, no panic, nothing. I feel like got to try one more time, work my way out. And finally, I made it out.

When I came out, I just jump on the next one [reed pad]. And then, when I saw this big wave, I just lift one end of that pad and just surf right up to one of those houses. They [the others] got on one of these reed things, you know, that were floating along. They got towards the road and from there, they walked. But I rode all the way up there.

My boss, Araki, I think he was cooking that morning, getting ready for me [to] come to work, you know. I called him. He started looking around, he didn't see me. Well, I don't blame him because I was all covered with mud, he couldn't see me. Yeah, afterwards, he took us in, and he said, "Go wash." And he give us these clothes which was like two-sizes big. But at least we were

Robert Kahele's taro patch, 1978 (Center for Oral History photo).

dry. We had wine to drink. But, gee, I guess when you shocked, bad shock, I don't think one gallon wine can get that thing out of your mind.

When the tidal wave hit, that's when it destroyed his [Araki's] taro field and his garden down there. So, I went [to] work for the county. [But] the county was sort of regimented, too. Then I came back and I go back to taro patch. If I work for companies, organizations, something like that, your time is theirs, not yours. But with taro, it's different. I regiment my own time. Raising taro is one way of expressing my freedom.

The person who own the land sort of opens up the place for you [readies the patch for planting]. He doesn't tell me when to plant, how to plant. I plant just like doing it on my own. All you had to do was get your seed [taro cuttings] together and start working on a patch. Each sharecropper, how you get your money [was] on percentage [of the harvested crop]. Included in that sharecropping is for your time harvesting [the landowner's share]. Backbreaking, you know, pulling [taro]. That's not easy, not mechanized.

[But] I wouldn't know how to live outside of Waipiʻo. Like in a big city, everything has to be bought. Most of your needs has to be [met] with money. Whereas, down here, you don't need to have that much. All you have to do, probably, is dig down in that soil and you get what you need.

I think [you] come to an age where the bright lights or whatever outside places doesn't mean much to you. [Waipiʻo] meant a place to stay, a place to work. But today, I have different ideas about what Waipiʻo means to me. [It's] a place to find myself spiritually. If you can find peace and calm, you can find yourself. And because I found peace and quiet here, it sort of changed my life.

GLOSSARY

ʻape	large taro-like plant
luna	overseer
poi	food staple made from cooked taro corm

Robert Kahele in his workshed, 1978 (Center for Oral History photo).

MOSES W. "MOKE" KEALOHA

PROUD TO BE PĀLAMA

Those days, ever since I could remember, I don't know whether we spent more time at Pālama [Settlement] or more time at home. I think we spent more hours at Pālama. You just went home to eat, and went home to sleep. The rest of your waking hours was at Pālama.

Moses W. "Moke" Kealoha was born in Honolulu in 1928. His mother, Maria Kekai Gardner Kealoha, was a homemaker; and his father, Enoka Kealoha, a carpenter and painter.

Moke Kealoha grew up in the family's North School Street home, in the rough-and-tumble West Honolulu district of Pālama. To Kealoha's regret, the home was sold to the territorial government in the mid-1950s to make way for the Lunalilo Freeway.

The youngest of sixteen, Kealoha attended Likelike School, Kawānanakoa Intermediate School, and Farrington High School. After his military service, he went on to the University of Hawai'i, University of Miami, and Columbia University.

As a youth he participated in activities at Pālama Settlement. Later he served on its board. Through the years he has maintained close ties with the settlement.

An automobile sales executive since the 1950s, he retired from Servco Pacific, Inc. in 1996. He and his wife, Ululani Baldwin Kealoha, raised three children.

The following narrative is excerpted from oral history interviews conducted in 1997 by Warren Nishimoto for *Reflections of Pālama Settlement,* a two-volume set of interviews featuring life histories of individuals recalling their life experiences and the role the settlement house played in helping them adjust and adapt to life's difficulties.

Aerial view of the Pālama neighborhood, ca. 1932; Pālama Settlement, fronting Vineyard Street, is the complex of buildings in the center of the photo (Pālama Settlement Archives, photo reproduced by courtesy of Pālama Settlement).

I met this lady, she's a personnel director—I forget where we met—through someone else. "Moke Kealoha. Moke Kealoha. Ey, Moke Kealoha, you Pālama?" "Yeah." "Ey, I'm from Pālama, you know. You know the fire station? I live right in back there. Iona Lane." "Yeah, yeah!" And you never met in your life. But that's the Pālama boy or the Pālama girl. Regardless of the age, regardless of what era.

I was born at 533 North School Street in 1928. The age difference between myself and the oldest sister in the family was like little more than thirty years. And then the closest above me was my brother Enoka. And he was four years older than me. And above him, my brother Tommy, he was like about three years older than my brother Enoka. So number fourteen [Tommy], fifteen [Enoka], and sixteen [Moses], as a result, became the closest, simply because we were close by age.

Being the youngest I'd have to get up at five in the morning. Clean the yard, rake the yard, pick up the leaves and do those chores. Then get to the corner of School [Street] and Liliha Street, sell the morning paper for about an hour so we can make that commission, eh? You got a penny for so many papers that you sell. That paid for my soup in the elementary school.

I should have be[en] home by the latest, four o'clock every day in the afternoon. 'Cause that's how long it takes to prepare the fire and get the hot water. Got to cook fifty-gallon drum water. So when he [my father] comes home by five, five-thirty, that water gotta be hot. And he does his things, put his tools away or whatever it is, and he takes a bath.

And then after that's done, then we gotta prepare for dinner. We eat poi every meal. Our family had taro patch in Kaua'i, but that mostly goes to commercial route. So we buy [taro] from See Wo Poi Factory.

Every Saturday in the afternoon, we going make our own poi. Make our own poi means you get the fresh poi, that from the taro you boil, and then you clean the skin, and then you smash 'em, you pound 'em, and you get the poi. And then you have to water that down, thin 'em out. And then you have to strain that to get the pu'upu'u.

To that now, we get some whole wheat flour and regular white flour, we mix that dry together. Meanwhile we cooking hot water. Hot, hot, hot, hot, hot. Once that water is hot, then you add this flour into the hot water and you stir 'em slowly, and pretty soon they come thick. And now we strain that, take whatever residues and stuff, we thin 'em out, and that looks exactly like the poi.

You put that two together and they get what we call, the Hawaiians call, poi palaoa, [pronounced] "plaua." So we get roughly about a hundred pounds of poi. That's not enough for one week. We still gotta eat toast with the meal.

And for food, we became very good fishermen. Net fishing, dive fishing, you know. Limu picking. Our parents used to take us to Waikīkī. Today you call it Halekūlani, those days we called it Grey's Beach. That's a favorite spot.

Because we lived on School Street, that's fronting Pālama, the closest was Sand Island. And Sand Island was very bountiful because you could get anything. Any type of fish, any kind of limu. Actually, you go anywhere in the island those days, depending on what you wanted. You see, we wanted a certain kind of limu, we go a certain place.

You know in those days, until I actually enlisted in the army in 1946, we knew how to cook or prepare fish only three ways besides raw. We either boil 'em, we fry 'em, or we dry 'em. (Laughs.) That's the only way we ate fish, besides raw. And everything, you salt 'em. That was the spice of all spices.

We used to raise [pigs] in the corner, in our yard. Or sometimes you go down and we kompa-kompa with somebody else. We get the pig at birth, and we send 'em down to the—right across, closer to the river by Kapālama Canal. Over there, you know, they get a pen, eh? Everybody kompa-kompa like. They share and raise their pig. Go down, feed 'em.

My father taught all my older brothers how to kālua pig, so we did that every New Year's Eve. We start about, maybe eight o'clock at night for New

Year's Day lunch with all the family come over. So we kālua the pig. Or two pigs, because the surrounding neighborhood, eh? They'd come, and you gotta have enough to take home. So we're diving the whole week, gathering limu, and get the chicken, and so forth, and so on. And then our neighbors would come over.

And the Japanese had their own [New Year's celebrations], too. Because, of course, that was big, eh, the Japanese. We want to get out of our house, and get to our friends' house, the Japanese house, sometime like around two, three o'clock, or four o'clock, or something, 'cause we gotta get that sushi, and the macaroni salad, and daikon (chuckles), and whatever else. You just go house to house.

And our parents used to tell us, preach to us, we were wealthy. We were wealthy because Hawai'i had everything we needed and more. You know, you could go anywhere, you never starve. The thing was to identify, recognize what's around you, and then learn how to prepare it.

Different kinds of plants were used for sickness, for colds, diarrhea. For example, banana. The leaves, we used every time we got injuries of some kind, or cuts. You know from the [tin] can cuts? Yeah, they taught us how to chew the old banana leaves with Hawaiian salt, and get all that juice, like tobacco. Then you put 'em on the wound, wrap it up with any kind of cloth. In twenty-four hours you take 'em out . . . and you have a nice-looking, clean-cut wound.

And the use of the aloe plant [used for] scrape on the skins, bruises, you know, all external stuff. Of course, the internal we used the bananas, and what we call the pōpolo tree. We boil the leaves like you do tea, and we use that when we get colds, or the flu.

Then, of course, you had the other plant [for sore throats], the 'uhaloa plant which they grow all over Pālama. Vineyard Street, School Street, Houghtailing Road, hey, you want it, just go out and get it.

Five thirty-three North School Street was about the fourth house from Liliha Street corner. When the City [and County] of Honolulu had those electric buses—you connect to the wire up above—that [corner] was a bus turnaround. Then directly connected to that bus turnaround, was the Funn family. Part-Hawaiian, Spanish. Next to the Funn family, had their cousins, and I can't recall that name. So that would be the second house. The third house was my father's brother's son, Seaweed Kealoha, he lived in the third house.

Then Tin Yao Goo family next to us going 'Ewa. And next to Tin Yao had another Chinese people, and then you had a small little lane that goes to the Korean elderly home. From that little lane, down to Pālama had all Chinese. The Chinn Sunn family, the Young family, the Tyau family, all in that area, and on the 'Ewa side of that little lane, that's where you had a lot of Koreans in the little camp. [There] was a fence that separated that [Korean elderly] home and Pālama Settlement on one side, and you had more Japanese going down towards Vineyard Street.

And going 'Ewa of the Korean home, you had Yamaguchi Camp—and we call it Yamaguchi Camp because it had more Japanese than the other ethnic groups—but scattered in there had Chinese, Koreans, part-Hawaiians, going on all the way down to Pālama Street. That [Yamaguchi Camp] leads on one part right to School Street, across St. Theresa's church. Then if you continued walking towards 'Ewa direction, then you would run into the concentrated [area of] Chinese people where Bobby Kau and Bobby Wong, those guys came from. Sing Loy Lane, [a.k.a.] Crack Seed Lane, and then you come onto Likelike School, that's where we went to school.

So, the proximity from our house to Pālama [Settlement], to Likelike [School], where we spent our elementary days, it's only like four minutes here, four minutes there. Everything was so close.

Pālama [Settlement is] right on Vineyard. The gymnasium was right along the sidewalk. The main building was in a loop. The [Strong-]Carter [Dental] Clinic was on the 'Ewa side of the loop, adjacent to Pālama Street, going up, connecting to School Street.

I forget whether [it was] fifty cents a year to be a member. You know, like 90 percent cannot afford the fifty cents. You go sell newspaper, you get lucky, okay, but, you could work it out. You could perform labor, and get credit towards a membership, and that's how we were able to do it for years.

Those days, ever since I could remember, I don't know whether we spent more time at Pālama [Settlement] or more time at home. I think we spent more hours at Pālama. You just went home to eat, and went home to sleep. The rest of your waking hours was at Pālama.

Now, the activities conducted in the gym included badminton, volleyball, basketball, indoor baseball, what they call BCA—Boys Club of America—activities, such as broad jumping, high jump. We had boxing room, we had weight-lifting room next to the boxing room. And we had a playroom [with] billiards, we had pool table, Ping-Pong. They made room for every kind of activities for the kids. No reason for you to get bored, see?

Of course, you had the swimming pool, we had a locker room. And most of us took shower at Pālama. You didn't take a shower at home because you go in the tub, you in the tarai. You know, get the pot, pour water over your head, rub the soap. Then get out of that, pour some more water, and then go outside the house, get the hose. Whereas if you went to Pālama, you get hot and cold shower.

Then in the main building we had arts and crafts. We learned about wood burning, like we used to go out and hustle dry coconuts, cut it on the top, make cigar man. You get a coconut, and you draw the face of a man on the coconut—the husk—and you draw the mouth, and you get a little hole on the side and you poke the cigar in there, like a cigar man. You know, they taught us all kinds.

Those days we had junior helper clubs. Whenever they had a function they called this club to do this, that club to do that. Anyway, we had carnivals, all that stuff, once a year. So, I would say there were about thirteen clubs, fourteen clubs. The name of our club was Pals.

In the evening we had dancing. Can you imagine? This is in the middle '40s. Naturally the classes got bigger and bigger. Like dancing, for example —ballroom dancing, jitterbug, the samba, the rumba, the tango—the classes got so huge they had to conduct 'em in the gym.

The kids hanging around Pālama, you drew from Farrington [High School] and McKinley [High School], primarily. 'Cause those are the only two [public high] schools [in the area], huh?

So all the kids, all the way into Kalihi, would be a part of Pālama program. As far down as Libby [McNeill & Libby] cannery. You know, Nimitz, Mokauea, Kalihi Street. 'Cause it's really a short walk, you know. You walk down Dillingham [Boulevard], along the train tracks, and the vocational school [New York Technical Institute], cut right through. And you in Pālama.

They had guys from Kaka'ako playing for Pālama. Yeah, like Boyd Andrade, for example. He's born, raised in Kaka'ako. For his age he was big. He'd come over to Pālama and play [basketball] for Pālama. So he'd come because Kaka'ako can only field one team. Pālama, we can field two, three teams. You see? That's the basic difference.

And when you did that, you didn't put all the good guys on one team. You try to split the good guys to balance the other teams. The idea is to share in learning, your abilities, to share with the next guy. So if you had all the good guys on one team, then forever and ever you only going get one good team, and you cannot develop. Pālama program was to develop people. The body, mind, soul. Really, athletics was just a secondary thing, just to keep 'em occupied, no get in trouble.

I rather go home, my parents give me licking than me getting suspended [from Pālama Settlement], 'cause I got nowhere to go. You going sit by the sidewalk, and watch everybody go in and out, and you say, "Nelson [Kawakami], can I play?" "Stay there." Or you hanging around outside the swimming pool, "I like swim." "Stay there." Oh, I tell you boy, that bugga hurt. I mean hurt! In the evenings you have club meetings, and then you have story-telling, you got share and tell. Every night something's going on in Pālama, and you cannot attend.

See, the old days, almost every store they get the bin right alongside the sidewalk. This one get onion, this one get, what do you call, Irish potato. So you walk by [in a line], you take one. Then we make fire, we throw 'em on the fire. We cook 'em. All black, eh? You peel 'em and you eat. Those menial [shoplifting] stuff. But after a while, you not kidding nobody. 'Cause the guy in line, that's his parents' store! (Laughs.)

Good for us we got caught. So they suspend us from the settlement and the police come down, they investigate. They gave us break, but you get good scolding. Can you imagine the Pālama Settlement suspending us, and we not even members! (Laughs.)

They just say you suspended, and they submit your name in to this guy, Nelson Kawakami. Any one of the counselors. One day, two day, not too bad. But you don't want to get suspended on a Saturday, because there's movies.

Pālama had a little theater, an auditorium, where we put on plays, they teach us how to act. So, they issue a little card like that, and that card is good for a month. Every time you go in the movie, you got to check in and they punch the card. There's two shows, one in the morning, one in the afternoon. The younger guys, between age here and age there can go in [the morning], and then the older guys go in the afternoon.

Health movie screening at Pālama Settlement, 1936; talent shows or other entertainment sometimes preceded the movies (Pālama Settlement Archives, photo reproduced by courtesy of Pālama Settlement).

The projector room, you know the kind—[count down] ten, nine, eight, you know, on the screen? So, by the time it gets to six everybody's yelling, "Five, four, three, two, yea!" (Laughs.)

She [Ragna Helsher Rath] used to bake cookies on certain days for the staff. But she make mistake, that wahine. She used to put 'em outside by the window of their place, to cool off. That smell travel all the way down to the swimming pool and gymnasium. (Laughs.) Then after she came back. . . . All gone. Yooohoo! (Laughs.)

I would have to say they [Pālama Settlement founders James Arthur Rath, Sr. and Ragna Helsher Rath] preached humanity to the counselors, understanding the importance of compassion, that kind of thing. Because Pālama staff people, they never ran out of patience. Down to the janitor, the night watchman even. That's the kind [of] people they had around there, and they all poor people. But the kids were first.

Like you know, you went to school, and you meet different guys—whether or not they take a bath, whether they wash their BVDs at night, or however they dress, you know. Pālama told us you take a bath, even if cold water, wash yourself good. Wash your clothes if your shirt dirty. And your shirt puka, they tell you, "Ey, go sew. You don't know how, Nelson going show you, get the needle and thread, and here, do this."

I think that's the most amazing guy I've ever experienced life with at the Pālama Settlement was Nelson Kawakami. He's a guy that was not formally educated, but he made sense. He got the respect of the parents, the kids, and he was a good teacher. Not certified, but he had compassion.

Nelson Kamakami (Pālama Settlement Archives, photo reproduced by courtesy of Pālama Settlement).

The Pālama kids were different. They listen, they attentive, but if the counselor got little bit out of line, the kids would let 'em know. Some [counselors] couldn't last, some couldn't take it. By that I mean, ey, anybody give us humbug, he got to deal with twenty guys, one time. (Laughs.) You take on anybody, and if you cannot do it, you just tell the guy, "I no think I can take care this guy, you better come help me." "Okay, shoot." Two against one, three against one, whatever it is. However, a lot of guys really straightened out the Pālama kids, and that's the good part.

I think I was the top candidate to land in jail, but lucky for Pālama. Lucky for me. See, I feel very strongly that as long as that boy, or that girl, attended Pālama Settlement, went through the activities, the chances of him [or her] going jail, getting in trouble, is almost zero. On the other hand, we had other people that left the settlement when we were in high school. They got into dope, they landed in jail.

All parents want their kids to go to school, but they used their best judgment. You don't want to go school, then you going work. "Ho, right on, I can go work! I don't have to study." Then comes the dawn twenty years later, fifteen years later, "I wish I wen study."

The relationship that Pālama had created with families and the students is that, "I don't want to see you regret one day you going land in jail because you don't know nothing. You go hungry. You going get a job, you don't understand the boss, what you going do, fight back? You're too young to work." Some parents resented it, but those were good advice.

You cannot be a good citizen without being a good academic student. They not saying now you got to make A [grade]. Meet the standards, that's all they're saying. Whether it's C or D, but certainly F is unacceptable. That's the message we got, is that you got to stay in there and keep plugging. You know the beauty? They had tutors. Whether it's another student or whether it's an adult, they always had somebody to help you out.

Everybody has some impression or story about Pālama Settlement. They can talk about their experiences at Pālama Settlement, and they so proud to be a part of it. And I really don't know, I cannot put a finger on—is it because they were poor, no place to go? Or because they learned something? I think it's the sharing that they learned. And then thereafter they had a measuring stick, they had a benchmark. And I think that's what happened. So then today, it's a treasure.

To conduct the program at the level of achievement that you had in the past, you gonna have to have more people. 'Cause today's people don't have the heart that they had in the old days. We did everything by heart. Today, you do everything by compensation. If big business can compensate those people, I think we could make the program go. They would be supplementing the staff.

. I'm not saying it's a perfect place, but it's very commendable for a non-government-funded agency. When I look at the future, I say, well, how long will this last? How long will the memories and the teachings, the doctrines of the Rath family, how long is it gonna last? That's a big question we have to answer ourselves.

I think you going find that anybody who was actively or inactively, with or without consent, associated with Pālama, they proud like hell, boy. "Ey, I'm Pālama." Man or woman, boy or girl, they are so proud it's amazing.

GLOSSARY

bugga	thing
daikon	turnip
'Ewa	direction west of Honolulu
kālua	bake in ground oven
kompa-kompa	pool efforts to share in benefits
limu	edible seaweed
poi	food staple made from cooked taro corm
poi palaoa	poi made with flour and taro
pōpolo	black nightshade, Solanum Nigrum
pu'upu'u	lumpy, as in poi
puka	hole
sushi	vinegared rice
tarai	galvanized tub
'uhaloa	a small shrub, Waltheria Indica
wahine	woman
wen	auxiliary verb indicating past tense

HELEN FUJIKA KUSUNOKI

FOND MEMORIES OF WAIKĪKĪ

There were about five or six of us who would go to the [War Memorial] Natatorium. Every Sunday, we get together. What we did was, put on our bathing suit and wear a dress over it. The Natatorium has chain links around. We'll tie our dress on the chain, and we'll swim all day. And I was real tan. My mother was quite angry at me. Some people called me a "water baby."

Helen Kusunoki was born in Honolulu in 1918. Her parents, Sakazo and Hisako Fujika, raised five children and founded the Unique Lunch Room, a popular Hawaiian food eatery on the Diamond Head end of Kalākaua Avenue.

Kusunoki attended Waikīkī School and Washington Intermediate School. She completed her formal education at Tsurumi Jōgakkō in Japan. She returned to Hawai'i in 1939 and married Jules Kusunoki three years later.

The Kusunokis resided in Waikīkī for thirty-four years. Since 1981, they viewed Waikīkī from their hilltop home in St. Louis Heights. Helen Kusunoki died in 1999.

Michi Kodama-Nishimoto interviewed Helen Kusunoki in 1986 for COH's *Waikīkī, 1900–1985: Oral Histories* project.

FROM HIROSHIMA TO HAWAI'I

My mother's full name was Hisako Fujika. She came from Hiroshima. Actually, her name was Yokoyama. And so, she was adopted by her aunt and uncle, the Fujikas. They didn't have any children, so she carried on that name. It was a custom in Japan to have someone carry on their family name in those days.

My father's full name was Sakazo Tahara. But because he married my mother to carry on the Fujikas' name, he took Fujika, as a yōshi as they say in

Japan. So his name was Sakazo Fujika. You know, it's kind of confusing because my mother had her natural name, Yokoyama, then her adopted name, Fujika (chuckles), instead of Tahara. But people called my father "Tahara" all the time.

I think my father came to Hawai'i about 1910—1909 or 1910. He's also from Hiroshima. His [sugar plantation] contract was to work in Kohala on Hawai'i. I don't know how many years the contract was, but after the contract ended, then he came to Honolulu and went to work at the hotel, Moana Hotel.

The thing I remember, he used to talk about being a waiter. There was a picture of him with white pants, and white shirt, and the bow tie, you know. There was a group picture, also—all these Japanese waiters. I think he mentioned Sato Clothiers [founder], Mr. Sato. And who else? There were a couple of other people who he mentioned and they were quite successful. So he always laughed and says (chuckles) he was the most unsuccessful one in the group.

Once in a while, they would get together at a certain man's home. My father loved his sake, so they used to enjoy having sake and talk stories. And then, he says they used to come home late at night. Of course, this is mostly on weekends. I remember my older brother, myself, and my younger brother—one night, my mother took us and she went looking (chuckles) for my father because she was quite upset.

I'm number two, the eldest of the girls. I had a brother above and a brother below, and two sisters below my brother. I was born in 1918 in Waikīkī. If I remember correctly, my mother said it was right near the store somewhere. So they must have had the store then—ice cream parlor.

FAMILY BUSINESS

I don't know if he had another name before that, but I only remember the Diamond Ice Cream Parlor when he had a little counter, and he had showcases with candies. And in a small little showcase in the front, he had some cigars and cigarettes and some candies. He had, I think, one or two tables, small table, where people can sit and have ice cream and maybe some sandwiches, something light.

And then, this man who was here from the Mainland, his name was Frank. I can't remember his last name, but he was a Scotch; he was a very good baker. He asked my father if he could go in partnership with my father, because my father was alone at that time. And so, they agreed to go into partnership.

He taught my father how to bake. He baked some delicious pies. I think he also taught my father how to make chili con carne and a few other dishes.

So they had those on the menu and they started making, I think it was hamburger steak and beef stew.

He stayed for a while, then Love's Bakery heard about Frank and came to ask him if he wanted to work for them. So, he went to Love's Bakery because it was a good offer for him. My father thought very highly of Frank, because Frank helped my father to expand the business, by serving lunch.

Naturally, Hawaiian people like to eat their Hawaiian foods. So, they suggested to my father, why don't he serve Hawaiian foods? They taught him how to make laulaus and things like that. So he started out small, and when people found out that he served Hawaiian food, the demand got bigger and bigger. That's how he got into the Hawaiian food restaurant and he changed the name to Unique Lunch Room instead of ice cream parlor.

The pipi kaula, the Hawaiian boys taught him how to make pipi kaula the Hawaiian way, which is, you salt it with rock salt and dry it. But the demand was so much, he didn't have time to dry it. He would cut the meat smaller and put shōyu and Hawaiian salt, just a little bit of sugar, and garlic. He would soak that, and then fry it because he didn't have time to dry it. So that was partly Japanese-style pipi kaula. But people didn't mind. Because it has that shōyu no aji. And they liked it. Even the haole people liked it, (chuckles) you know.

After the ice cream parlor, he had one, two, three, about four tables and about four chairs to a table. So people used to wait outside in front of the store when it's full. (Laughs.) And of course, some of them would come and say, oh, they want sandwiches or if we could fix lunch so they can take it with them and eat at the beach. So my father would put it in the paper plate—beef stew and rice, hamburger steak. And even the poi and pipi kaula, later on, he made it so they can take it out.

She [my mother] opened a little dressmaking shop in Waikīkī, right near Fort DeRussy. But after Frank left, she decided she would help my father in the store. We all (chuckles), in shifts, we helped. My brothers helped, also. So it was a family business. And of course, later on, they hired couple of women to help.

Most of the customers are the very faithful people who came all the time. So they all come into the kitchen, say hello to my parents. And (chuckles) they know him by his name, too, Tahara-san, and it was a very friendly atmosphere, like a family, which was real nice.

Because it was a very small, very simple, informal place, people could come in their bathing suit, you know. They were mostly local people, people who go to the beach, and lifeguards. And Duke Kahanamoku and his family,

Left to right, Hisako Fujika, Helen Fujika Kusunoki, Eiko Yokoyama (Kusunoki's cousin from Japan), Lillian Fujika Sakamoto, and Yokoyama's friend, in front of the Unique Lunch Room, Waikīkī, 1959 (photo courtesy of Helen Kusunoki).

most of his brothers, used to come, too, because they liked their Hawaiian food, so they would come.

You know, the beach boys and the Stonewall boys, they used to come and eat. They [Stonewall boys] played music on the stone wall [beachside of Kalākaua Avenue] and entertained themselves, entertain the people who's passing by. And so, they would all sing in harmony. Tourists used to pass by and they used to stop and listen. Even we would go out of the store to listen to them because they really made good music.

Naturally, sometimes, they [beach boys and Stonewall boys] would overspend, so they didn't have enough to pay. So, they would ask my father if they can charge, and my father would let them charge. But they would always come and pay what they owe. So (chuckles), that's the way it was. I mean, you know, those days, everybody trusted everybody else.

Oh, those days, the poi was ten cents a bowl or fifteen cents a bowl. And pipi kaula was about fifteen cents or twenty cents a dish. The lomi salmon was about twenty cents a dish. My father and my mother figured that because people who come to the beach want to eat something simple and nothing expensive.

IBARAKI STORE

[The Great Depression], that's one time they [my parents] really tried to keep their business and tried to make it so they can support the family, keep the family going. Because a few times, they would ask me to go to Aoki or Ibaraki Store to buy certain things for the day for the store. You know, get couple of loaves of bread or maybe buy so many pounds of hamburger and buy a few, maybe, lettuce for the sandwiches and things. That's how they managed because they didn't want to charge or buy too much at a time and not be able to pay. So, I know it was kind of rough for a while. But somehow, they pulled through.

See, Ibaraki Store, way back, when we were about five, six, seven years old, Ibaraki Store was right nearby our store. Mr. Ibaraki used to make ice cakes to sell. We used to go over and help and watch how they make those ice cakes.

And he also had Japanese furo in the back of the store so the people in the community would go into that furo. There was Mrs. Ichida who used to work part-time for Mr. Ibaraki. She used to take care of the bath.

She had to put wood sticks to burn to start the o-furo. And it's the real Japanese-style from Japan, that wooden o-furo. She had a little stool to sit on, and so you can step on it to climb in and out. And she had a little pail so you can scrub outside, and scoop the o-yu, and then wash yourself before you go in to soak yourself. That was another pleasant thing that we used to enjoy, especially after we came home from swimming.

THE NATATORIUM

You know, there were about five or six of us who would go to the [War Memorial] Natatorium. Every Sunday, we get together. What we did was, put on our bathing suit and wear a dress over it. The Natatorium has chain links around. We'll tie our dress on the chain, and we'll swim all day. And I was real tan. My mother was quite angry at me. Some people called me a "water baby."

We joined this swimming group while we were in Washington Intermediate [School]. And the swimming team trained there [at the Natatorium] with Mrs. Flint. She was a very good swimming teacher and diving coach.

Then they had a swimming meet where they had some real good swimmers from the Mainland and divers, too, quite well-known divers from the Mainland. And I remember Johnny Weismuller. He acted in *Tarzan*. And Duke Kahanamoku. Of course, they were known as great swimmers at that time, so they were special performers.

War Memorial Natatorium, a salt-water swimming pool built as a World War I memorial, Waikīkī, ca. 1930s (photo courtesy of Fannie Harakawa Kono).

[At the meet] I didn't come in first, but, I guess, we came in about third. I remember, at that time, we had the bronze medal. So it was a big thrill. But actually, I really wanted to see all these people, too. That's why, our parents were excited, too.

GOING TO CHURCH

The Hongwanji [Buddhist] Mission used to send teachers and have Sunday schools outside of the main temple. They rented Aoki's porch. It was a nice, roomy veranda. And so, they had hanamatsuri there. So, we would join that. And after hanamatsuri, we would go down to ʻŌhua [Avenue]. On ʻŌhua, there was a Baptist church towards right near Ala Wai Canal. So we would join that church because when Christmas comes, they'll give Christmas candies and gifts.

Well, our parents were so busy with their business. They knew we were going to the Hongwanji Sunday school. So, as long as we were going to church, they didn't mind. I mentioned to my mother that I needed something to wear for the Christmas play. She wondered because Buddhist churches don't have any Christmas plays. So I had to tell her, we all went to the church down the street. Oh, she was pretty upset for a while, but she thought, since all the other children were going there, too, (chuckles) she didn't want to discourage me. We went there for a couple of years, and then we stopped going later on.

BUDDHIST SCHOOL IN JAPAN

I went to Waikīkī School, and then to Washington Intermediate. That's when a few families sent their children to Japan. My mother asked if I wanted to go and visit my grandparents and go to a school in Japan. Because Mrs. Komagata from Soto-shū, she taught at Tsurumi in Japan. So, she said she would help make the arrangements.

So, I decided I'll go and visit my grandparents and go to school, although it was very, very hard because it's not like here. They have their strict rules and regulations, being a Buddhist school. At age fifteen, to go (chuckles) through that, you would think, "My goodness." But because there were other girls from Hawai'i and from the other islands, it wasn't too bad.

It's completely Japanese. They don't want to put the girls from Hawai'i together, so they put all the girls in different classes, separate classes, so we don't get together and try to speak English all the time. Of course, when you get back to the dormitory, most of us are from Hawai'i, so we would speak more English.

The hardest part is, being a Buddhist school, every morning we had to get up early, we all go in the cafeteria and before we have our meals, we pray together. Then when we go to school, again, we all go in the auditorium and we have a short service. Then, the principal will come and have a short speech. Then, we go to our classes. You sit on a hardboard floor. You have to sit Japanese-style. I guess it's part of discipline.

At that time until we came back, I always thought, "Why did I come?" But now that I'm older, I see the generation changing so fast, I don't regret it. In fact, I feel very thankful. I'm lucky that I was able to go and experience all that and see my grandparents because they're gone now. If I didn't go, I don't think I was able to see them and see where my parents had come from and where they lived. Because these are the things that you cannot buy. You cannot learn from books. It's something I had experienced directly.

See, I left here in 1933, and I came back in '39 because it was getting pretty bad. The China-Japanese war had started. They were rationing things and they were questioning foreigners, especially students from foreign countries. Every once in a while, they would come and question us—why we came to Japan, are we planning to work in Japan or are we planning to live in Japan, and if our parents are sending us our money to support us. So, I decided that if anything, I don't want to be stuck in Japan. So, I better get back fast. So

I came back in [19]39. See, the [same] ship I came back on, the ambassador of the United States was leaving, too. And so, I sensed there was something going on.

MILITARY PEOPLE

When I left, it was the old store. When I came back in '39, it was the new store. Now, they had rebuilt the store so it was a nice big change.

I think the [civilian] defense workers came from about early 1940s. Because a lot of them moved in[to] the Waikīkī area. So, they used to come by for their meals. Well, they had shifts, so the ones who would start late would come for lunch or maybe late breakfast. And then, they would buy maybe lunch to take with them or dinner or whatever.

See, the Mossmans' [Lalani Hawaiian Village] moved out. So, that place became a military post for recreation. It was a place for the military people to come and change to go to the beach. And so, lot of servicemen used to come by truckload so they can go down the beach. Of course, they used to come to eat, too.

But because the Japanese attacked Pearl Harbor and we, being Japanese, a few customers—seeing us, being Japanese, they got pretty mad, so they call us names. Or they would have a cold drink or something and they refuse to pay. So they had the MPs [military police] patrolling around. We would call them and have them come and take care of the soldier. But, you know, we don't want to cause any trouble because, after all, they are soldiers. They're doing their duty for the country. But that doesn't mean they can go ahead and call people names or harass us.

But other than that, most of the soldiers there were real nice people. I remember there was an Italian soldier. One day, he asked my parents, he says, "Oh, someday when you're not too busy, can I come and prepare the real Italian spaghetti?" So, my father say, "Oh, that would be nice. Sure, you come."

So, he would come with all the ingredients. He fixed a nice Italian dinner for the family and, of course, for the soldiers that [are] on duty. They have soldiers who are on duty to take care of that [recreation] place.

They [my parents] used to invite a few of the military people up here on weekends or on New Year's and Christmas. Because they're away from home, and so they felt that it would be nice for them. A few of them remembered. They used to write and ask about my parents. And I think, too, that these were the things that we learn from our parents. To respect others.

NO-FRILLS WEDDING

I got married in '42. This was right after the war [started] so we didn't have time to plan anything big. My husband said he may be drafted. So he says, "Well, let's get married before I go." And so, we just made up our mind, we'll get married, never mind all the frills.

I helped my parents half a day on a Sunday because they were really busy. So we went to the church in the afternoon, we got married, and we came home because it was blackout. You know, after the war started, so you can't have anything elaborate. So, we brought some food home from the store, and his parents came over. We had family dinner together and that was it.

Because the military disregarded his draft call, he wasn't called. So, after working at the post office, there was an opening at Barber's Point. So he decided to go work at Barber's Point. And because we couldn't find a place to rent right away and since my parents had an extra bedroom, we stayed with them for a year. And I continued to help at my parents' restaurant.

We bought this place in Waikīkī [Paki Avenue]. Because I was born and raised in Waikīkī and we always liked (chuckles) Waikīkī, we thought it was a good idea. We had our children there, which was really nice because it's right around the zoo area and the beach is close by. We lived there for thirty-four years.

GOOD BUT TIRING

Well, my brother was on the Mainland. So when my parents wanted to retire, they asked us if we wanted to take over the business but we didn't want to. So, they asked my brother [and his wife], so he came back and they took over. I think they stayed there about ten years.

The hotels were coming up, and so people say, "Why don't you folks open someplace in Kapahulu?" But they didn't want to. And so, people asked us, too. When they saw us in the shopping area, they say, "Why don't you folks start a restaurant, you sisters?" I guess we had enough. It's a good business, but it's a tiring business. Lot of responsibility and lot of work because you're on your feet all day.

LEAVING WAIKĪKĪ

I'm sorry we had to move. We wanted to rebuild because that house was getting old. But the city decided that they'll acquire all that area, so they didn't want us to rebuild. So, we had no choice. I guess, in a way, at this age, anyway, we wanted to be settled and have a peace of mind. But now we can see Waikīkī from here, so that's not too bad.

I think it was one of the best parts of my life in Waikīkī. I mean, the people, the place. Oh, I have many, many fond memories.

GLOSSARY

furo	bathhouse; hot tub
hanamatsuri	Buddha's birthday festival
haole	Caucasian
laulau	baked or steamed pork, fish, and taro tops wrapped in ti leaves
lomi salmon	seasoned raw salmon mixed with onions
ne	you see; isn't that right?
o-	honorific prefix
o-yu	hot water
pipi kaula	beef jerky
poi	food staple made from cooked taro corm
sake	rice wine
-san	Mister
shōyu	soy sauce
shōyu no aji	soy-sauce flavor
shū	sect
yōshi	adopted son-in-law

FREDERICK P. LOWREY

BUILDING A BETTER HAWAI'I

One of our many good Japanese contractors must have had about twenty men on the job painting the roof that day. I'll never forget this picture of these guys, up on the roof, with the shrapnel falling, and they all started climbing off. I called them together and told them we had been attacked by the Japanese, and that I thought the best thing for them would be to go home because I didn't know what the heck the army was going to do.

Frederick P. Lowrey, the oldest of Frederick D. and Leila Lowrey's six children, was born in 1911 in Honolulu. He grew up in Mānoa and was educated at Punahou School, Phillips Academy, and Harvard University. In 1934, Lowrey started as an inventory clerk at Lewers & Cooke, Ltd., where his father, and grandfather before him, served as president. Lowrey left in 1935 to attend Harvard Business School. On his return to Lewers & Cooke, he worked in various capacities, including personnel department manager, manager in charge of operations, manager in charge of government sales, and corporate secretary. Lowrey was appointed vice president of Lewers & Cooke in 1953 and president in 1956. In 1966, when Lewers & Cooke merged with U.S. Plywood, Lowrey resigned from U.S. Plywood but stayed on as president of L & C, Limited, a holding company. He retired in 1968 after overseeing the merger of L & C, Limited with Dillingham Corporation.

Lowrey married Janet Meyer in 1937. They had a son and four daughters. Lowrey was active in the Outrigger Canoe Club, city planning commission, Young Men's Christian Association, Honolulu Chamber of Commerce, Rotary Club of Honolulu, and other community organizations. Fred Lowrey died in 2002 at age ninety.

On December 7, 1941, during Japan's attack on Pearl Harbor, stray American anti-aircraft shells landed on the Lewers & Cooke headquarters, lumberyard, and warehouse. No one was hurt, but it signaled the beginning of major changes for the company as private construction diminished and military construction boomed. Because he possessed unique knowledge as a department manager of Hawai'i's largest lumber and building supply store, Lowrey was interviewed in 1992 by Warren Nishimoto for *An Era of Change: Oral Histories of Civilians in World War II Hawai'i*. Lowrey's interviews highlight the stark bureaucratic realities the territory experienced under martial law between 1941 and 1944.

FAMILY AND BUSINESS

My father and mother had been married very early in 1911. They were married in Santa Rosa, California, and then went down to the Grand Canyon for a honeymoon, then came right to Honolulu. They stayed with my grandfather and grandmother [Frederick J. and Cherilla Lowrey], who lived at Lunalilo and Victoria Street. Anyway, I was born in that house, in November of that year. They had already drawn plans for a house up Mānoa. This was an interesting house; it was built on the side of the hill, which was fairly steep there, so it had a fairly big basement in it.

Sometimes when my family would go off to the Mainland and take the younger kids, they'd leave John and me—we're the two oldest—with my grandfather. His sister [Ida Lowrey Castle] had come down to Honolulu when she was sixteen years old. My family were staunch Congregationalists, and of course, the missionaries down here were staunch Congregationalists, so she got to know a lot of the kids of them. And I guess among those that she met was W. R. Castle [whom she married in 1875]. She kept writing letters back to the family in Oakland, saying what a wonderful place it was, and what the opportunities were here. So my grandfather decided, gee, maybe this was the place to come to.

He started in as a bookkeeper at Lewers & Cooke in 1879. He was a whiz at figures. He could take a column of figures, and go down it like this, and add it up, and come out (chuckles). As a matter of fact, I can tell you a story, that when Lewers & Cooke bought their first adding machine, he wouldn't trust it. (Laughs.)

He taught me my first lessons about the use of debt. He made the remark that all debts are always repaid. He meant by this that if the borrower does not repay the lender who loans the money, then the money is not repaid and the lender pays the bill to balance his account.

Another very clear recollection I have is his telling about how they paid the bills in the early days. They put either gold or silver coins in a wheelbarrow and went around from place to place and paid their bills that way. This was a very interesting memory of the days from late 1880s when he started until banking and checking and so on became a lot more acceptable.

Many of his stories also were related to the Lewers & Cooke sailing vessels. After the [First World] War, needing a greater lumber capacity, the company bought a used four-masted schooner, the *Commodore,* in about 1920 or '21, and the *Commodore* was quite a bit larger than either the *Robert Lewers* or the *Alice Cooke,* carrying approximately a million and a half feet of lumber against the million feet that the other two had carried.

[When] my father told me that he could no longer cover any further costs on my college—I guess it was after my first year [at Harvard]—I looked around to see what I could do about earning my way through. I thought, well, the better thing to do at that time was to come back to Honolulu and try and get some sort of a job here.

I went down to Tacoma where the *Commodore* was loading and had already made arrangements for me to come down as a working hand, ship's boy or something. Spent quite a bit of time in the mill that was cutting the lumber for the vessel so that I learned something about logging and lumber operations of milling, and the loading of the vessels.

And very late [on a] Saturday afternoon, probably four or five o'clock, the tug cut us loose about thirty miles off Tatouch Light, which was the marking point for the south shore of the Straits of Juan de Fuca. And the following Saturday night, we could still see Tatouch Light, which meant that we had moved in and out with the tides for seven days and made no progress whatsoever toward Honolulu.

Fortunately, however, the winds came up that night and we were off to Honolulu and had a pretty good trip until we got off the north coast of Moloka'i, north of Kalaupapa, at which point we ran into another case of no wind. Of course, Lewers & Cooke in Honolulu knew the ship was there and they (chuckles) at this point needed the lumber bad enough so that they sent a tug out to pick us up. And it was a very enjoyable moment to have the *Mikioi,* or whichever one of the other tugs it was, come alongside and have Jack Young, who was skipper of the tug, wave to us and get their line aboard and tow us from Kalaupapa into Honolulu.

I remember when I finished college, I definitely had the idea that I was going to stay there. I remember going to dinner one night with my aunt and uncle, in Boston. He said, "You were told by your father three years ago that he couldn't afford to give you any more money, and you've been on your own and working your way through." And he says, "Your father needs your help." All of this guilt sort of came back, as if, you know, well, gee, it's my obligation, maybe, to go back and help my dad.

We had so many items of merchandise—it was in the thousands—because we had hundreds of tools, or literally, maybe a thousand different tools. We had plumbing supplies, we had all builder's hardware. All the things that made up locks. And then, we were in the lumber business, we were in the glass business. We even had wallpaper. We sold Persian rugs, and so on. So for the first five quarters that I was at Lewers & Cooke, I did nothing, really, but take inventories. But it was one hell of a good way to get experience in knowing something about the materials and what we carried and what I was going to have to sell for the rest of my life if I stayed at Lewers & Cooke.

But things were very, very slow when I came back in '34. I spent a lot of time studying where Lewers & Cooke could go, how soon we were gonna come out of the depression, how best to try and bring it out of the depression. So I immediately talked to Dad about bringing in new, younger guys who had good experience and had capabilities of moving ahead and moving up the line. We hired several very capable guys who later went on to become vice presidents and actually presidents of subsidiary companies.

Main floor, Lewers & Cooke, Ltd., Honolulu, 1934 (photo courtesy of Fred Lowrey).

One other very important improvement which developed out of taking inventories for a year, was the realization of how little we knew we had in stock, or how much we had on order and on the way, and sales of each item in inventory. So, during 1935 we began the development of a perpetual inventory and daily sales card record system.

We also completely modernized the whole first-floor sales display. Oh, and the other thing that bothered me was that our equipment, I felt, was old, and not really up-to-date. And so I put in an argument that we increase our equipment and try and get some more modern equipment, which we did.

Here I was, a fresh, young kid, and the boss's son, which made it all that much more difficult. I got myself into trouble with a lot of the guys up the line. So I put in for a leave of absence and I left in December of '35 and went back to [Harvard] Business School. I couldn't afford to come home that short one month summer, so I made a trip West and called on several Lewers & Cooke suppliers. And then, went to business school again and finished in 1937, but I did not graduate. They flunked me out. (Chuckles.)

I think the reasons were twofold. One was that I sort of thought that I had an idea as to what I wanted to do, because of my Lewers & Cooke work, and the things that I wanted to spend my time on. And then also, I met a girl that I was quite interested in. We got engaged sometime in 1937. And then we were married in September of '37. We drove across the continent, got back here in November.

PREWAR PREPARATIONS

And so we kept right on where we'd left off in 1935. They gave me personnel, and then they formalized the planning group, which went along nicely with personnel. We leased the headquarters here at King Street. Kawaiaha'o and Cooke Street was the warehouse, and, let's see, Queen and Punchbowl was where we had our lumberyard. But we were limited there, because everything had grown up around us, and the civic center was moving right into us. And we knew if we didn't get out, that, you know, they'd condemn the property. So besides building personnel to take care of the future, I saw the need of building capital and also expanding our land.

So we now added much needed warehouse space fronting Kapi'olani Boulevard, Kawaiaha'o, Cooke, and Queen Streets. This was in 1938.

We found, about one half mile Waikīkī at the end of Kawaiaha'o Street just beyond Kamake'e Street, nine acres of partially coral-filled swampland. This would be sufficient for our lumber operations. In the Waikīkī direction there was another several parcels which, if we could get them land courted, would give us another four-plus acres which would front on a future extension

Lumberyard, Lewers & Cooke, Ltd., Honolulu, 1934 (photo courtesy of Fred Lowrey).

of Pi'ikoi Street makai to Ala Moana Boulevard. But we were not able to buy this parcel making up the full 14.7 acres until 1942.

We had Farrant Turner [treasurer of Lewers & Cooke], a year before, being called into the guard [298th Infantry Regiment]. [We] had our own watching what the Japanese were doing in China. You know, they were bragging that they were going to take the whole of the Orient. And the fact that somebody had called out the troops to—or national guard, or whatever troops they were—to defend the pumping stations indicated that they were afraid of the possibility of sabotage here.

In August of 1941, we took out with Lloyd's of London, war risk insurance on all of our operations. So we were fully covered against war risk on December 7, and we collected on it.

Our inventories were high because we knew the army, navy was going to need all of these materials to continue building, not only here but whatever forward bases that they might build. All you had to do was drive by Hickam Field to see that Hickam Field and Pearl Harbor were being expanded terrifically, and they needed housing for all of these Mainland workers they were bringing down. They needed housing for the enlisted men and officers who were going to be here.

The other thing we did was, every location had its own block warden-type organization, the same way the neighborhoods had them. For instance, my job was the warehouse, and I was responsible for the warehouse.

DECEMBER 7, 1941

Sunday morning of December 7, Janet and I—we had two children at that time and one was on the way—we had had breakfast, and I was sitting, reading the newspaper. And I got this telephone call from one of the Japanese-American boys who had driven by 177 South King Street [Lewers & Cooke headquarters], where the Bishop Bank [now First Hawaiian Bank] building is today. And he was very excited over the phone, and he says, "F. P.," he says, "there's been an explosion in the building, just when I went by. The fire alarm's gone off." And I said, "Well, if the gong's gone off, the fire department will come down there very shortly," knowing that our alarm system was tied in with the fire department.

As soon as I got my call, I turned my telescope—which I had up on the hill on top of Maunalani Heights—I turned my telescope to see if the building was on fire, and as I brought the telescope down, I could see there was no smoke from the building, but I could see the smoke at Pearl Harbor. And as I trained the telescope on the channels running into Pearl Harbor, I saw ships trying to get to sea. I saw planes above. I saw plumes of water jump in the air, where bombs had hit alongside of the ships, and these huge spouts of water going up, you know, fifty to a hundred feet in the air. And then as I turned the telescope further mauka, I could see the fires at Hickam and Pearl Harbor. So I guess it didn't take me more than, you know, two, three seconds to put two and two together, and say, "My god, we're at war!"

At that point, I had the responsibility of letting the senior officers of the company know. And so, I went back over to the telephone, and I couldn't get any response [from the telephone system]. So I felt that it was necessary for me to get down to the warehouse as rapidly as possible and do what I could down there.

She [Janet] was then seven months hāpai, and so I wanted to see she was all right, and the two other kids were all right. There was no way for a carrier air force to drop hundreds and hundreds of attackers. So I felt that my family was safe where they were. And at that time I had a .22 Colt automatic, which was small caliber. I think I left the gun with her and showed her again how—filled the thing that held the shells and the bullets and so on. And my daughter remembers that.

I got down to the warehouse building, and just as I drove in through the warehouse gate—you came in from the Kawaiaha'o Street side, the main warehouse was on the right—I heard this terrific explosion, oh, I don't know how far above us. And then I could hear shrapnel come down on the corrugated iron roof. None of it hit me or my car. That shell had had its time fuse set, but unfortunately for too long. The U. S. gunners were all inexperienced and wrong fuse settings were common.

So we had one of our many good Japanese painting contractors working for us on that job, and he must have had about twenty men on the job painting the roof that day. And so, I'll never forget this picture of these guys, up on the roof, with the shrapnel falling, they hearing it, and they all ran for the edge and started climbing off the roofs. They were painting all the one-story corrugated iron sheds so it was not too far to the ground. I called them all together and told them that we had been attacked by the Japanese, and that I thought the best thing for them to do would be to go home and stay quiet, because I didn't know what the heck the army was going to do, you know, in the way of rounding up people like they did on the Mainland.

I did go up to King Street and saw what had happened there. The shell exploded on contact because of a faulty fuse setting in the shell. It then hit a pipe, which I imagine was at least an inch or an inch and a quarter in diameter, ruptured the pipe, and as soon as the pipe ruptured, water flowed, then the alarm went off. The water probably prevented any fire from breaking out.

A crew had assembled and were mopping up the water damage on all floors and the basement. I went up to the third floor and was greeted by a fantastic sight. The shell had exploded in a bay maybe fourteen feet, U-shaped, where most of the hanks of cotton sash cord were stored on shelves which went to the ceiling. On explosion the shell broke up into many small sharp pieces. The velocity of these many pieces cut the hanks of sash cord into hundreds of lengths from a few inches to several feet and blew them all over the place. The whole wooden roof structure looked like it had big cobwebs hanging from the rafters.

Next to the sash cord was one of three freight elevators. Shrapnel went through the sash cord in two places, went through the steel sides of the elevator and into other parts of the building, and, unbelievably, did not touch either of the elevator repairmen working there at that moment. At the top of the elevator, four steel cables held it up. Three of these cables were completely severed; one cable was strong enough to hold the empty freight elevator, very lucky again for the two men at work.

A shell also came down and hit the lumberyard, but it came down between stacks of lumber and just drilled a hole in the ground, about four feet deep, and about four feet wide at the top, so that there was a big puka in the ground, and that's the only damage it did.

DECEMBER 8, 1941

I think we started at 7:30 [a.m.], and we were all there. And a good number of the Japanese boys came to me, being personnel manager, and they were all upset. And I said that we were going to do the best to keep Lewers & Cooke going as an operating organization to help in any way we could, but we had no idea what the military governor—who had already been appointed, I think—what they would do, whether we'd be taken over and so on. I said, "You know, there's no question in our minds about your loyalty or anything like that. They can't pick you all up, where are they going to put you? If you are concerned, it might be worthwhile to think about writing a letter stating the fact that you are an American citizen, not Japanese."

Later, I suppose it was about maybe 9:30 in the morning that this army officer walked in the front door, and went into my father's office—this was Colonel [Charles] Marek. And he gave my father a purchase order from the corps of engineers for all the materials we had in stock, and it was written in such a way that we couldn't sell anything without their approval, because they'd already purchased it.

So I called Captain [John] Gaffney [navy supply corps officer], I got an appointment with him right after lunch, and I showed him this purchase order, and he really blew his top. I don't remember his exact words, but they amounted to, "They don't have authority to do this, and we are equally important and maybe more important than the corps of engineers is in getting forward bases set up for the navy."

I got the impression from Captain Gaffney that the corps of engineers may have gone off, you know, half-cocked, and made the decision, which might not be approved, and so he told us to just sort of forget the thing until we got further instructions. And as I remember it, within the next couple of days, we were told to honor army and navy orders, until formal regulations were issued.

Well, my father put out a memorandum the following morning [after the outbreak of war]. He said, "No increase in prices," until the imposed government sets up an approved new price structure for all. And then it was followed up very shortly by the military governor's office freezing all prices. And so all our prices were frozen periodically all during the war.

The first convoys didn't come in to replace any of our inventory until about the first week in April, 1942 and that had only parts of what we had ordered and needed. We immediately started to think, how are we going to survive?

And so we worked out a contract with the navy supply corps to run a big lumberyard for them during the whole war. We leased a piece of property where the present [Central] YMCA is, out on Atkinson Drive. We also had the Queen Street and Pi'ikoi Street lumberyards. So we had three yards.

Even with more people for the lumber operations, our staff dropped by about a third. Some were drafted, some volunteered. And all during the war we had problems retaining enough to keep surviving under the changing conditions.

We [also] acted as warehouse and storage areas for the government. We felt we could help them and help to survive if we tried to do everything we could to facilitate their getting goods from the Mainland and the docks.

We were extremely fortunate in having a very capable man [Mowatt Mitchell] start a San Francisco office for us. Now, in the northwest on lumber, we had had a very capable buyer [Newton Jernberg] up there who was sort of an agent for us, he wasn't an employee. He now took on the problem of getting the lumber forwarded to us here to handle for the navy, et cetera, and alleviate the extra problems of government bureaucracy.

MILITARY COURT

Well, I would say it must have been within a matter of two or three weeks after the war started. One Friday noon, while I was in the office there—the others had all gone to lunch—and in walked these two huge military policemen. And they asked for the manager. Well, in a sense I was the manager on duty. And they said, "You're under arrest." And I said, "What for?" I'm not sure whether they told me or not. But anyway they said, "Come on with us. You're going down to the police station." So I had to walk through town with these two military police. (Laughs.) One on each side of me.

Apparently it had to do with them claiming that we had broken a rule of the military governor. That we had sold some Black Leaf 40, which was an insecticide for flowers, and it was poisonous. And under the rules we were allowed to sell it, providing we had authority and providing that we sold it to somebody who had gotten permission to buy it. And [it was sold to] this elderly Japanese man who grew flowers, I think, up on the top of Maunalani Heights. Up in that whole area was all carnations in those days.

And so I tried to explain the whole thing to the guy at the booking desk. But you know, these were young junior officers or enlisted men. They didn't want to make a mistake so they took me downstairs and put me in the Bastille that was down in the basement—their cells down in the basement. It's in the old police station down at Merchant and Nu'uanu. And they wouldn't let me make any telephone calls.

It was dark in there—no lights. When my eyes got used to the dark, I saw this man lying on the floor. And I tried to talk to him, but he didn't talk very good English. But I got the impression that he might have been the guy we had sold the stuff to.

So somebody else, late in the afternoon at Lewers & Cooke—I hadn't come back—went down to the police station and somehow found enough money to put up enough bail. Then a couple weeks later, I was taken to military court. Roy Vitousek—that's the father of the present Roy that's here now and grandfather of the youngest one that's here—he was Lewers & Cooke's attorney. And we had quite a battle explaining the whole thing to the military judge, but they finally let me off. And then I think we helped get the Japanese man off, too.

You had a single military judge who was often untrained and he just made automatic decisions. And you know, you could be madder than hell at him, and yet looking at the other side of it, the community had to have some law and order because some guys were always trying to break rules. The local courts couldn't have handled it. The normal laws wouldn't have handled the situation. So like it or not—and I didn't like it particularly, none of us did—I think it was something we had to put up with. Now maybe they kept it on longer than necessary [martial law in Hawai'i lasted until October 24, 1944], but as time went on they got people that were better in the job and understood things better.

LONG HOURS

She [Janet] was hāpai for the first several weeks of the war there. And we had a heck of a time getting her to the hospital the night that she thought the child was going to be born because it was a blackout. And god, we eased our way down the hill—top of Maunalani Heights—and we got down to the bottom. And we were very fortunate in that as we were about to turn out onto Kaimukī Avenue and head down toward the Kapiʻolani Maternity Hospital right across the street over here, a policeman came along. He says, "I'll take you down." As it turned out, it was a false alarm and we had to do the whole thing over again two weeks later. (Laughs.)

It was a strain because of my hours. The army was working twenty-four hours a day during all of the first year of the war. Somebody was in the warehouse and the lumberyard all night long to fill any orders that the armed forces might want. We started work at 7:30 [a.m.]. So that meant leaving the house really very early. And I had to drop the kids off at school. And then it was sometimes very late when I got home.

And then the blackout, of course, really disrupted things. For several months there were no parties. Husbands and wives couldn't get along with each other because their social relationship had been changed. I remember several of our friends got divorces. And then when there was room on some of the clippers going out, several of the wives who were afraid of being here, they left. And then they couldn't get back.

WARTIME VOLUNTEER WORK

Well, they [the businessmen's military training corps] rode sort of shotgun. (Laughs.) That's not a very good word, but they rode as a second to a police officer. And they were given training and were able to assist. They all had uniforms, they all carried guns, you know. It made the police not have to send two police officers out.

My father came to me—I may have gone to him and said, "How about me joining that?" And he turned to me and he said, "Fred, I wish that you wouldn't do it. If you go, there isn't anybody of officer or junior officer status that I have left that I can count on if something should go wrong." So I didn't ever have that fun of being in it.

I sort of felt guilty about it, as if I should be doing something else. And that's one reason why I did get into a lot of things that could be done during daylight hours. I must have been doing quite a few community-service type of things from early in the war and perhaps before. I don't know which paper [article] it was in. I guess it was in both. But it was headed, "Frederick P. Lowrey Honored by Junior Chamber of Commerce for Outstanding Service During 1944." So this would have been as the war was tapering off.

THE 1949 STRIKE AND UNIONISM

After the war I would say from the financial point of view, certainly we were getting back to better profits by 1948, but only $268,000 versus $422,000 in 1941. But we still were way, way below profits before the war, even at that point.

The major problem that we faced was that unionism had begun to start, and unfortunately the union leaders felt that they had the right to demand more and more and more in wages, but they didn't seem to have the feeling of responsibility to the community to produce and justify the higher costs.

The strike started and we thought it was going to come in April but it started in May. And it lasted until November. [The strike ended October 23, 1949.] So we did not get one single bit of merchandise [through West Coast shipping] in from April to November.

We took the position at the beginning of the strike that we hoped that we would be able to ride it through and keep everybody employed. So we'd been on a forty-hour week and we cut to thirty-six hours. And then within another month things were getting worse so we cut to thirty-two hours.

So it was a devastating thing to us. Much, much worse than the war. During the war, you know, if you go to a guy and he had a problem, why, you could say to him, "Sure you've got problems, we all have problems, all your friends have problems, but we're trying to win the war against Japan." But when it came to 1949 you didn't have that argument.

Because of the strike following the war, we did not get back to 1941 profits until 1958. Now, there are other factors other than the unionism in this. Housing was being built individually, single story, and so on. Then the trend shifted toward building houses in tracts, but they were single-family houses in tracts. Then the next trend was toward building maybe two-story buildings, and so on. And then you got into multistory buildings. We were doing our best to meet these changes because they meant changes in the type of building materials we handled, it meant changes in organization, it meant changes in the way we handled sales—who we bought from. We had to think in terms of joint venturing with tract developers. We even thought of buying land ourselves and developing it, and then building houses on it, and selling a house and the lot together.

We gave up the leases or the fee simple title to all of our properties during the latter part of the war to concentrate on and have the capital to move to [Pi'ikoi] Street. And then '49 comes just when we need the capital and we lose $100,000 because of that strike and not being able to finance it.

Dad had reached retirement age. And [Paris Lewers] was president '53, '54, and '55, but Lewers was not a very healthy guy, and as stated in his annual report for the year '55, in the next-to-the-last paragraph, "My health has not been good for some time." Paris's annual report is dated March '56, so I would imagine that I came in as president at about that time.

I felt that we needed right off the bat, a statement of purpose. I said, "Our job is to bring together a team of four—what I call people groups." There were 700 stockholders at that time. There were 400 Lewers & Cooke people, approximately. There were 500 suppliers we were dealing with. We had to have their kōkua. And there were at least 20,000 builder customers that we sold to. And we had to organize these groups into a team that would bring about a vital balance between the interests of all of these groups.

[But] the union guys were thinking only, to a great extent, only of themselves because [former head of Local 5, Hotel Employees and Restaurant Employees Union, and Hawai'i Teamsters Union, Arthur] Rutledge and the union leaders would keep drumming into them, you know, "More money, more money, more money." The most memorable union meeting that I ever remember was one night we were discussing wages. And the union, they had asked if they could bring, oh, as many as ninety guys or a hundred guys to the meeting. And we thought it was a little unusual but we said, yes, it would be perfectly all right, because we thought and I thought that we could have them understand at least that there was more than one side to the problem.

So they asked if they could leave the room. And then about fifteen minutes later Rutledge brought them all back into the room. And do you know that every single one of those guys—and there were over eighty of them— came back into the room with a pickaxe handle over his shoulder. And then they set the pickaxe handles down between their legs—these [handles] were all wooden—sat back down in the room. And this shocked me.

I talked to the mediator and I said, "I think that we should just adjourn the meeting at this point." And he said, "You feel that this is a demand against you—you're being held hostage to pickaxe handles with an implied threat to use them if you don't move in their direction." But he said, "I think you'd do much better to just ignore it. Not even comment on it. And just go back into the meeting."

It took me several minutes to do that. We always had an attorney there because a legal problem would come up. He didn't like it. And our guys—all our negotiating team—didn't like it. Being responsible, I had to more or less say to myself, well guys, it's more important that we have a good contract and win these guys over to do a job than we antagonize them in a way that will make things worse.

MERGER WITH U.S. PLYWOOD

The big piece of property that we had at Pi'ikoi Street became a problem for us in that it was too expensive to do just the type of business that we were on. We had to develop that piece of property for highrises or some other development which would properly recognize the value of that property, because that was an underutilized resource of the stockholders.

We did have some preliminary discussions in '64 on a potential merger [with U.S. Plywood]. And we ran into a stumbling block because we felt that the Pi'ikoi Street property was more valuable, quite a bit more valuable, than they did.

And what we decided to do was to put all of the merchandising operations into what we called the Lewers & Cooke Merchandising Corporation. And then we took all of our types of operations and activities that involved land development, tracts, joint ventures, and that sort of things, and we put that into what we called the Lewers & Cooke Development Corporation.

And those were the two corporations that held all of the operating assets of Lewers & Cooke, Limited, with the exception of the land.

And so that gave us the opportunity—and for them—to reopen negotiations in 1965, after these corporations were formed, where we could say to them, "Well let's talk about merging the merchandise corporation and the development corporation into U.S. Plywood."

I also felt, from the point of view of the former Lewers & Cooke—which they asked we rename L & C, Limited, or any other name we wanted—it was going to be great for our stockholders because Plywood, gradually, over a period of time would go up in price. It still left the holding company a chance to develop the Pi'ikoi Street property the way they felt best.

I was walking along Merchant Street. And I was on the mauka side, walking along, and Hung Wai [Ching] was on the other side. And he hailed me across the street. He said, "Hey F. P.! I want to talk to you." And he put out his hand to me and he said, "F. P., you one goddamn good Pākē!" (Laughs.) What he was saying was, "You kept the land, the most valuable asset."

We signed all the papers in Dudley Pratt's office and then I was to take them to the airport. And we hadn't been in the car for five minutes on the way to the airport when this financial vice president, who was the senior one, turned to me and he said, "Fred, we like what you've done." And then he said, "But." And I thought, oh my god, we've been married for ten minutes and the "buts" have started. And I said, "What are the buts?"

He said, "We feel that you really have had, as president of Lewers & Cooke and these companies, more authority than we feel that you should have under us. Number one, you will have no further right to hire anybody at the $10,000 level or higher without our authority." And then he said, "You have no right to give a raise to any person at the $10,000 level or higher without our authority."

And then he went on down another list, about eight or nine things that I couldn't do. And I thought to myself, well, you still have done the right thing for your Lewers & Cooke people, you still have done the right thing for the community, you still have done the right thing for all of the people you buy from, and you still have done the right thing for your stockholders. The only guy that you haven't done the right thing for maybe is yourself. (Laughs.)

RESIGNATION

I talked over my decision to resign from Plywood with my directors and my father, feeling as I have indicated that they were going to assume most of the real top management in New York City and the West Coast. My directors and my father agreed.

After all, Pi'ikoi Street and L & C, Limited were a very major responsibility and an important challenge, too. And so I kept an office down at 404 Pi'ikoi Street. I had one secretary and then I would hire the consultive help here or on the Mainland that we needed. And I had an architectural group that was working on developing plans for the property, if we could find the means to develop it ourselves and show to potentially interested people.

[But] if I didn't bring about a good merger, and get my stockholders a tax free exchange, I was not doing my job fairly to the stockholders. Because the company that came along might have offered cash and/or bonds, and these poor stockholders, who had costs of two and three dollars a share, would have had to pay the difference between two and forty dollars in capital gains. In September of 1967, I approached Lowell Dillingham and in November we wrote to the stockholders of their offer of merger of L & C into Dillingham. Our stockholders agreed and the merger took place in March 1968.

A possible explanation of Dillingham's changing and growing interest in the L & C property was its size and proximity to the Dillingham Corporation [Ala Moana] Shopping Center. They did not want an adverse competitor across the street, and so Dillingham bought it up. For me, I was this time really out of a job.

My stroke in early 1969 and Janet's illness put off any thought of any full-time job during those years, and I am glad that I spent them with her.

U.S. Plywood did liquidate the Lewers & Cooke companies in 1978, twelve years later. They had merged with Champion Paper Company around 1966–67 and Champion came out on top.

There were two paintings of two sailing vessels of Lewers & Cooke. And I'd seen these paintings since I was, you know, old enough to remember them. They were done by a Mr. [William] Coulter, who was a very prominent marine artist way back in 1889 and 1891. I had told Champion that I wanted these paintings if they were ever going to give them up. And I got this telephone call one day, the president said, "We're going through the final liquidation of the company. You told me at one time that you'd like to have first crack at the paintings."

Well, I got the price, it really knocked me over. (Laughs.) I didn't argue with them on the price of the two paintings, but there were actually three. The picture of the *Commodore* had hung in Jim Lovell's office for many years. And so I said to him, "Look, they valued that painting less than the others. I'll pay you your asking price for the two Coulter paintings if you'll give Jim Lovell that painting that was in his office." So anyway, Jim has that picture.

LEWERS & COOKE'S LEGACY

Up to the time of the war, Lewers & Cooke produced a substantial part of the housing inventory and much of this still exists today, serving its owners as it was built to do. The war years, and the strike which followed, interrupted this addition of new housing inventory. But as Lewers & Cooke was able to reestablish its residential home building organization and cooperative contracting functions for the individual home builder, and also begin the joint venturing of tract developments, they again played an important role in building Hawai'i's housing inventory. Lewers & Cooke also sold many kinds of building materials to nonresidential structures, office buildings, hospitals, most kinds of building structures.

I am proud of the part the Lewers & Cooke people played over many years, and the satisfaction of those who are left knowing they contributed in this effort. In 1956, we established our basic mission: "To Build a Better Hawai'i through Service to Builders." Together we met that objective. Together we accomplished much for the satisfaction and happiness of the community, but much will remain to be done as housing demands increase and change over the years to come.

GLOSSARY

hāpai	pregnant
kōkua	help
mauka	inland
Pākē	Chinese
puka	hole

ERNEST A. MALTERRE, JR.

SUGAR PLANTATION MEMORIES

We were allowed a nickel a day for milk, or maybe ten cents with the ice cream. We'd save—in fact, this carried on through practically all my life that I used to do something like this—we saved the nickels. And then after you had four nickels, you could buy the dry abalone. Looked just like a bar of soap. That was our candy.

Ernest A. Malterre, Jr., of Portuguese, Hawaiian, and French ancestry, spent most of his life on sugar plantations. He was born on Hawaiʻi Island, in Onomea, a community eight miles north of Hilo, where his father worked as a plantation overseer.

When the family moved to Waipahu, Oʻahu, Malterre joined Oʻahu Sugar Company. Over the course of forty-nine years, Malterre was a pump worker, field supervisor, irrigation overseer, assistant housing administrator, and employee relations supervisor. He retired in 1979.

Volunteer work with the Waipahu Community Association, Waipahu Cosmopolitan Senior Citizens' Club, St. Joseph's Church, Boy Scouts, and Friends of Waipahu Cultural Garden Park, among others, led to his nomination as Outstanding Senior Citizen in 1983. Parents of three and grandparents of seven, Malterre and his wife lived in Waipahu. He died in 2000.

Malterre recounted his life experiences in tape-recorded sessions with interviewer Warren Nishimoto for COH's *Five Life Histories* in 1983.

AN ONOMEA CHILDHOOD

There were eight of us born, one died at about eight months. I was born in Onomea on the island of Hawaiʻi in 1915.

The time I was born, my father was an overseer for Onomea Sugar Company. He had people spread all over the Onomea section that he had. He had charge of all the plowing, cultivation, which involved all the mules and horses that they used on the plantation. You must remember, there were no tractors so they did all the plowing with mules.

My father bought what was formerly the Onomea School prior to getting married to my mother. He bought about three acres of land that belonged to the territory at that time. When they moved the school, that's when my dad bought the property. He sort of renovated the building and that became our home.

Left: Ernest Malterre, Jr., and his brother Leon in chair, 1918 (photo courtesy of Ernest Malterre, Jr.). Below: Malterre home, Onomea, island of Hawai'i (photo courtesy of Ernest Malterre, Jr.).

It had three bedrooms, a large living room, a dining room, and an immense kitchen. I remember the icebox was one of these old boxes where you bought the ice in blocks. We had maybe several, I think, of these big crocks in which we kept the salt pork and stuff like that. The big leg of cured ham would be in a sack on the beam on the ceiling.

For the wood stove, the plantation gave us 'ōhia wood. They came in big logs that were, oh god, from about six feet in length, some of them. So we had to saw the logs into sections of about one and a half to two feet. That was every Saturday, when my brother and I used to get on one of these big logging saws.

Then for water, we originally had a water tank that got its source of water from the rainfall which fell on the corrugated iron roof. It went into a flume, and from the flume, into this tank. Now, water standing in the tank would accumulate mosquitoes. On the faucet, we'd tie the [Bull] Durham bag. You know, tobacco bag (laughs) to get all the impurities out of the water.

Our [outdoor] toilet facilities were just a hole in the ground with a shanty on top of it. When that filled, all they did was dig another hole and move the shanty.

We sold chickens and we raised for our own use. Every week we had to clean out all the coops and refurbish with dry grass for where the hens laid their eggs. We raised a couple of pigs. We'd pick breadfruit, and we'd carry it home, and cook it up, and feed the pigs that breadfruit.

And then we raised some calves and we had them in paddocks. Us kids used to like to go jump from the railing, top of the paddock, onto the calves and play cowboy on the calves. After the calf was of certain age, we'd let them run out in the pasture till they were big enough to breed.

These plantation areas, people either owned or leased sections of property [for cane cultivation]. Like my father owned his own three acres. We did the work, or if he needed plowing or anything, he hired from the plantation, you see.

Every weekend or even after school—all depended when was necessary—we'd go out into the fields and work. We had to weed. Then as the cane grew, we had to strip all the leaves off the cane, so by the time they harvest, all that remained would be the cane with the top on it.

When it came time to harvest, he'd hire these people, the [work] gangs. They cut the cane and they had to bundle it. And they tied it with the cane top because it's green and it's still pliable.

After these bundles were weighed, then a sled driven by two mules would come along. They piled these bundles of cane onto the sled, and the sled would take it to a flume. These flumes were portable flumes, put into the fields to transport the cane from the field to the main flumes. And that's how [the cane] went to the factory.

The plantation would charge him for all the different services, and what was left over was his profit, you see.

I was born clubfooted, both sides. They put me in the hospital for I don't know how many months. What happened was that they left the cast on so long that I don't have a normal leg. You see how this [thigh] is big and this [calf] is small.

I went to [Onomea] School a year late because I had to use braces to walk. After I got rid of the braces, I had to have special shoes. You know, was built up on one side, and built up inside, in front.

Of course, we walked to school. Every so often, us kids, instead of going to school the regular route which was the winding road that went down the gulch and up the other side, we'd go on the railroad [tracks]. The railroad had two tunnels that we had to go through. So what we'd do, we'd get down and put our ears to the rail and listen, you know. 'Cause you could hear the train coming for many miles. And we'd scoot through before the train would come through.

I tell you the story of the day I was walking home from school and I thought I['d] cut across the field that was harvested. And [as] I jumped over the flume, I fell into the flume with the water running. And it carried me down for a little while until I finally caught on the side of the flume, able to climb out. I thought I was gonna go to the mill. (Laughs.)

We were allowed a nickel a day for milk, or maybe ten cents with the ice cream. We'd save—in fact, this carried on through practically all my life that I used to do something like this—we saved the nickels. And then after you had four nickels, you could buy the dry [abalone]. Looked just like a bar of soap. That was our candy.

And we played a lot of marbles. We had the wiliwili red beads. And one of those red ones was worth ten Job's tears. Every kid [who] went to school had wiliwili and Job's tears in his pockets. If he didn't, he wasn't (laughs) going to school.

MOVE TO HONOLULU

We moved [to Honolulu] in 1928. That time my dad was forty-two years old. His boss used to give him a bad time. So my dad got fed up with him and he just quit.

So, we came to live there. And then I went to Lili'uokalani [Elementary School], and my brothers and sisters went down to Liholiho [Elementary School].

I was only thirteen at that time. I was too young to go to work in the pineapple cannery. So I went up to something like a cash-and-carry [store]. A dollar and a quarter a day for, at that time, I think it was ten hours of work. I'd sweep up the store, and I'd bring in the produce and put it on the shelves. Then since I worked there, I was able to have a discount on the groceries I bought for our family, at which time we were having a difficult time.

Then in 1929, the store went out of business. [My brother] was younger than me, but he had been a caddy at Wai'alae Golf Course and [I] had three cousins that were caddies. So I joined them. Saturday morning, Sunday morning, we'd be out there four o'clock, bright and up to get in line to caddy. You go with these people and you carry the bags. And they paid us seventy-five cents a round. But the fellas that were generous, they'd give us a dollar per round.

My father, in the early part of '29, got a job at O'ahu Sugar [Company] in Waipahu. He started as what they call a foot luna for seventy-five dollars a month. [At first] they could not give him housing for his family, which was part of the benefits for all the employees, but they put him up in what they call the bullpen, which was a bachelor barracks, sort of, for supervisors.

So what he used to do was, every Saturday night—'cause they'd work six days a week—every Saturday night he'd get on what they call the Honolulu Taxi. You paid fifty cents, I think, for a ride from Waipahu all the way to 'A'ala Park. And when he got to 'A'ala Park, he [caught] the streetcar and came up to Kaimukī where we lived.

That went on for over a year until he finally got a house in Waipahu in 1930. The plantation sent a big Mack truck, I remember, to pick us up with all our furniture in Kaimukī. And we moved to the camp area called Pump 4.

[There] was a whole big camp they called the Pump 4 Camp. They had a mixture of irrigators living in one little section called Camp 17 or something like that because the people that lived there worked in Field 17. And then there was the pump people that was divided into two sections. One section was all the engineers and the assistant superintendent live there. One end was the Chinese bachelors, and they lived in these U-shaped buildings. There were a few Filipino workers in the pump department at that time. They usually commuted from Waipahu town down to the pump.

That summer I started looking for work and I applied at the pump department. So June 29, 1930, I started working for the [O'ahu Sugar Company] plantation. In that particular section there were five pumps that pump irrigation water up to the fields. My first job was to chip the rust off the big pump valves—they weighed about 300 pounds each—and then paint them with red lead.

We had beautiful green lawns all around the pump departments. Was maintained, mowed, and trimmed, and irrigated. There was no such thing as a pension plan in the early days. So when a guy got to the degree where he couldn't perform certain jobs, then they say, "You going to be yard boy now."

As I continued in school, I went to Central Junior High. Then I graduated from Central and I went to McKinley [High School]. I finish high school in '34. My dad got me a job working in the fields with him to learn to be a supervisor. And he was the strictest guy that ever was and ever will be. What happened in the field, he'd take home with him. See, he couldn't forget because I was new and, by god, I made mistakes.

WORKING FOR THE O'AHU SUGAR COMPANY

After I learned the ropes, they gave me my own gang. So I had a gang of young people. First was with what they call li'i kō, picking up the cane left in the [harvested] fields. Then I got a gang that used to cut the cane and I used to teach them how to cut cane.

From that, I had a Chinese gang that did the seed [cane] cutting. And in seed [cane] cutting, they used mules. So what we'd do, we haul the seed cane [on mules] from where it was cut and bagged, out to the road either to where the cane cars were, or there was a truck waiting that we had to load.

I was assigned these Chinese and Korean men. They lived in quarters assigned to them in one particular area of the camp. They called it Chinese Camp. And they had a family that looked after them. They did their laundry for them, they cooked for them, and they sent out the food to the field.

They [the laborers] spoke English, but was in a jargon that I'd never known. It was pidgin, but the pidgin included Hawaiian, Chinese, Japanese, whatever else there was, all together. I learned it from them eventually, but it took me a while.

They [also] used to converse in their own language. Of course, they had their spats among themselves. Sometimes they'd threaten with the darn cane knives they used. I let them fight. Half the time I didn't know what they were saying, anyway. But then nobody ever chopped anybody else that I know of.

When I started they paid me forty-five dollars a month as assistant supervisor. Then when they made me a full supervisor, fifty dollars. It kept going up until the time I was about to get married in 1940, I was earning ninety dollars a month and I was already a relief irrigation overseer at that time.

I met my wife [Angie Ornellas Malterre] in the 'Aiea gym in 1937. While she was in school, I only corresponded little bit with her but not much. Finally, I started courting her in 1939. Married in 1940.

Ernest Malterre, Jr., as a field super-visor for the Oʻahu Sugar Company, ca. 1930s (photo courtesy of Ernest Malterre, Jr.)

[Oʻahu Sugar Company] must have had about twelve irrigation overseers. We had about 12,000 acres, 1,000 apiece. I'd take one irrigation overseer's place while he went on two weeks' vacation. I'd ride around with him, and then I'd take over, and I go to the next one. We had a Korean overseer that kept all his records in Korean. So before he could go on vacation (laughs) he had to translate to me what was what.

WORLD WAR II

When I became a full-time irrigation overseer in 1940, I had 1,300 acres 'cause I had the section that's the west side off Mililani. We used to leave home, god, 4:30, five o'clock in the morning. Saddle our horses and get up to the camps. I had only two camps to contend with in my own section. But some of the other fellas had sometimes three camps. So what it is, you rode up to the camp and you give the men their orders for the day. So by six o'clock, they had to be out in the field.

I was overseer during the war. When December 7 [1941] struck, I was at home. We didn't know what was going on. Finally a friend of ours came by, "Eh, there's a war, war!"

"What!"

"Yeah, the Japanese have attacked Pearl Harbor. It's war."

We were part of the OCD, the O'ahu Civilian Defense. We had formed a group and we had gone out, practiced, learned from the police department what to do, what not to do. We had been preparing for about a year at least. Right away, they congregated the OCD. So I went over to the ballpark and there's a little clubhouse they had there.

I watched the Zero [Japanese aircraft] going right around, and the guy was looking right at us. He was so low, we could see him and he could see us. After that, I start thinking, by god, good thing he didn't let loose. 'Cause we had no uniform on, you know, but here we were gathering.

We sort of organized ourselves, and then right that night, they started already putting people looking out. For instance, the filters where the water came into town, around the mill, all these different strategic areas, they had people on guard. And remember now, we didn't know whether they going invade or not. So everybody was on pins and needles.

We patrolled the town every night after curfew. And [if] we came to a house, we saw lights on, we just walked in the yard, we hit on the wall, and, boom, you'd see the shades would come down fast. Passed by the nurses' quarters, they tell us look in first, then you knock. (Laughs.)

The plantation sent out Filipino people to go help with the defense construction, and I went with them. We put up pillboxes, we put up barbed wire. Up in the hillside, we put up gun emplacements. We put in command post, you know, for all the communications.

I had experiences with riding to work when they had encampments within our plantation areas. One morning, I remember distinctly, Japanese irrigation overseer and I were riding our horses and this is pitch dark in the morning. And we going up, tong, tong, tong, all of a sudden I hear click!

I told my partner, "Stop."

"What's the matter?"

"Try wait!"

Ernest Malterre, Jr., in O'ahu Civilian Defense uniform, 1942 (photo courtesy of Ernest Malterre, Jr.)

The guy [the sentry] say, "Halt! Why didn't you stop the first time I said halt?"

"I'm sorry, I didn't hear you."

I couldn't see the black guy, pitch black in the morning! All I could see were his white teeth when he finally talked.

I got acquainted with these military people from the South. These were white men, though. We couldn't get butter, we couldn't get corned beef, we couldn't get any of that kind of stuff. So they'd say, "Eh, you want some butter?"

"Oh, sure, why not!"

So in return, I'd go down the store with my liquor permit and buy my quota. I'd buy me Three Feathers whiskey and take it to them, make them happy.

THE 1946 STRIKE

In 1946, the union [International Longshoremen's and Warehousemen's Union] had come in. They tried to negotiate with the plantation and they often had difficult time. So on Labor Day, I think it was, in 1946 [September 1], they decided to go on strike. Everything just closed down, tight as a drum. We were patrolling, the supervisors. We had to go out and check our fields because cane was just drying up. We afraid of fires, besides.

The workers in the field, irrigators, had a contract with us. They were paid a daily wage. But over and beyond that, when the cane was harvested, they got a percentage paid on the tonnage of their fields. They would sneak out into the fields and open up valves on the reservoirs, whatever source of water, and let it run into their fields. You know, was to their benefit, to our benefit, also.

Well, the union hierarchy, as we used to call 'em, the chiefs around here, didn't want them to do that because just like strikebreaking, you know, as far as they were concerned.

I don't know whether they picket other people, [but] they picket me because they knew I was going out [on patrol]. So I got up in the morning, what the heck, whole lot of voices. I go out to my front gate, god, must be about thirty, forty guys all in front of my gate!

After a while, I walked outside and said, "Good morning."

"Oh, oh, good morning."

Lot of them were ashamed, but they were given orders. They had to picket, see. They stayed there several hours. Then they finally gave up and went home. But just to show the unity, see.

Ernest Malterre, Jr., with plantation mules, 1946 (photo courtesy of Ernest Malterre, Jr.).

It's a funny thing, but some of the folks that did all this kind of stuff—they used to threaten me even, you know—became my good friends after the strike. In fact, I had to work with them.

Prior to 1946, they had free housing, free electricity, free medical for the workers, free water. [After unionization], we charge them rent. Charge them for medical, charge them for water, charge them for electricity.

Then we started selling different camp areas. What we did, we went into an old camp and kind of move the houses around and would install maybe new bathroom facilities if need be. We put in streets, put in new water lines, sewer lines. We sold the houses and lots to the employees. All the way through, all our subdivisions, the whole idea was to get [the company] out of housing.

By the time I retired [in 1979], I had the housing, the medical plan, the trades progression, the workmen's comp, what else did I have? I don't know what else, but (laughs), anyway, I never had just one thing that I was doing, was always several.

In the meantime, I was always in activities. With the church, you get involved in certain things; with the community, you get involved in something else. With my senior citizens, lot of them, we worked together and we can reminisce once in a while: "You remember when . . ."

GLOSSARY

li'i kō	picking up small pieces of sugar cane in the harvested fields
luna	overseer
'ōhia	type of tree
wiliwili	indigenous type of tree

STANLEY C. MENDES

TOGETHERNESS WAS THERE ALL THE TIME

Even from the young time, when we were still going school, we wanted to go work with the mules. I'm thinking one of the best jobs they had in the plantation was mule gang. 'Cause you go to work in the morning, you harness those mules up, ready, they gotta eat, ready for go. Put two, three burlap bags and tied it together. Was your saddle, that. Play cowboy, race-horse, take longer to get to the field.

Stanley Clifford Mendes was born in 1931 in Āhualoa on Hawai'i Island. He was the only child of John Mendes, Jr. and Josephine Souza Mendes. The family moved from Āhualoa to Kapulena, then to Pa'auilo into a housing area called New Camp. Stanley Mendes attended Pa'auilo School until the eighth grade.

In 1944 he began his forty-year career in the sugar industry, first with Hāmākua Mill Company and later, through company mergers, with Laupā-hoehoe Sugar Company and Davies Hāmākua Sugar Company. He retired in 1984.

In 1952 he married Kathleen Doris DeRego of Haina. They raised five children.

The closing of the three remaining sugar plantations on the island—Hāmākua Sugar Company in 1993, Hilo Coast Processing Company in 1994, and Ka'ū Agribusiness Company in 1996—dried up the area's major source of employment. Two of Stanley Mendes's sons lost their plantation jobs due to the slowdown and eventual closure of the sugar companies.

Stanley Mendes died in 1998.

COH's *The Closing of Sugar Plantations: Interviews with Families of Hāmākua and Ka'ū, Hawai'i,* is a collection of oral history interviews with dis-placed workers and their families. In 1996 COH director Warren Nishimoto talked with Mendes about his youth in the plantation community of Pa'auilo, jobs on the plantation, and feelings about the end of this way of life.

PARENTS AND GRANDFATHER

My grandfather was John Mendes, Sr. And then my father was John Mendes, Jr. Me, I get Stanley. My oldest boy [Stanley "Butch"] is the fourth generation of the Mendes family [in Hawai'i]. His boys is the fifth generation of the Mendes family.

[Grandfather] was not a very smart man. (Laughs.) He was a wise man in other ways, but really not a reader, you know. He could take care of his business because he always had something in his head to do. He took care of his family, built nice home, all of that. He was appointed to all kinds of community services and even during the war [World War II], he was the CD [Civilian Defense] person up Āhualoa, all those areas there.

He used to supply the plantation with firewood, the camps. They get a big—what they call ox. And he had big trailer, you know, wagon, for supply the wood to the plantation.

My father was [also] a wise man. He was a workingman. A man that was skilled doing anything. Wake up in the morning, go to work, and work till dark again.

He started out with T. H. Davies Company. And he used to work with a portable track. You take 'em [i.e., tracks] in the field and lie 'em out in the field, so that they could take the cane cars into the field, and they load 'em up with cane. Throw [cane] inside the car. That's what they call hāpai kō. Then, after that, the mules pull that cane car out [to the main train line]. He was with the mule, you know, the steersman of the mule, just like the driver.

He was a serviceman for the plantation. He go and put fuel for all the equipment get there at that time. Sometime the equipment no start. He go check the equipment out in the field, start the equipment.

And he used to supply the camp, the houses, with kerosene. You know, they go around the camp and they fill up the kerosene for the people in the camp, 'cause the plantation supply the kerosene. You get your own five-gallon can. The kerosene usually is for cooking. Because they use firewood [to] make hot water, things like that.

When the union came to Hawai'i, my father was the first president in Pa'auilo. That's the CIO [Congress of Industrial Organizations] union. Then, little by little, the ILWU [International Longshoremen's and Warehousemen's Union] came inside, squeeze him out.

Then afterwards, he became supervisor during the war [World War II] years. He got this lift of being top man, supervisor and superintendent. One section Pa'auilo, one section is Kūka'iau. Till he died [in 1955].

My mother was Josephine Souza Mendes. She was Pa'auilo-born. Mother was the cook for the plantation supervisor. And at the meantime, young boys from different parts of the island used to come work. They used to come eat our place, and she make the lunch for them.

GROWING UP IN PA'AUILO

Pa'auilo was a very popular place in the old days, because they had hotels down there, and the train used to come all the way to Pa'auilo from Hilo. They pick up the sugar from Honoka'a, Pā'auhau, and all those kind [of] places, go to Pa'auilo on the train.

You know, the train used to come till there, and whatever groceries used to come through there. Da kine guys who go [to Pa'auilo as wholesale] salesman, salesperson, they stop. They live in the hotels.

Nakashima, he used to cook for the Japanese. Nakashima Bar. Old guy, get hotel above, too.

And right next, had one more hotel. Arita Hotel. [During World War II] Arita Hotel had one big wahine over there, you know. Regular whore, that. Live downstairs. And you can open the door, she stay with one guy inside there. Go talk story, she no care. You like kaukau for eat, she making all the time.

They had car garage over there. They had tailor. And they had a movie house over there, and of course, several stores. One Filipino store run by Filipinos, and Japanese store, vegetable stand place, where you get vegetables. And they had two pool halls there.

And they had one small—you would call that hotel or motel or whatever. And they had the Japanese graveyard, church, above that side.

Pa'auilo was a popular place, because they had parties, they had dances, and things like that during the weekends, yeah? Sometime family kind, sometime occasional get-togethers, things like that. Some religious parties. The Filipinos famous for that.

And of course we had Hawaiian parties. Hawaiians [there] was more famous making laulaus than kālua. In fact, the kāluas was the Portuguese, mostly. The Hawaiians, they go make one party, they call my uncle for make kālua. My uncle Walter, he used to be the kālua man. Or other uncle. All the Mendes boys could handle one kālua.

Pa'auilo was quite a big place in its day, you know. Above that was Japanese Camp and Filipino Camp, Puerto Rican Camp or Spanish Camp, they used to call 'em. They had mixed variety there anyway. They had the Stable Camp. They had mixed variety up there. And Japanese Camp, they had mixed variety there, too. All kind [of] people.

Up high, there, where the camp is now, that's where it [New Camp] was. They just build the homes right in the cane field, laying on the cane, you know. You had all those furrows.

We was the first people to move into the house. Three-bedroom home. Bath inside the house. You had to take two steps go down to the bath. Toilet down there, and everything all enclosed.

Not da kine you gotta go outside toilet, like the Japanese Camp. Each house you get toilet place, you know, where you wash clothes, but [to] take a bath, a big [community] furo house.

My neighbor below was Japanese. He's still there, in fact. The one above me, that pau, no more. Well, that was Portuguese, but the original people that was there, not there anymore, was Japanese, Filipino.

My mother and father, I was the only son. No brothers, no sisters.

[But] you have bunch of guys. Portuguese, Japanese, Filipino boys, all. Had plenty Japanese boys, they don't want to hang around with their own Japanese kind. Young ones, they didn't care [for] the style of Japanese, you know, old people. Had to do this, had to do that. So they hang around with the Portuguese boys, or the Filipino boys, eh?

Before, we used to make our own yo-yos. You know the ladies get the sewing thread? The spool. Then you cut that spool in half, and you put one pencil in between the center, you make your own yo-yo. My grandson, now he get yo-yo. Only now, they make 'em little bit more fancy, noises and lights.

Our slingshot was the guns we had. You get guava stick, you know the guava stick with the V-[shape]. Those days, there was no synthetic rubber. Was real rubber tire tubes, eh? When you pull 'em, it goes back. Of course, we get the small guavas like that, too, [for ammunition]. The guavas or marble, something that's completely round, you get more accuracy.

That was our living, then, go hunting, shoot birds. Cook 'em in the [open] fire, regular way. Eat that, salt and pepper. Mynah birds was good, really good. Sometime, we no come [home for] two days. See, as long as get enough rice, eh. You stay, cook our rice with da kine coffee cans.

Pa'auilo had lot of spring-water catchments. You had even caves in the ground. Yeah, the spring inside there, plenty water. This was drinking water. So people no make trouble, they put cement and put steel doors outside. And then they have pipes coming out from there. Where the water come out, leaking, it's dripping, out of there.

Kūka'iau side had more places than Pa'auilo side. In fact, there was one spring up there, way up in the forest there, [you could see] my grandfather's handprint.

[But] Paʻauilo was a poor [cane-growing] place because of [lack of trench] water. No had much trench water strong enough to do all those kind [of] irrigation, or fluming.

That's why [they] had tin bins. Cable from down the bottom of the train track, go all the way up the mountain, this cable. And in between, they get power to help the thing [i.e., tin bin] go up. Down, no problem, but go up, they had to have little more strength. 'Cause they supply anything from cane to fertilizer, poison [i.e., pesticide], that's how they ship 'em up to the [cane fields]. They had certain place where they would do that, supply that, that way.

That's how they harvest. The cane inside bundles. And they sling 'em on those [cable] wires, they send 'em down, and then into the cane cars, and the cane cars take 'em to the mill.

Along the coastline they had soldiers, or marines, sailors, worked the ocean [during World War II]. They get their guns, machine gun, stuff like that, watching the oceanside. And they always end up down Paʻauilo, (chuckles) so they always getting into one fight.

Mostly the Portuguese boys used to make money with [servicemen]. We go shine shoes. Japanese kids no used to go, you know. But even Filipinos very scarce, you know.

Of course, they [the servicemen] used to chase the Japanese around the place, or the Filipinos. The Filipino's walking with his bottle, one gallon of shōyu. They thought was wine. Oh, they chase 'em, they bust 'em up, boy. 'Cause they come back from the war front, eh?

Each place had their own school. Kūkaʻiau had their own, Paʻauilo, Pāʻauhau, Honokaʻa, Kukuihaele. Pretty rough teachers we had.

I don't know if you see in the paper had one guy, just passed away. He was one agriculturist teacher and math teacher. Pilau buggah, that. He come down there with the chalk and broke your head with the chalk. Hard, you know, the chalk. Sometimes he stay by the blackboard, writing something. He turn around and he see you playing around or doing something. He get the eraser, throw the eraser at you.

When you stay inside the classroom, you watch out. But you go outside, good. He used to take us park, [play] basketball like that, eh? In his own car, you know, go.

Yeah, and had wild kind [of] principal, too. I swear at the teacher. And he [the principal] put chili pepper in my mouth. Bumbai I stand up and tell him, "Thank you." I used to eat chili pepper all the time. Round chili pepper. Red, green, yeah? Ho boy, he get mad. He get the hose pipe, give me licking with the hose pipe.

PLANTATION WORK

We get the summer job, work plantation. Hoe grass in the cane field, so they call 'em hō hana. Go in one gang, regular workers, you know. They give you kaukau, too, eh? You take our own lunch, but the rest you get there.

Sometimes the Filipinos, they bring two varieties of stuff. Portuguese, very seldom that you see 'em with two variety. [If] sausage, only sausage. But the Japanese people, ladies, plenty food they make. When they go in the field, they open up the bag, it's just like one table of food, yeah. You get daikon, da kine cabbage, and the red fish, and the long skinny fish with seaweed, and stuff like that, you put on top the rice. Little bit, little bit, little bit, you get full, boy.

Then they give me one job in the [Hawaiian Pineapple Company] cannery. Honolulu scary place to live. I went Kaimukī with one of my aunties up there. I never like 'em. I went with one of my aunties down Damon Tract, and from there, I went straight back to Pa'auilo.

I wen move back over here to attend Hilo Technical School. We had several guys from Pa'auilo used to go school there. Two, three Japanese boys used to go. We went on the bus. At the same time, I could get job, plantation.

Nineteen fifty, that's when I was hired full-time for the sugar company. Oh, cover [cane] seed, hō hana, plant [cane] seed, all those kind of work.

Even from the young time, when we were still going school, we wanted to go work with the mules. [They] said, "No, that's man's job, that." I'm thinking one of the best jobs they had in the plantation was mule gang. 'Cause you go to work in the morning, you harness those mules up, ready, they gotta eat, ready for go. Put two, three burlap bags and tied it together. Was your saddle, that. Play cowboy, racehorse, take longer to get to the field.

When you reach the field, after a while they [workers] waiting for you over there. Pull the plow. Doing the cultivating, you stay in the back of the mules. You have this long rope come around your neck. The rope is to be there if you want to control the mule. That's the steering, in other words, yeah?

One time we was working in Kūka'iau, high by the forest. Lunchtime, you know. Oh, we go play inside the forest. We come outside, who stay waiting? My father waiting outside there for us. The other guys didn't catch hell over there. But me, when I come home, I catch hell.

Then, they had opening with the tractors. I get job driving the tractors. It's just like same kind [of] job as the mule, that, but you sit down and ride the tractor and go. They still used to use the mules on the palis, hills, you know.

Like the cut-cane guys, they used to cut the cane and pile 'em in the ground, and these tractors used to come and rake 'em, put 'em into piles.

Left to right, John Mendes, Jr., John Mendes, Sr., holding Butch, and Stanley Mendes, Pa'auilo, Hawai'i, 1953 (photo courtesy of Stanley Mendes).

Then the loader come around and pick those things [the cane piles] up. They didn't have no hāpai kō man, you know, da kine guys [who] make bundles and carry the cane. They didn't have anymore.

They had one rock in the cane field over there, even one tractor no can move 'em. Huge rock. And if you plow the field, that always in the way. And everybody say that was a kahuna stone. If you move that thing, something [bad] happens to you, or to the machine. Finally somebody went ahead and dig one hole in the ground there, dig, dig down, and put the stone underneath the ground.

I can say for myself, whenever I see one job, I learn to do the job by myself. That's the only way you're going to learn—to do and try. Some people, they no want to teach other people jobs. They figure they be the important one, not you. But I never was that style. What I was doing, I always teach somebody what to do.

I wen work inside the mill. Off-season basis when we had to repair the mill. And, well, most of the time, I worked with the electricians there. Helping them repair motors, you know, take out the motors from the mill.

Like I say, I can do anything on the plantation. Except for office work. But I was doing some office work one time when I got hurt and was laid up for a while.

I was looking for job with the state. If I could have better myself, I would go. [But] if I would join the state, I had to pay my own medical. That's little bit too much, eh? Like this girl [his disabled daughter] here, the plantation cover her for all the medical expenses.

They retired me 1984 or somewhere around there. I went to the doctor, catch cold, sick. Had pneumonia. Put me in the hospital. I stayed in hospital about one week or so. Then, after I get out, I went back work. Oh, but not feeling good. I went back, and I still get pneumonia yet. [X-ray] picture no was looking too good. Get emphysema, that's why.

There's quite a few people that quit the plantation. Some of them made it pretty good. And some, I guess, they sorry that they quit the plantation. In other words, if you bred to be a plantation worker, you might as well not pack up, because you might as well stay here. (Chuckles.)

While they was growing up, I always told my kids to do anything. Tractor driving or try to get their nose into everything else. No try to say, "I like only this job," or "I like only that job." Take what you can get.

Like Butchy [oldest son], he had these chances of staying in the plantation, but he didn't have the heart to lay off other people. Because, "Aw, I no like go bump off this guy." After he was laid off, he was driver for some business people down Kawaihae, truck driver. Then, he waited eight years before he could get into the state job. He still with the state, working as a parks keeper or something. But he lives over here. And he goes all the way to Kona every day.

[Younger son, John], he stayed on till the last harvest [the final harvest in 1994]. He work on and off, different kind of jobs. He was another one that he want to drive truck. But I told him, "You have to learn to do other jobs."

Actually, you know, when this [decline] started, it was before [Francis] Morgan [acquired Davies Hāmākua Sugar Co. in 1984 and renamed it Hāmākua Sugar Co.]. He improved the plantation. But his own family, they the ones made the trouble for this plantation. They bought equipment that anybody in their right mind wouldn't buy. You know these big, what they call top cutters. Cut the cane underneath the ground, root and all, dirt and all. Those cutters never did come out right.

They wanted to get the dirt out of the cane [coming] to the mill. What they had to do was get one helicopter, haul the cane up, and something cut 'em underneath, away from the dirt, then they take 'em to the mill.

Environmental people never like the dirt in the ocean. Okay? They go ahead and pump the dirt out in pipes to pile up someplace else. One time

Stanley Mendes sits on porch of Honoka'a home, Hawai'i, 1996 (Center for Oral History photo).

they pump the dirt, next day the pump no can work. The dirt no can go through. All plug up inside the pipe.

They blame the workingman bin broke the plantation. It's not the workingman. If they listen to the workingman, all of that, plantation would still be going.

Tell you the truth, even till the last harvest, I think I still had hope for the sugar to come [back]. That's right. I never believe anybody when they told me sugar was going to go out the door.

I feel hurt because when I was driving cane truck, hauling cane, you go to the field, you come back with a load of cane, back and forth, you know. In the eight hours shift of work, only one, two cars you see during the night. Then the last hours in the morning hours, then you start seeing the cars coming alive, people waking up. You know, because we used to haul cane near the camps, and you see the lights coming on. Then you begin to know that there's people living around there.

I wanted to go up [to Honoka'a town to witness the final harvest parade of cane trucks on September 30, 1994]. I had my jeep parked right there in the yard. But as I got out there, I couldn't go. I didn't have the power to drive up see them. Plus they blowing the [truck] horns. Can still hear that horns, you know, it blow. Sad.

GLOSSARY

bin	auxiliary verb indicating past tense
buggah	person
bumbai	later
daikon	turnip
da kine	unspecified referent
furo	bathhouse
hāpai kō	load harvested sugarcane
hō hana	weed
kahuna	in this context, spiritual force
kālua	roast in underground oven
kaukau	food
laulau	baked or steamed pork, fish, and taro tops wrapped in ti leaves
pali	cliff
pau	over, finished
pilau	rotten, stinking
shōyu	soy sauce
talk story	casually converse
wahine	woman
wen	auxiliary verb indicating past tense

FRED HO'OLAE PAOA

MY KĀLIA HOME

I miss the area very much. I miss the fishing. I used to get my fishing gear—small pole with a reel—leave it in my car. I used to get up at 5:30 in the morning. And I used to go to DeRussy. There was a little pier that went out. Catch two or three pāpios. Come home, cook it for breakfast, then go to work. What the hell's better than that? You tell me.

The seventh of twelve children, Fred Paoa was born in 1905 to Henry Ho'olae Paoa and Florence Bridges Paoa. The Paoa family residence sat on an approximately one-acre lot—now part of the Hilton Hawaiian Village hotel grounds—in the close-knit neighborhood of Kālia in Waikīkī.

After attending Waikīkī and Ka'ahumanu Elementary Schools, Paoa entered St. Louis College, a preparatory school, graduating in 1924. He earned his bachelor of science degree from the University of Hawai'i in 1928. Paoa joined the Honolulu Police Department in 1932 as a patrolman and retired in 1968 as assistant police chief. At the time of the interview, Fred Paoa and his wife Madelyn, who were parents, grandparents, and great-grandparents, lived in Foster Village. He died in 2002.

Paoa was interviewed in 1985 for COH's *Waikīkī, 1900–1985: Oral Histories,* demonstrating a ready memory for the people, places, and events in his life. Interviewer Warren Nishimoto noted at the time: "Mr. Paoa was hesitant at first to be interviewed, but as I asked more questions and mentioned more names, he became supportive and open."

* * * * *

My dad, he had nets. He was quite a fisherman. Catching kala, mullets, weke, et cetera. Sometimes we catch about a hundred, a hundred fifty kala, and we never sold them. We gave it to the neighbors, Hawaiians, whoever. That was the custom in those days for the neighbors to share their catch with their relatives and friends.

My father worked as a laborer at the old U.S. immigration station out here on Ala Moana Road. He worked there, I guess, all his adult life. Naturally, working there, he got to meet these people—Filipinos and Japanese immigrants, and I remember South Americans. He used to bring one or two to the house and tell us that these people would like to fish. On weekends they'd go out there with a small spear. They'd dive for uhus, kūmūs, oh, big fishes. Then he take 'em [the immigrants] back on Monday morning. You see, they were in his custody and he used to take 'em back there. He did that quite a bit. (Chuckles.)

He's pure Hawaiian. My mother was half. Her mother was Hawaiian and her father was Yankee. (Chuckles.) She [Paoa's mother] spoke fluent Hawaiian. And we answered in English. I'm sorry she didn't force us to learn Hawaiian. We had all the chance to learn the language.

I was born in Kālia, on the corner of Ala Moana and Kālia Road. It was a property there of about at least 45,[000] or 46,000 square feet. Quite a big old rambling house [with] the old type lānai that went about three-quarters around the building. There's twelve in the family, six boys, six girls. You can imagine how many bedrooms we needed.

"Boy" is my [nick]name. My parents called me that when I was so young. My nephews call me "Uncle Boy." They see me in town, they yell, "Hi, Uncle Boy." When they say that, I know it's a relative, see. But I sometimes don't know who they are. (Chuckles.)

We used to have lū'aus on New Year's Day [for] the relatives or friends of relatives. My dad used to buy a big pig about three days before. Big live pig,

Paoa children in their backyard, ca. 1912 (photo courtesy of Fred Paoa).

maybe 200 pounds. Every year, New Year's Eve, [the pig] would get out. And it was all over the neighborhood. Everybody's chasing him. And everybody knows the Paoas are having a lūʻau.

So they finally catch up with him, and we dress the pig in the morning, cook it. We had a big backyard, and we made the imu in the backyard [with] stones and rocks, and everybody chipped in.

We had all types of raw fish or cooked fish. Everybody catches squid, and they catch fish, and prepare for the lūʻau. Everybody takes a hand in cooking laulau, make things like that. It's a big job. Mixing the poi. All by hand.

In those days, no [serving of alcoholic] drinks. He was very religious, you know, my dad. He wouldn't allow any drinks. [Instead,] he used to mix [syrup] up, put into gallons. Cool it. Like Kool-Aid, something like that. (Chuckles.)

Piʻinaiʻo Stream flowed from Mānoa Valley, through the duck ponds across Kalākaua Avenue, along Ala Moana Road near our home, and ended at the area where the ʻIlikai Hotel now stands. We used to get underneath the shrubs and weeds along the side of the stream. Then you catch ʻōpaes, [or] shrimps, ʻoʻopus, (chuckles) anything you can find in there.

We used to catch also another type of ʻoʻopu for bait. They were very small and they live in the mud off the shore. They form little holes in the mud. So, by inserting your fingers in the tiny holes in the mud, this type of ʻoʻopu is easily caught. We put [it on a hook] on a long cord with a little weight on it. Just throw it and then retrieve the line to catch pāpios (chuckles) that way.

Just off the shoreline at low tide, we dug up coral sediment with picks and shovels to get the clams that were embedded. There was actually a lot of mud in the bottom there in that area, but I think it's the result of the stream that enters [the ocean] there. We found clams there for several years until the entire area was dredged [in the 1920s].

Then we used to go in front [offshore] of [Fort] DeRussy and Pierpoint. That's where we used to get all these different types of limu. Get lot of wana out there, just inside the reef. We used to put them in a bag. As the waves come on the seashore, we just roll them to break off all the spines. And then, break open the shell to get to the meat by using either a spoon or your thumb.

[At Pierpoint], Duke's father [Duke Paoa Kahanamoku's father, Duke Halapu Kahanamoku] taught me to swim. Duke's father was a captain of police. Big guy. See, Duke's mother and my dad were brother and sister. You know how he taught us? He tied a rope around us [at the waist]. He'd throw us in the water from the pier. That's pretty deep, wasn't shallow. About fifteen feet at least. So, he says, "Okay, you want to drown, you can." Then he pull us up. Take a rest. Next one, bang. (Chuckles.) That's how we learn.

We used to surf there on these waves about [three- or four-feet] high. Catch 'em out by the point to the pier, come on in with the surfboards. It was one small board like an ironing board. Not the regular redwood boards.

And as we got older, we went [farther] out with (chuckles) the big boys. I remember going out there with a surfboard. My cousin Sam [Kahanamoku] took me out. I was about fifteen then. So I paddled out. Before I got out to Canoe Surf—that's at the Moana—I hear this whistle. Chee, I turn around, look. Duke's on the board. He says to me, "Get inside."

That's how they operated out there. The big guys didn't let any of the young kids out there. I'm glad they did it, because when I got to do better, surfing bigger waves, then I gradually went out. You gotta really know how to handle it. (Laughs.)

[Surfboard polo] is a rough game, very rough. We played it quite a bit. It's just like water polo, except you're on a surfboard. You have the ball, you throw it from the board. They have a goalkeeper there. He's sitting on the board and he's reaching for it [the ball]. You could sit up or you could paddle [in a prone position]. If the ball is thrown at a distance, you just go for it and paddle. But it's dangerous because these boards are pointed and they're heavy.

Oh, three teams [were] there [including Hui Nalu, Paoa's team]. There was Outrigger [Canoe Club], Queen's Surf. We used to beat 'em all the time because we had some (chuckles) rough guys there.

We used to hang around there quite a bit at Mochizuki [Tea House in Kālia]. They didn't have a baseball field, but they had an area big enough

Hui Nalu surfboard polo team, c. 1925: (left to right) John K. Kaupiko, Jr., Sam Kahanamoku, Sargent Kahanamoku, Louis Kahanamoku, Fred Paoa, Kekona, and Fred Steere (photo courtesy of Fred Paoa).

where these fellas [Japanese college teams] played. It's a big open grassy area. They came to play baseball with the local teams here.

Later on, we played baseball [ourselves] as I grew up—Kālia Athletic Club. We played the army teams, [Fort] DeRussy. And we used to play teams from Schofield Barracks. We're all bush leaguers. Sweatshirt, dungarees. We didn't have any uniforms. (Laughs.) But we played for several years.

When they [Mochizuki] have festivities, like some Japanese event, some big deal, they'd have tents out there. Then, they had a beautiful pavilion in the back where they had shows. You know, Japanese dancing, and sumō. We'd sit on the lawn on the side, big gang of us, just watching. (Laughs.) That's where we learned to eat musubi. I used to shine shoes down at Pierpoint, from house to house. Most of them were haole people. They say, "Oh, just a minute." They leave their shoes out. Then I do my job, go the next one, all the way down. I made a few—I forget what the heck it was. Two bits, I guess.

We used to walk—Sam [Kahanamoku], Louis [Kahanamoku], my brother Gilbert [Paoa], Sargent [Kahanamoku], myself—from home to the *Honolulu Advertiser* to pick up our papers. They were two for nickel, those days. We used to sell papers where the streetcar used to come down from McCully [Street], and hits Kalākaua [Avenue], and makes a left turn. Oh, it's wide open, both sides [of the streetcar], those days. [We'd get] on the back of the transit [the streetcar], and make that turn, and get off. That's how we sold the papers on the streetcar. Catch another one back. We used to catch hell all the time from the conductor.

And we sold—we didn't sell, we swapped—'o'opus for ice cream cones. (Laughs.) And we swapped coconuts. There's a man that came out and sold ice cream in a wagon. We give him a whole bunch of coconuts for one cone or a string of 'o'opus for one cone. Big deal, we made. (Laughs.)

I think I was out [at] the beach there as a beach boy, [age] fifteen, sixteen, [with] my cousins Bill Kahanamoku, Sam, Duke, David. When they went out on the canoes, take the tourists out—this is summertime—I got to get on the canoes with them as a second captain. We'd charge the tourists for going out, [about] dollar a head. And then, we took [gave] surfboard lessons. I think we charged two dollars or two and a half [dollars] an hour.

We made our money teaching surfboard lessons, swimming lessons, 'ukulele [lessons]. We went out to the Kamaka studios on King Street. The old man [Samuel Kamaka, Sr.] made 'ukuleles there. In those days, they sold these pineapple-shaped 'ukuleles. I think they cost about three and a half or four dollars or five dollars. We sold them for seven dollars for (chuckles) one of those, seven and a half, then taught them lessons. We show them how to hold it and how to finger the 'ukulele.

We would have these people here [and be] in charge of their vacation for, say, a period of two weeks, three weeks. A family—husband, wife, and their kids, maybe. We take these people out on the surfboard. They stand, and they fall over, and they like it. We made sure they're not in the sun too long because they get sunburned, and then you're going to lose your business. So, we tell them to stay out not more than ten minutes. Or we'd bring a white shirt, cut the sleeves off, and make them wear it. Or we'd get coconut oil and rub it on them, things like that.

The people enjoyed their vacation because we did things that ordinary tourists would never think of doing. We'd get an old jalopy that one of the guys owned. They [the tourists] would bring their cars down from the Mainland sometimes. These big cars—limousines. And all these (chuckles) Hawaiians sit there with bare feet and everything.

First, we'd go to People's Cafe. That used to be on Kukui Street, in that area, where they have poi and fish, and stuff like that. We'd go and eat with the tourists. Walk Chinatown, through the slums, and all that. And then, we go to the Empire Theater. I mean, these people are well-to-do people, but they did something that's unheard of, something different, and that's what they liked very much.

Usually, we receive tips at the end of the vacation—let's say, the day before they leave. So, [the next day] we go down to the decks where the ships are leaving—the *Lurline, Matsonia,* the *Maui.* We buy a lot of leis out there, and go down there, and we take our 'ukuleles and guitars. When we get in the staterooms, we have a terrific party there. Well, I didn't drink in those days. But the older fellows bring their bottles and they have a good time. Put the leis on the [tourists], they cry like hell, you know. (Laughs.)

[In 1932] jobs were scarce and because I was married and needed regular income, I joined the Honolulu Police Department as a rookie. I could tell you the things I learned from these old-timers. These guys were all big guys —six feet, three [inches]. All pure-blooded Hawaiians.

There was one of 'em who took me in the back of the—you know the fish market, Kekaulike Street? There used to be a little alleyway from River Street in the back. So, [we] walk in there. There was a box there. So, he says, "Sonny, you get tired, you sit right here. You sleep, rest." I said, "How? What do you mean?" He said, "Well, you hold"—you know what a baton [police club] is?—"you hold the baton like this [propped up against your forehead], you sleep." Well, doesn't have to be on your forehead. But the fact is, when it hits the concrete, it wake you (chuckles) up [like an alarm].

Another guy says to me—I think it's Nakea. He says, "Say you see a fight over there on the sidewalk, what do you do?" I said, "Why you ask me? You're supposed to teach me." He said, "I just asking a simple question.

What do you do, you see a fight?" I said, "Go over there and stop the fight."
He said, "No, no. You don't do that. You wait. Everybody fall down, then
you call the [paddy] wagon." (Laughs.)

Domestics [domestic violence cases] are the most dangerous type of cases.
Had a case up Kalihi. This Portuguese fella fighting with his wife. Second
floor, and you had to walk up a stairway. When I got to the top of the stairs,
the door opened. Here's a guy facing me with a German Luger. I didn't ex-
pect it. My gun in my holster. I was really a rookie in uniform.

He says to me, "Get out of here, you cop!" I say, "Hey, brother, what's
the matter?" "Oh, my wife!" I say, "You know, those wahines, they always
give you trouble." He said, "Yeah." I say, "Gee, my wife's the same way. The
wahines, I don't know what's the matter, they always give you trouble. Is that
right?" He say, "Yeah."

As he turned facing his wife, I gave him a shove and I grabbed the gun.
And the gun was loaded. All he had to do is pull the damn trigger and I'd be
gone. But that was a close one.

I went in on June 15, '41 to the Navy intelligence as an investigator, you
know, as a civilian agent. [Governor] Jack Burns was a detective with us at
the time. He told me that they wanted somebody from the force and asked if
I was interested. I stayed in the service till the end of '45.

Then I went back to the police about November of 1945, the start of '46,
to the detective division as a detective. I think the following week, I went into
crime prevention as a lieutenant. And then, Captain Madison resigned, oh,
about five or six months later. I got his job in the same division.

Then I got promoted to assistant chief. I think it was '56. Mostly administrative work. You know, technical services, personnel, records division, finance
division, had our crime lab, the radio communications, the maintenance of
the blue-and-white cars, and so forth. Later on, we acquired the county jail.

I came out [retired] in '68. 1 loafed for almost a year, playing golf, fishing.
The latter part of '69, I think, I started [working for the "Hawaii 5-0" televi-
sion series]. Like the beginning of the season, I'll go to the police station and
get a list. Find out who was interested in working. Police officers, detectives,
motorcycle officers. These fellas have to be off-duty officers only.

And then, I rented all the blue-and-white cars, motorcycles, wagons, and
hired the fingerprint officers, crime lab, and the panel truck. And then, I got
permits for "5-0" from city and county, state, and federal to shoot movies on
these respective highways. I assigned officers on security patrol when they're
shooting. And then, I did a lot of [consulting for the] crime scenes where they
would like to know what the detectives did at the crime scene or what the lab
people usually did. [I did that for], oh, about nine years, I think. I left there
about two years before they quit [making the series] altogether.

When Henry J. Kaiser purchased property in Kālia in 1954, the value of adjacent properties began to skyrocket. After leasing it for ten years, we sold the [family] property to Hilton Hawaiian Village [in 1965]. I figured it would be better to sell it and we split [the proceeds]. Each individual [sibling] could invest that money or [do] whatever they wanted to do with it and enjoy it. People say, "Why don't you save it?" Save it for whom? Sure, the property [value] has gone up. So what? My dad and my mother didn't enjoy it. My oldest brother, another brother, two [other brothers], and three sisters didn't enjoy it. [Another sister, Mary Paoa Clarke, also a Waikīkī project interviewee, died in 1988.] They get nothing out of it, they're dead.

But the biggest headache that would come about is the fact that your family will expand—you have in-laws—to the point that when you negotiate and transact business, that means everybody has to sign the papers to approve they going to do this. Only takes one person to jam up the pie, right?

I mean, I don't regret it. [But] I miss the area very much. I miss the fishing. I used to get my fishing gear—small pole with a reel—leave it in my car. I used to get up at 5:30 in the morning. And I used to go to [Fort] DeRussy. There was a little pier that went out. Catch two or three pāpios. Come home, cook it for breakfast, then go to work. What the hell's better than that? You tell me. (Chuckles.) That's what I miss.

GLOSSARY

chee	mild exclamation
haole	Caucasian
kala	surgeonfish
kūmū	red goatfish
lānai	veranda
laulau	baked or steamed pork, fish, and taro tops wrapped in ti leaves
limu	edible seaweed
lū'au	feast
musubi	riceballs
'o'opu	goby fish
'ōpae	shrimp
pāpio	young jack fish
poi	food staple made from cooked taro corm
sumō	traditional Japanese wrestling
uhu	parrot fish
wahine	woman
wana	sea urchin
weke	goatfish

IRENE COCKETT PERRY

INTERWOVEN MEMORIES OF LĀNAʻI

Come rainy time, you know, the time when can't work outside, then the ladies would get together and clean the lau hala and soften them and put them in pōkaʻa. Pōkaʻa is rolls. When that's all done, they get together and they weave. . . . All the ladies, like the Kahaleanus, and I think Cousin Hattie [Kaopuiki] all get together and they make it a nice time.

Irene Perry is the sixth of eight children born to Robert Cockett and Rose Kahikiwawe Cockett. At the time of Perry's birth in 1917, her father worked as a foreman for Lānaʻi Ranch, overseeing the cattle in Keōmuku.

Perry attended Keōmuku School until the family moved permanently to Kōʻele in 1928. She completed her education at Kōʻele Grammar School. In 1934, she married Dick Perry, a Hawaiian Pineapple Company employee.

Irene Perry worked at the company's daycare center and also operated her own bake shop, supporting her two daughters and parents after her husband's death in 1950. When her daughters joined the military service, Perry followed them to the Mainland for a year.

She then moved to Honolulu and worked for the Moana Hotel. After retirement, she returned home to Lānaʻi, where she enjoyed weaving and other Hawaiian crafts.

Irene Perry was interviewed in 1989 by Hermina Morita, a longtime Lānaʻi resident who later became a representative in the Hawaiʻi state legislature. The interviews were part of COH's *Lānaʻi Ranch: The People of Kōʻele and Keōmuku,* a project conceived after Castle & Cooke, Inc., virtually sole owner of the tiny pineapple plantation island of Lānaʻi, decided to transform the island's economy by closing the plantation and constructing two major resort hotels: the 250-room Manele Bay Hotel and the 102-room The Lodge at Koʻele. The latter hotel, which was still under construction at the time of the interviews, stands on the former site of Lānaʻi Ranch. The site is historically significant because the ranch represented the island's major commercial activity prior to the beginning of pineapple cultivation in 1922.

The oral history project came about when the County of Maui Planning Department, which oversees land use for the county (which includes Lānaʻi), approved Castle & Cooke's request for land development and hotel construction provided that a comprehensive oral and written history project be undertaken. This was in congruence with an archaeological reconnaissance survey conducted in 1986 that recommended that oral history information should be collected from a number of older Lānaʻi residents with special knowledge of the island since 1900.

KEŌMUKU: CLOSE AND NICE

For me, Keōmuku was the best. I just loved it, even if you were much to yourself and all, but there was so much that you could do and enjoy.

We'd go crabbing and a little fishing, even if you don't get much, and pick limu and all that. Saturdays we'd go out and catch fish and we'd bring home. That was fun because we kids would go in and swim and splash water so that the fish would run into the net (chuckles). We would eat some fish and dry some for the winter months.

Every week, we'd go out and get enough firewood. We had to go out in the kiawe and pick up little twigs. Three different sizes, we'd get. We'd bring them home and we'd stack them up.

When there was plenty of lau hala, we had to go and help pick, the children from around there. Like the ones that can do the gathering of the lau hala, we'd do that, and the older ones would maybe strip the kukūs.

Come rainy time, you know, the time when can't work outside, then the ladies would get together and clean the lau hala and soften them and put them in pōkaʻa. Pōkaʻa is rolls. When that's all done, they get together and they weave. I don't remember seeing my mother weave a hat, but I know she weaved mats. All the ladies, like the Kahaleanus, and I think Cousin Hattie [Kaopuiki] all get together and they make it a nice time.

Summertime, before then, we used to plant watermelon. We would have a patch right in Keōmuku, right in the back where the big windmill is. And after school, or on a Saturday, we'd get together and we'd go up to the different places that needed to be weeded.

When that's growing and the vine starts getting longer, we had to go and peg them because the wind would blow on the vines, and then it ruins the

Keōmuku Beach, 1921 (Kenneth Emory, Bishop Museum).

plant. We would do that for this family, and then we'd go to the next [fami-ly's] watermelon patch and we would do that.

Then when the watermelon was ready to be shipped to Maui, we'd go and gather the watermelons. The parents would get the ripe ones ready and then break them [off] and put them in piles. And then the children used to have to carry them to the beach, so that they could be put on the boat and sent to Maui.

One time we had a nice crop that year. Big ones. And they were sweet, sweet like sugar, and red inside. They passed the watermelons down, and just where our place [was], we had a fence that you had to cross [in order to] go down to the beach.

I took this huge watermelon. My mother said it was too big [to pass down] so I carried it. And as I was going to put it down to open the gate, I dropped it. All the kids came running. We all dug into it. And, ah, it was a feast.

Anyway, that's what we had to do, all the kids, you know. We all worked together. It was really close, real nice. We had the Kahaleanus and we had the Japanese, Nishimura. And, of course, Kaopuiki children. But they lived in Ka'a. We'd walk and go up and see them, and play with them.

We'd go to church on Sundays. We'd all get together and go to the church down there, Ka Lanakila [O Ka Mālamalama] Church. And whenever they would have something big, maybe a convention, they would make a party for the church. All the ladies would make cakes. No measurements, you know, they'd dump flour and eggs, and just get going. And boy, I used to love to watch them mixing up their cake.

My mother used to make hers at home, if she's not with the ladies. Then when she gets through, I'd go get an empty coffee can cover, and I would make my own batter, dump some eggs and flour just the way she did (chuckles). And I would put it in this coffee cover, and I'd stick it in the oven. And at the end, it would be like pancakes.

We had a Rev. Alexander [George]—Alika, we called him. He comes from Moloka'i. He'd come, I think, once a month. I know he used to come to Keōmuku for church.

Oh, I loved that old man. He was real nice. He's blind, but he's sharp. You can't fool him. He'd ask you what time, and we tell him a different time. He looks at his watch and he said that we were wrong. "It's certain-certain time." "Gee, how can? He's blind. How can he see his watch?" But he just feels, I think.

He'd come and he would stay with us down Keōmuku. My father strung a wire from the outhouse to the back porch. And whenever he would want to go to the bathroom, he would just go with his cane and touch the wire, and he used it as a guide.

I used to take him from Keōmuku to Ka'a. And walk with him, and we'd talk, and he'll just follow you. You don't have to hold his hand, 'cause he'd just listen to your voice.

This is what my mom told us. When they were down in Keōmuku, my dad got real sick. He went to doctors, [but] something was wrong with his leg. It couldn't heal.

So he [Alika] came and talked to my dad and he told my dad that he can be cured if he joined the church. So my dad joined the church and he got well.

From that day, he said that he was going to learn about the Lord. He would read the Bible and he would go to church, and it was all in Hawaiian. My dad [at first] couldn't speak Hawaiian, he didn't know Hawaiian. Of course, my mom spoke Hawaiian. So after that, it was only Hawaiian. He kind of forgot his English. (Chuckles.)

I'm really ashamed of myself because I could have really known the Hawaiian language and speak it like my two sisters. Mary and Mikala, they're crack at it, they're good. And I could have been if I would have just used it. But, we didn't, because we were told at school that you don't speak Hawaiian. So, when we went home, "Oh, teacher say we speak haole [i.e., English]."

There was an old school, a big schoolhouse, but I never went to that school. I remember the new one, the nice small school that was built right below [the old one]. From the windows, you could look down into the ocean, you could see Maui. But it got you away from your studies, because you're thinking of going to the beach to swim.

I started in first grade, and I was in the first grade for I don't know how many years (chuckles). Because we would have teachers come over to Lāna'i. Haole teachers [saw] just nothing over there. They would come and stay about a month or two months and leave.

I was in the first grade, and when the [next] teacher came back again, I was still in the first grade.

PĀLĀWAI: TŪTŪ MAN AND TŪTŪ LADY

When my mother got worried, maybe they're not well, we'd get on horseback and come up and visit her tūtū [grandparents David and Makaimoku Keliihananui] down Pālāwai.

We would come from Keōmuku. We would go on horseback down Kahalepalaoa side and come up to that area where they lived. I would say about two hours by horseback, maybe longer. We'd bring fish or whatever we had.

My mom would get the he'e from [atop] the horse. I remember I was with her one time and we were coming up. And on the way, when the tide is low, she would see the [octopus] and poke it [with a stick]. And you could feel the tentacles climbing up. Sometimes she'd get a good-sized squid.

We'd stay with my [great-] grandparents, maybe several months. Tūtū Man must have been about eighty and Tūtū Lady, maybe about in the seventies.

David and Makaimoku Keliihananui flank Jean Munro, Pālāwai, 1921 (Kenneth Emory, Bishop Museum).

They had a nice old shack, a regular wood building, something like my garage out there. And then on the side, they built another extension without a floor, just the hard earth, [for] the cooking area. They had that with the iron roofing. And they had wood stove.

It was divided, just the living room and a little portion in the back. Just one window in the living room, and then from the entrance, the front door, you'd go right through to the back. Just two doors.

They had a back room [where] they had this bunk. You know, wooden planks and then they put this mattress on, and inside they had all this fibrous things. Must be lau hala shavings or whatever, I don't know, but it's all stuffed.

They'd have a sweet potato patch and we would go and work in the potato field. We would help harvest.

They had a big tank and when it rained, we'd get all that rainwater. It was for drinking. But there wasn't any running water.

We would take five-gallon cans, put all our clothes in there. We'd take it down almost to the piggery where they had troughs for the water for the animals. At that time, that place was full with pāninis. And the pānini plants were, I would say, just as high as this ceiling [ten to fifteen feet]. They would get the water from the trough in those cans and take them to the rocks, and then we'd wash all our clothes. Just imagine, all that work!

[In 1928] when we moved up [to Kō'ele], well, my tūtū them was gone by then.

KŌ'ELE: MOVING UP

My sister Mary said something about they [the Lāna'i Ranch Company] were thinking of closing out the ranch, Keōmuku side. They cut down the [number of] men so we were all to come up [to Kō'ele]. They weren't having the cattle [graze] down there anymore. They were only having [cattle] up this side, Kō'ele.

I think our things came through Kaumalapau [Harbor]. And we got off [the boat] and we wanted to come up to the city, to Kō'ele. So three of us kids, we were going to walk. So we walked up and we walked and we walked. And then finally, we sat down and waited for the truck to come. We got on the truck with all this piled up ukana. Oh, if we walked we would have died. (Laughs.)

When we moved up, that was something for us because it was indoor lua, and you didn't have to go outside. They had a nice, big bedroom, and a nice, big living room, and nice kitchen, and everything.

We had some fruit trees in the yard, like lime trees, and we had papayas. I think we had an orange tree, too, and mulberry. At home we didn't have any garden, but some of the neighbors had, like the Japanese and all, and they'd give us some [vegetables]. We got some of our vegetables from school. We had a garden at the school at that time.

When we came up, there was no church, but there was [James] Kauila. Kauila was kahuna pule, I think, for the Keōmuku church. I know we used to go down to Keōmuku to [Ka Lanakila O Ka Mālamalama] Church. Then when we moved up, we didn't have any church so we would hālāwai at home, have our services at home.

My dad and I think all the other Hawaiians there that wanted a church, I think they all got together because it was hard to go down to the Keōmuku church. Or the ones up here decided they wanted to have a church and so they got together and talked to the [Hawaiian Pineapple] Company, and the company told them they could use that land.

My father was ordained minister for [that Ka Lokahi O Ka Mālamalama Ho'omana Na'auao O Hawai'i] church [in 1930]. I have it written up.

Rev. [Andrew] Bright from Honolulu and Rev. [John] Matthew, they'd come over and work with the people here. I guess to show them the ropes and help them with the work.

Way back, we used to look forward to when we have that Sunday school. And then the different groups would come and they have their songs, and then we have like a contest. That's about the biggest thing that we have at the church. And then, of course, the special Christmas services that we have. But, Easter and all this other kind [of special services] that these churches have, we don't. Simple, it's very simple.

It's sad because Tūtū Hannah [Kauila Richardson] them and all of Kauila them [were] all in that church. It was for all the people at the ranch. The Kauilas, Kaopuikis, and Manos and everybody. But then [there was a] disagreement. And then they wanted to be by themselves and have their way. That's why now they call this the Cockett church. There's [now] just four of us going to church, you know.

So they got my father up, and then he took over the old [ranch] store over there. My father was doing the bookkeeping and tending to the cowboys that did the work outside. I think [James] Kauila was the foreman for the outside work.

Did they tell you we had that bell for this store, and that every Friday, once a week, they would open in the evening, I think it was something like three to five, and they would ring the bell, then people would come with their bowls or whatever for their poi? And they would have these huge barrels of

Buying poi at the ranch store, Kō'ele, 1921 (photo by Kenneth Emory, courtesy of the Munro family).

poi. One guy would scoop it up and put in your container. We'd wait for that day and then we would ring the bell.

I don't think there was much change. Not for me. I missed Keōmuku more, though. I just loved going out to the ocean for a swim whenever you wanted to and to just sit on the beach and enjoy. But the friends that were down at Keōmuku moved up, too. We were there together and then we got to meet a little more of the people up here.

I remember when we came from Keōmuku up there, and come December, it was so cold we had to use heavy jackets. So my dad had to go buy some thick, heavy sweaters.

We'd order from Sears Roebuck or Montgomery Ward [catalogs] at that time and come to Maui and get it. We'd go to school with these thick, heavy sweaters or overcoats.

Kō'ele [Grammar School], that was the one at the [present Cavendish] golf course. I started in the sixth grade and, boy, I did have a hard time. It would have been worst for me if my dad didn't help us with our schoolwork. Because we didn't have much at Keōmuku.

My family, [they] were so strict we couldn't go out and play with other kids. I don't know why, but my mom said that we're supposed to be home. We do our chores and we stay home. We don't bother anybody.

So we'd stay and just from the fence watch Hannah and (chuckles) all the other kids playing. And so, the only time we got to meet the kids is maybe Saturdays. After we get through with our chores, we can maybe go out and play with them until a certain time, then we had to be home.

And we couldn't go to the movie with the kids. The kids were all free to go and we just couldn't. And if there was something special, a special movie that was extra good, we had to beg and my dad would take us.

That's why I figured, oh, heck, because I met Dick [Perry], I may as well get married and I'll be free, and do what I want. Dick came from Pā'auhau, Hawai'i. He came here to work in the pineapple fields. I think he came in the '30s. And then I met him. I got married in 1934.

LĀNA'I CITY: IN A HOLE

I like Kō'ele better. I like Kō'ele because I like the hills and when you're up there you can see the ocean and those mountains down that north end side. Over here [in Lāna'i City] it's so cooped up like I'm in a hole. You can't see much.

I started [at the daycare center] in 1936, that was with the [Hawaiian Pineapple] Company. The company would get the kids to a place like that because the parents went to work. We had it down at the [Lāna'i] Baptist Church.

It was just from 8:30 [a.m.] to 12:00 [p.m.]. They would have the bus to go pick up the children. They would come over and get me when I was down that side, pick me up, and then we'd go right around the city and get all the kids.

They started from [ages] four, five, six. Everything was furnished. Papers, pencils, colors. And they would get their milk and their good lunch, you know, rice and meat.

I worked from '36 and then when I had Moana, I stayed home for a year and then I went back to work. Then I had Momi, and I was home for another year, and then I went back and I worked until 1957, 1 think, when the company did away with the daycare center. I'm not sure what year.

Dick passed away in 1950. When I was working for the preschool, I was only getting eighty dollars a month and I had the two children.

I [also] had my parents to care for because my father was paralyzed. It was after, in '56, I think, he was paralyzed. I had him and Mother move down and they stayed with me.

When the daycare center closed—before they closed—I opened up a doughnut shop. Irene's Doughnut Kitchen. Let's see, I think, '51 to '57. Right down in that little garage, I had my shop and had doughnuts and pies and pastries. I enjoyed it.

I had that special doughnut machine, greaseless doughnuts, it's called. just like a waffle iron. You just put your batter in and close it. And in about five minutes it's done. You can make dozens of it. So, I used to have that and I'd sell it to Richard's [Shopping Center].

And when we'd have blood donation time over here, I used to give some to the hospital. You know, donate some doughnuts. Sometimes they'd buy it, but I'd donate a little more.

It was good, but at the time there weren't too many people. And you know how Lāna'i is, sometimes they get tired of eating the same things. It's not a big profit. I couldn't make a living on that.

[Then] I went to visit Moana and Momi. They were both in the service on the Mainland. So, I went there and I worked one year down in the St. Francis Hospital in Colorado Springs. And then my dad passed away so I came home. My mother wasn't too well, so I thought I'd better stay close to home.

There wasn't anything here [on Lāna'i]. I wasn't going into the pineapple field. I [once] worked in the pineapple field for three months in summer. I'd come home and my [feet] would be swollen every day and I had to soak them in hot salt water. And every day like that, it was too much. I thought I was stupid, too. (Chuckles.)

So, I figured, well, that was too much for me and so I went to Honolulu, instead of going [back] to the Mainland. Here, I can come home and visit Mama. So I went to Honolulu and got a job at the Moana Hotel, 1959. I was working in the pantry.

I worked until 1978, then I decided I want to quit. Time to retire and come home. I came home and then in 1981, '82, I worked part-time at the First Federal [Savings and Loan], just cleaning.

Then I decided I think I want to go and learn to weave hats with Tūtū Mahoe [Rebecca Mahoe Kauila Benanua]. I always wanted to learn to weave. We used to make fans, when we were kids, for the church. But I wanted to learn to make hats.

So we went down [to Keōmuku] and got some lau hala and came back. We all made our own box [hat block],

Lau hala weaver Rebecca Mahoe Kauila Benanua, Lāna'i, Hawai'i, 1989 (Center for Oral History photo).

you know. What do you call that? Anyway, for the shape of our head. We made our own and then Tūtū Mahoe came and she taught us how to weave.

We started with the harder things. We should have started with fans or with little mats. The big weaves, you know. The hat was a fine weave. But, we learned to do it.

While I was working, I said, "Gee, I don't have enough time. I'd like to be home where I can get to Tūtū Mahoe and sit down and work." So, I decided to quit my job.

Just before I retired, I would take her some weekends, Friday, Saturday, and we'd come home Sunday. We'd go down to her place down there [in Maunalei] because she was good [well] at that time. And we would go and spend the night down there. We'd sit and weave and talk, you know.

LĀNA'I: RED DIRT

I'd like to see the old ranch, just the way it was. You can just picture—oh, before, the house was here, we were here. You can see that and then now you see this [hotel]. But, actually, I think it's really nice. You go up there and look, beautiful hotel right up there. I think it's good for us. We can see that little difference than just plain Lāna'i. That's the way I feel, but some people, I don't think they like it.

Like the Mānele one [hotel], I hope they don't cut us off from using the beach. You know, that we cannot camp there, or we cannot go into the place. That's the only thing that kind of worries me. So far, we can go and we can enjoy. So, I think it's all right.

I just hope they don't lose the specialness. Lāna'i cannot be like Kā'anapali [Maui resort] or all those other big places. You know, Lāna'i is different. Yeah, Lāna'i has red dirt. (Chuckles.) Lāna'i, you get dirty and you enjoy it.

GLOSSARY

hālāwai	meet
haole	Caucasian
he'e	octopus
kahuna pule	preacher
kiawe	algaroba tree
kukū	thorn
lau hala	pandanus leaf
limu	edible seaweed
pānini	prickly pear cactus
tūtū	grandparent
ukana	baggage

ALFRED PREIS

INTERNED: EXPERIENCES OF AN "ENEMY ALIEN"

No light. No reading matter. No writing matter. We decided, on the first evening, that we've got to do something. So I proposed that we would form University of Sand Island, in which each of us who had anything particular to offer would act as discussion leader. And that is what kept us not only busy but learning new skills.

Alfred Preis was born in Vienna, Austria in 1911. After graduating from high school in 1929, Preis traveled throughout Europe and later returned to Vienna to study architecture. In 1939, he and his wife, Jana, left Nazi-occupied Austria for Hawai'i—a destination they chose after seeing movies about the South Seas.

Upon his arrival, Preis worked as a designer for Dahl & Conrad, Architects. Following the Pearl Harbor attack, he and his wife were interned in Honolulu for several months as enemy aliens. In 1943, Preis opened his own architectural firm. Alfred Preis is perhaps best known as the designer of the USS *Arizona* Memorial at Pearl Harbor. Preis died in 1993.

The first executive director of the State Foundation on Culture and the Arts, Preis was interviewed by COH's Joe Rossi for *The State Foundation on Culture and the Arts: An Oral History* (COH, 1991). The four-session interview covers his youth in Austria, immigration to Hawai'i, and career as an architect, planner, and SFCA executive director. This edited narrative focuses on his World War II internment.

SUNDAY, DECEMBER 7, 1941

Connie Conrad was the second boss, the designer of Dahl & Conrad. It was he who brought me to Honolulu. I was with them from 1939, June—we arrived, by the way, on June 22, 1939, in Honolulu on Pier 17—until the day Pearl Harbor was attacked and most architectural offices had to close shop.

At that time, Pearl Harbor was rebuilt. And a great number of people were there. It was quite obvious that there would be a war, more to me than to other people here because I have seen some of the war preparations of the Nazis. We lived one whole year under the Nazis in Austria.

Jana is my wife's name. We went Christmas shopping and went Downtown to Thayer's Music Shop. And I found there the Fifth Symphony by Bruckner.

The next day was Sunday morning. I had to persuade my wife to let me open this Christmas present, I couldn't wait. I put the record on. We had a console radio/record player, a Philco.

We listened to the Fifth Bruckner—which I still have, that album—and we heard shooting and felt the impact of bombs or shots. And I turned to my wife and said, "That's a very realistic maneuver today."

At 10:30 [a.m.] we turned the record player off and turned it to radio. KGU every Sunday at 10:30 had a symphony concert, which we turned on. There was no symphony. There was a man who said, "This is not a maneuver. This is the real McCoy." We were all prepared for it, but we couldn't believe it.

There were two people living on the second floor, and we had the studio on the first floor. So we went up to them and said, "Did you hear that?" Both of them were green in the face. They were public health officers. And they were just called to Pearl Harbor.

When they came back in the afternoon, they had aged twenty years, each of them. They had to, with bulldozers, shovel the corpses, and with rakes and shovels to pick up arms and limbs. They helped prepare a temporary burial place at the entrance to Hālawa Valley—a big hole. The corpses were thrown in—and parts of corpses—and they put some chalk on it and then earth.

I had some courses in Vienna in civil defense. It was fairly new here. Nobody had worried about that. Sometime before—it happened to be that [Vladimir] Ossipoff was president of the [American Institute of Architects] chapter at that time—I said, "Maybe I could be of help. I learned how to design bomb shelters. There will be a war, and maybe you ought to do something about it."

He picked up the suggestion and arranged that if the war would break out, we would meet in the office of the doyen of Hawai'i's architectural corps, whom we called Pop Dickey—Charles Dickey, at that time the biggest architect in town—and there we would decide what to do.

I was assigned to a group of three, four architects—I don't remember, really, who they were—to blackout the YWCA [Young Women's Christian Association]. And this is what we did.

PICKED UP

The evening before—that means the evening of the day of the morning attack—we left our studio apartment in Waikīkī, put a sign there [indicating] where we were going to be, that we will be with friends on Pacific Heights. There were instructions that all people living near the ocean had to evacuate inland and uphill, either to predetermined centers or to friends.

Both my wife and I were fairly sure that we would be interrogated or something like that. We would have felt very insecure if we would have been accepted as refugees without being questioned.

About seven o'clock in the evening following the attack, two men in civil[ian dress] came and said, "We have to ask you to come with us. We have to ask some questions. You will be back very soon."

But it was seven o'clock in the evening. Somehow my upbringing under the Nazis made me skeptical. I said, "Do you mind if we take some toothbrushes along?" "Well, you don't need them, but okay, if you want to." We were the only people with toothbrushes.

We drove very, very slowly at that time through the darkened streets. The headlights were blue—later on red—painted with a tiny slit for the light to shine through. I recognized—it was dark already, it was December—that we were driving to the [federal] immigration station.

When we got out of the car, we entered a large, dark room. We could not see anything. Then we stood at a counter or a desk, and both of us were asked to empty our pockets. And my wife was moved to one side [of the room], I was moved to the other side.

I felt something cold and sharp in my back. It was a bayonet on a rifle, [by] which I was guided—or pushed—towards a steel stairway of steps, which I went up. The bayonet disappeared.

I was alone, in front of a steel door. I waited. I waited. I thought something will happen, but nothing happened. So finally I opened the door. I looked in—full of cigarette smoke and the smell of fish and a glow of cigarette [Preis points] here, and here, and here.

I stood at the door and waited until somebody will instruct me where to go. And I asked, "Isn't anybody going to show me a place?" When I [had] entered there, it was absolutely quiet and nobody said a word. But when I spoke—and some of them knew me and recognized my accent—they roared laughter.

Mario Valdastri, a plastering contractor and cast stone specialist with whom I worked quite often, recognized me. There were other people who knew me. And that broke the ice.

On the bunks were Japanese fishermen. They were just taken out of the boats the way they were—full of stink and smell, you know—but they were the first, so they had the bunks. The people were sitting around the walls.

So I found a little slit of space under the lowest bunk, on the floor. And I could at least hide my face, so they wouldn't step on it.

Next to our room were the women and our wives. We were separated by a metal wall, and on top there was a grill, so we could hear everything. The wall was so high we couldn't look [over].

There was one woman who cried, who was completely hysteric. She and her husband were also picked up the way we were, assuring that we would be [returned] there in a few minutes. She had a baby. They urged her to leave the baby, alone, which she did. But that was already near midnight. She didn't know what happened to the baby. She cried the whole night.

The next morning a Viennese doctor who happened not to be interned was able to arrange for her liberation. She was permitted to go home. And I learned, later on, that the baby was all right, fortunately.

The baby's father was a born American, not a naturalized citizen. She was a born American. And they were interned. Why? Slowly we found out that there was a certain pattern, that anybody who was in the "old country" during the last year and a half was drawn in. He was a jazz musician and traveled in Germany, but an American citizen, and they still picked him up.

We were for not quite two weeks, maybe a little bit more than a week, at the immigration station. We had to be lined up to get breakfast down in the court. We got an aluminum can, and we got some cold scrambled eggs, some cold prunes on top of it, some cereal on top of it, and a spoon that we were supposed to eat with. We ate. We were hungry.

From the first night on when I came to Honolulu, I discovered I was susceptible to sinus headaches. Sleeping on the concrete floor [of the immigration station], I got a vicious headache. I asked a man in uniform—in an army uniform—where I could get an aspirin.

He mumbled something and again with his bayonet pushed me into a direction, opened the door—we were in the toilet—and said, "Clean it." "Clean it?" I never in my life cleaned a toilet. "With what?" "Don't you have any hands?" They didn't even give a paper towel. I was alone. I thought I better not cause him to use his bayonet.

I had no idea how people in a situation like this could be. I knew how Nazis would be. I had a different expectation of America. But the people were angry, edgy, and almost hysteric. An attack on Pearl Harbor was considered impossible. The only explanation was that there must have been treason. So everybody was suspect.

And people were trigger-happy. All through the nights we heard shots. Wherever there was noise, you know, people were shooting in the direction of the noise.

UNIVERSITY OF SAND ISLAND

We were there for just a few days. And then we were moved to the harbor and put into a motorboat and crossed the harbor to Sand Island. And there, again, I was separated from my wife. I didn't see her since we arrived at the immigration station.

We were lined up and walked in line. We came to a one-story building which used to be a part of the quarantine station for immigrants.

The man in charge, a major who was originally a customs officer, was evidently overanxious and strict. He made us strip off our wedding rings, which made me break down. Not even the Nazis took my wedding ring. I was very nervous. I was worried about my wife. I made such a scene there that he returned all of our rings to all of us.

We were moved to an open area. There was a bunch of rolled up tents, and they said, "Erect them." So we built tents. Somebody came and said, "Take the tents off and move them over there." They did that three or four times, perhaps just to be kept busy. We finally had tents, no floor, just cots without mattresses.

I was extremely fortunate that in my tent was not only Herbert Walther —the friend, you know, who took care of us—but Konrad Liebrecht, who was the first violinist of the [Honolulu] Symphony; Ernst Orenstein, a Viennese banker who was a music lover; and educated people like that.

No light. No reading matter. No writing matter. We decided, on the first evening, that we've got to do something. So I proposed that we would form University of Sand Island, in which each of us who had anything particular to offer would act as discussion leader. And that is what kept us not only busy but learning new skills.

There was a Viennese. He worked on a book on the history of the occult sciences. An enormously erudite man with a fantastic background. I learned from him that he had to leave Vienna because he, a stage designer, designed [Arthur] Schnitzler's *La Ronde*. *La Ronde* was a play—we have seen it in Hawai'i as a French movie later on—and it simply showed one young officer who moved from girl to girl, from woman to woman, and each of them had a particular angle. Well, that was too much for Vienna at that time.

The Sand Island internment camp was set up shortly after the start of World War II (U.S. Army photo, reproduced by courtesy of the U.S. Army Museum of Hawai'i).

He lectured about the Bible—assuming that all or most of us would know the Bible—and related it to ancient history, that means the history of the ancient religions out of which the Bible really was created. I was spellbound.

I remember that I asked, naively, "Mr. Tauber"—Harry Tauber was his name—"how come that you speak such a marvelous English?" He said simply, "I read only good books."

There was Ernst Orenstein. He was a banker in Vienna, but he was an expert musician. He played piano, belonged to every avant garde music club in Vienna—Arnold Schoenberg, Alban Berg, and so forth. He knew all nine symphonies of Bruckner by heart and hummed them, analyzed them, showed us how Bruckner developed musical themes and ideas, all in a dark tent.

There was a short, vivacious man—I don't remember his name. He was a surveyor who spoke with a North German accent. He was an accomplished amateur astronomer. At that time, I began playing something of a leadership role, to which I'll come back later. I went to the major and asked for permission to be able to be longer out of the tent at nighttime to watch and study the stars, which was granted. To see the sky at a blacked-out city, where the stars are doubly and triply as bright as they ever have been, was really a sight. Well, this is the way that we spent our time.

CONTACT MAN

But let me come back. That same major—ever anxious and nervous and so afraid that we would be rebellious internees. In our group was a professional wrestler, also the owner of a massage parlor. So he was assumed to be strong enough to control us. He [the major] asked him to become our camp captain.

The major also had the idea to keep us busy, that we are men, that we ought to exercise. He asked him to conduct physical education classes.

It so happened that I paid for my college tuition partly by conducting gymnastic and physical education classes with my future wife. She was a gymnast, and I was a gymnast and acrobat, that means gymnastics without bars and rings.

So I stood there and waited until that hunk of a man will start the class. He seemingly didn't know how to start. We became bored and restive. So I started to exercise. And the others behind me, next to me, followed me. Fortunately, the wrestler was bright enough that he did the same thing. So instead of he being the strong man, I became the strong guy now and the fellow in charge. So I became the contact man with the major.

Meanwhile, our wives, or the women, got a wooden house built on the other end of the space and outside of the fence where our tents were.

The house was constructed by a sculptor with whom we were earlier befriended—Roy King was his name—who didn't know what to do when he saw me. Here I was, a prisoner of war, a traitor, or something like that. He didn't know whether he should even greet me. He was patriotic. He didn't.

Soon after that, every Sunday morning the married men were invited to share breakfast with the women in their house.

One Sunday we were lined up to go there, but didn't go there. The major came and accused us that somebody of us has stole some knives and forks, and that's dangerous because we could make weapons out of them and escape. We had to undress—stood completely naked.

There was a young lieutenant of the national guard who served under him. He was in charge of that search. They couldn't find anything.

So the major finally reached up to the gutter of the mess hall and pulled the knife—or knives—and forks out. He said, "Here, you couldn't find even that," embarrassing his men in front of us. He was hiding them simply to demonstrate a case.

We were guarded by people from the national guard, local people. Some of them we were befriended with from before. They were tired, and they didn't have any sleep, so they begged us to let them sleep in our tent and that we would watch them so they wouldn't get caught, which we did.

CAMP FOOD

In the beginning, we had only canned food. There was no meat, no vegetables, but pears and pineapple in cans. But we had every single chef of every hotel—they were all Germans—in the kitchen. They concocted, out of canned things, some interesting meals.

By that time, I was starving for vitamins. We had no vegetable, no fresh fruit, nothing. I ate leaves of bushes, and blossoms.

The first major shipments came—that was before Christmas—of ships which could not land in the Philippines. They were on their way to supply the armed forces there—at that time the American army was in retreat—so we had certainly enormous amounts of food. We had turkey, of course, for Christmas.

There was an old German who had KP with me—kitchen patrol—too. And here I had the opportunity to get a slice of bread and butter. I was so starved for butter that I virtually put butter on thicker than the bread was. That old German was so outraged at my waste that he berated me.

JAPANESE CAMP

There were two camps side by side, separated by about a twenty-feet wide maze of barbed wire. We, the haoles, were about fifty men. The Japanese camp had about 2,500—we thought 3,000, but I learned later on it was a little under 2,500.

In the middle of the space between the Japanese camp and ours was a raised platform in which our only captive mini-submariner was kept. He was stripped except for a loincloth. He was the one who, in the attack on Pearl Harbor, came with his mini-submarine and was caught in the submarine net.

We were ordered not to look at or talk with him or we would be shot. Now, how can you not look at the prisoner of war virtually exhibited on the platform? Regardless of which direction we wanted to look, we couldn't miss him. Nobody was shot.

My cot sank deeper and deeper into the rain-soaked mud until my mat-tress-less cot was touching the wet mud. I was really sleeping in the water. I got backache. We had no doctor in our camp, but there were several very well-known doctors in Japanese camp. I was permitted to go to the Japanese camp.

The difference between the Japanese camp and ours was striking. Every tent—they had tents, as we did—was adorned with tiny pebbles, shells, and coral splinters. They picked them up, and they made patterns like stone gardens out of it—neat, beautiful, clean, with an innate genius compared to us. We at most picked up cigarette butts which our men just threw away.

Well, Dr. [Iga] Mori was the doctor who saw me. He couldn't do any-thing for me because he had no medication. But we had a long talk and be-came friends, and we were friends afterwards.

PAROLED

Finally we were asked to go back singly to the immigration station to be interrogated by a commission. They knew a lot about me because I came late to the United States. At that time, they were already alert, but before, everybody could come in, so they really knew nothing about them. Anybody could have been fifth column or worse.

We saw that from our fifty people—Germans, Norwegians, Italians, Austrians, and Hungarians, all people whose countries were invaded and occupied by the Nazis and therefore suspect—small groups were leaving the camp. Among them, Konrad Liebrecht and Ernst Orenstein were released. The others, we later learned, were shipped to the Mainland. My wife and I and two others were left over.

We had to be released into parole, that means we had to have a respected citizen who was willing to sponsor us and vouch for us. Connie Conrad arranged that the owner of a quarry [Chester Clarke] would vouch for us—I designed his house on Hālawa Heights. Eventually we were released on parole on March 28, 1942.

GLOSSARY

haole   Caucasian

ALEX RUIZ

ALWAYS A REBEL

When I first came here, (laughs) I came under contract, see. I promised my mother after the contract, I'd come back. It was three years, three-year contract. Then you get a free passage [back home]. Come three years, my mother write to me, "When you coming home?" I said, "Oh, just a little more." (Laughs.) Keep on going on like that until today.

The second of ten children, Alex Ruiz was born in 1914, in Laoag, Ilocos Norte, Philippines. His parents moved to Manila when Ruiz was still an infant. Ten years later, the family returned to Laoag, where Ruiz continued his schooling.

In 1930, at age sixteen, Ruiz immigrated to Hawai'i. He weeded fields at Kōloa Plantation on Kaua'i and lived in the plantation's Filipino Camp. He soon transferred to the sugar mill as a machine operator and later worked in the laboratory.

Ruiz switched to order taking and delivery for Kōloa Plantation Store in 1933. After a stint in the U.S. Army's Filipino Infantry Regiment during World War II, he returned to the store. He married Janet Fukumoto in 1946. The couple had two children.

In the late 1950s, he went back to the mill first as a steam-generator operator, then as a journeyman welder. Retired in 1978, he died in 1999.

Chris Planas and Warren Nishimoto interviewed Alex Ruiz in 1987 for *Kōloa: An Oral History of a Kaua'i Community,* a project focusing on the historic town located near Kaua'i's southern shore, approximately ten miles southwest of Līhu'e. The site of Hawai'i's first commercial sugar plantation, founded in 1835, Kōloa's fields and mill continued to produce sugar for 161 years. Even before the plantation shut down in 1996, emphasis had shifted to developing resort hotels, condominiums, golf courses, and upscale boutiques and restaurants catering to tourists and wealthy newcomers, bringing about large-scale and irreversible socioeconomic change to the Kōloa-Poʻipu area.

FROM ILOCOS NORTE TO HAWAIʻI

I was born in the city of Laoag, Ilocos Norte. I think I was an infant when my father, my family, moved to Manila.

I went to school there in public schools. Schools in the Philippines, there were no dialect schools, only English. If they catch you speaking your dialect in the school grounds, you get suspended. At that time I speak only Tagalog. Then we moved to Laoag, nobody speak Tagalog there, only Ilocano.

So we moved to Laoag, my father put up a bakery. Any kind [of goods] you see in the bakery, he makes it. And the amazing part of it is, no recipe.

My mother was a jeweler. I think because one of her distant cousin, or something, was a jewelsmith. See, we don't have a jewelry store, so she carry jewelry, she go house to house. Just like peddling jewels.

In Philippines, we had maids, we had a cook. My father had a driver and he had horses. So our chores was we helped every one of these people. My mother used to always tell us that, "You folks not going to stay with us forever. You have to learn how to do that job."

When the maid wash dishes, you help wash the dishes. You help the yardman clean the yard. You help the guy take care of the horse. We help the driver wash the car. (Laughs.) Those days, you know, I think in that city that time, you can count how many cars there was.

We lived right beside the river. Just one block away from the city market. Down there they build houses that's always two story. It's a big river. That river, when you flood, you flood the whole market. That's why they built those two-story buildings.

My mother's cousin, he was a sea captain. He came back to Philippines to visit. And he told my mother that he wanted to take me with him back here [to Hawaiʻi]. I was in school then. When I went home, that was a mistake my mother made by telling me that.

So I say, "Oh, where is he?" "Oh, he went back." So I says, "I'm going." My mother said, "No, you're not. You have to continue your studies." "No, I think I better go."

My brother was here [in Hawaiʻi] already. And he writes back that plantation life is very hard, he cannot take it. So my mother said, "Your brother cannot take it. I don't think you can take it." I told my mother, "My brother is a silk [a softy]. I'm not."

Then one day when that HSPA president [probably Hawaiian Sugar Planters' Association secretary-treasurer John K. Butler] came to visit immigration, my father mentioned to him that I want to come down here.

He liked my father's cooking, so every time they come and visit immigration he send telegram down at immigration telling all the agents that he's coming for a visit, you know. So my father prepare lunch for him.

Well, matter of fact, I'm also involved on that because my father look at that Filipino dish they call adobo and then that omelet. My father cannot make the taste just as good as the way I make it. So when he comes, my father come and take me out from school, excuse, I cook the two dish, and go back to school.

But he's the man that give us the recommendation. Myself, my late cousin—he died recently—then David Cayetano, and another guy they call Juan, I forget his name. Once we came to Hawai'i, we got separated.

TRIP TO HAWAI'I

We came under the steamer *President Wilson*. Took almost a month, I think. You know when you come to Hawai'i, they put you steerage, no more first class.

They had a Chinese cook in that. And when it's ready for lunch, all he had to say, come inside the room and start yelling, "Lice, lice, lice." (Laughs.)

Well, it's not too bad until I got seasick. It was my fault, too. Because I was not feeling sick in the boat. And then there were people with boxing gloves. And then I went and box. After that I get seasick.

We were quarantined in Sand Island for two months because somebody in our group died of meningitis. We were supposed to be quarantined one month. Before we could finish that one month another one got sick. So was another month. It was luckily that after the second month nobody got sick. Otherwise we would keep on going one month, one month, you know.

One day I had a temperature. So they tell me, "You better go in the hospital." The nurse told me, "Hey, you get the highest temperature in the hospital." That scared me. Because if you have a temperature, by ten o'clock in the evening those doctors come. There was about five of them, and they [would have] taken fluid from my neck [with a needle]. So that scared me, so when I found out I had the highest temperature, I took [to] my bed, and cover myself with a blanket. I wanted to sweat it out.

By ten o'clock in the evening, that haole nurse came and wake me up, and put the temperature in my mouth, thermometer. Then she came back and snatch that thermometer from my mouth. Then she tells me, "You are dead."

"What you mean, 'You are dead?'" "It says you get no temperature." Because the fever went down.

And then I felt my back, my pillow, wetlike. I turn around and look at my pillow, it was a green sweat. The first time I see that kind of sweat. So, (laughs) I was ashamed of it, I turned around the pillow.

Then in a few moments, the doctors came. One of the boys had a temperature, and so they took that [fluid], as I said, take it right behind the neck. One of the doctors was kidding me, he says, "You want to have that?" I said, "No, I don't." "You're going to get it." "No, I don't want that."

He must have been here long time, the doctor, big haole doctor, even talk Ilocano little bit. He said, "You're lucky. Your fever went down so we don't have to take [fluid]." So I was happy.

KŌLOA PLANTATION

When I first came here [to Kōloa], there was a Filipino Camp over here. All single men, there. Just like one warehouse, you know. Divided into rooms. You got to room with somebody else. Get two army bunk, army cot.

And they have a long porch. You know this people that carry the cane, hāpai kō? And you know how dirty their clothes is, eh? That's all hanging on the porch. You look at that and say, "Oh, no." When you first see that, you don't feel like coming to Hawai'i. (Laughs.)

And you go toilet, you got to go outside, eh. (Laughs.) They used to have a box, you know, under the seat, and that is being collected every day. Then when a man used to collect that—and they used to call him "Kūkae Joe" or something—he used to collect all those. They dump it [the waste] way up in the mountains.

First day I went they assigned us to the field, kālai. I didn't stay pretty long, because I go out in the field, and then I cannot take it, I lay off.

[Camp policeman] Gavino Kilantang was Filipino man. Somehow he wanted me to stay back in the plantation, because he knew that I came as a student and could speak pretty good English. So he figured that I would be a leader, you know, around the community.

He tell me, "You go to the mill." Then he give me instruction, "Tell the guy that you used to work in a mill." I forgot all about it, you know.

He told the chemist that I used to work Philippine mill. And the chemist asked me, "Ruiz, you used to work in the Philippine mill?" I said, "No, I never did." "You never did work in the mill?" "No." He smiled and go away. So they caught the guy lying. That's another thing. I couldn't tell the lie.

They start me off with the number two machine. They call it massecuite, that's a mixture of molasses and the sugar granules, there. You drop that molasses. Then what I do is dig the sugar, drop it in the conveyor, and then it goes to the crystallizer, to be crystallized again. I did that for one year. It was pretty easy, because most of the workers was coming to help me dig the sugar.

[Later] I was a sample boy. You take samples of the syrup, the bagasse, the juice, all the things that's in the mill. You take sample of how much lime they have in the juice. So we analyze all that.

I was always a rebel. And when I started working in the mill, after harvesting season [when the mill stops processing cane], all that non-skilled laborers, like us, sent to the field, kālai. About four o'clock in the afternoon, we're supposed to pau hana.

Then Mr. [Norman] Deverill was the field supervisor, he came to the field and he saw kāpulu. He came and he said, "Everybody go back in the field because you folks made kāpulu." But that was four o'clock already, you know.

So we had to jump out from this truck. And I jump out, I told the other boys—the other men, they were all old men, local folks here—"You folks want to go back, you go back. I'm not going back." Then they decided nobody go back. "So, okay if nobody go back, tomorrow he going ask where is the leader. You have to tell him nobody lead." They said, "Okay."

So the next morning, they put us into something just like a skirmish formation. He suspected me. But he cannot do anything. Now, I didn't let nobody boss me, I boss myself.

Then, the second year, that chemist send us again to the field. He was Mr. Wickey, Samuel Wickey, he was the head chemist. I went to see him.

Kōloa Plantation's New Mill Camp, Kaua'i, 1926 (photo courtesy of the Vicente Amoroso collection).

I explained to him, "You know, I came to the mill to work because I could not take the work outside. But if you keep on sending us outside, maybe after season, I might as well get out." So he said, "Well, okay, Ruiz." He said, "You come back. You work here." If he leave me back he have to leave the other guys.

I notice about the haoles, you show to them that you are not scared to them, they respect you. Something like Deverill, when he found out, he knew that I lead that strike against him. He caught me talking story with another fellow in this field here. All of a sudden, hey, here comes a horse, and was Mr. Deverill [riding]. So he started scolding the other guy, you know. And went away and we went back to our work, and this guy said, "Hey, how come he only scold me? How come he no scold you?" I said, "You ask him." But I notice that's how they are.

STORE WORK

Well, there was an opening at [the plantation store] that time and I applied for it. That was between '33 and '34. Because that time they were paying us only a dollar a day in the plantation, and the store was paying by salary. They were paying at that time $35 a month, which is more than what we earn outside.

And there were several of us applied to it, but the plantation used to pick who has the best record in the plantation. At that time I already had the best record because I used to work even Sundays to earn more money, you know what I mean. So I was picked.

I go to Japanese Camp and Filipino Camp like that, taking orders. Groceries, rice, whatever they needed for the house. Those days they used to buy rice by 100-pound bag. A 100-pound bag of rice, it cost you about $5.00 or $5.50 or something like that. And those $5.00 that they order is five days' work, right? (Laughs.) Dollar a day. Until the union.

I take their orders, and then as soon as I go back to the store in the morning, I make [gather] their orders. After I make all their orders, maybe after lunch, I be able to deliver. We used to have a truck, canopy truck, where we load whatever we order and deliver with the truck. After I deliver I go back to the store. Then in the evening I go back [to the camps], take their orders again. Going on like that like a routine.

In the Japanese Camp is mostly families. In the Filipino Camp there were only about, let's see, four or five of them. The rest is single men. I used to have over 250 single men [customers], and we have to memorize all of their bangō numbers. And their bangō consist of about five digits. If you are going to take orders and you ask them, "What is your bangō number, now?" they don't like that. "Oh, what's the matter with you? You long-time store boy and you don't know my number." (Laughs.) So my head was full of numbers, that time.

Those Japanese families are charged on a regular charge slip. Not only Japanese, but the rest of the nationalities, whoever. And they are not being collected in the office [through payroll deduction], they come and pay their bills.

Except Filipinos. That's the discrimination. Well, Filipinos come in the office, and they are issued maybe three dollars worth of coupons. And that is automatically deducted from their paycheck. In order to buy anything from the store, they have to use the coupon.

Because of the fact that those days was mostly single Filipinos. They can work [Kōloa] today and work Līhu'e tomorrow. So by issuing the coupon from them, they can collect whatever they issued before they go anyplace [else]. [According to a former Kōloa Plantation store department head, coupons were issued to high-risk customers—mainly, but not limited to, single Filipinos—who didn't pay their store bills regularly.]

At that time, the very beginning of the store, the store was making all right, because so many plantation workers, and they monopolize to buy at the store. So the store was making money and every year we celebrated by having a store party. And that kept going on like that until the war started.

When the war started I went in the service. And when we came back after the war, the store was not making too good then, because it [the Kōloa Plantation] was already unionized, and our buyer, Mr. [Mitsugi] Nishihara, was running the store just like the way they was running way before the war.

"Your price is too high. You supposed to lower your prices and sell in volume. Today if you cannot sell in volume, you are out of business," I told him. And he didn't believe me.

Then they started to negotiate to sell that store because that store was not making money. And then the bigshots, the executives of the Big Save Store, came down. They was talking to him in the warehouse for oh, almost four hours.

He said, "Alex, you know who these people are?" "They are that Big Save executives, yeah?" "Yeah, that's right," he said. "They was telling me about volume sales, exactly what you was telling me." "Well, Mitsugi, I told you so. Now too late." "Yeah, yeah, yeah." (Laughs.) [In his interview Mitsugi Nishihara points to the rise in store wages after unionization as the main reason the store folded.]

When they started to give us notice that they're going to sell the store, I went to see Mr. [William M.] Moragne. At that time Mr. Moragne was the plantation manager. And I asked him if he can return me to the plantation.

MILL WORK

I applied for that [mill] steam-generator operator and I got accepted by [taking] a test. Then the regular operator got sick, he went to Mahelona [Hospital]. So I trained only for a couple of weeks, and they made me operate solo. And then I stayed steam-generator operator for a couple of years. So when that fellow came back from Mahelona, that means I have to go out from there because that was not my regular job, so they released me from the job.

At the same time our engineer was Mr. Vic Vargas, a Filipino man. He asked me if I wanted to go to school. I said, "What kind schooling?" He said, "You go learn welding." I said, "Yeah, I go." So the plantation organized several boys to go to that welding school. It was during the nights after work. And that's when we become welders.

All tradesmen grade five and up have to go and take trade progression. And you pass that, then you advance every six month to another grade until you go to the top grade, grade nine. So I passed that again. I came grade-nine welder, that's already a journeyman.

Mr. Moragne did not believe in contracting, he wanted us to do it. Everything is just like the shop boys and the carpenters do all that, whatever improvement in the mill. In the carpenter shop there're about, oh, about a dozen of them, and all the mill shop boys—machinists, welders, plumbers—all connect.

Well, at that time, the plantation wanted to change the washer where the cane goes and then create that flume where the cane being washed. Mr. Moragne was also a technical engineer, just like Mr. Vargas. So the two engineers formulated that, made up that washer that they have in the mill now.

They have a mud bath where the cane fall in the mud bath. [In the bath, the cane floats but the debris sinks.] And then they have a sprayer where the cane pass there, and they have drums where they can stir the cane before it falls to the carrier that is going to the mill. And Mr. Vic Vargas was so clever that when the truck dumped the cane in the first room, it's all automatic into the mill.

All we had to do is be given a drawing, and we weld that thing. We made the rollers, everything that went in there is fabricated by us. Steel and pipes, like that.

I retired as a welder [in 1978]. Well, I wouldn't say it's a better job physically [than the store job]. But moneywise it's better. Because in the store I was only grade four [job classification]. And if you work in the store, a grade four outside makes more money than the grade four in the store. I don't know why. The same plantation.

As I say, when I was working in the store I had a debt until my neck. (Laughs.) And I went to work in the mill, then I started to come up from that hole. That's when I was able to make this [second] house and all that.

I used to live in the [New Mill] Camp, after the war, you know. And the people have been moving all outside [to Kōloa], one by one, until we almost were the last ones to move there because my wife didn't like the idea of going toilet outside. Because all the Kōloa homes, those days, you have to go outside toilet. So we told 'em, "Oh, if I cannot find a house where we can have our toilet inside the house, we refuse to move."

And then one day they call me at the plantation office. [Personnel director] Mr. [Fred] Weber called me, "Alex, I heard you looking for a house." "Who, me? Looking for a house?" I said. And then I think back and I said, "Yeah, that's right."

He said, "Well, there is a house down in Kōloa we are renovating, we just finished renovating it. Tell your wife to go and take a look at the house. If you like the house, then you can live there." They renovated it, they made toilet inside, and dig another new cesspool, and all that, you know. So I came to see it, and I told them, "Yeah, I like to live there."

I was renting it from the plantation until I bought it. Plantation decided to get away from that renting business. [Eighteen hundred dollars] for the lot and the house. So nobody believe it.

All those mill people, Japanese families living in that [New Mill] Camp, are all around Kōloa side, now. That camp is not there anymore, only cane field.

GLOSSARY

adobo	a meat dish
bangō	worker's identification number
haole	Caucasian
hāpai kō	to load harvested sugarcane bundles
kālai	to weed with a hoe
kāpulu	careless, slipshod
kūkae	excrement
pau hana	end of work

JOHN SANTANA

YOU'RE YOUR OWN BOSS, NOBODY BOSS YOU

*So I rather work in the coffee land,
take contracts, you're your own boss.
If you want to work hard, you work
hard. If you want to work slow or
whatever, you're your own boss, nobody boss you. So when I came from
Union Mill, Kohala side, to Kona, I
started to pick coffee. Hundred-pound
bag, fifty cents.*

John Santana was born in 1906 in Kohala, Hawai'i Island. His father, Domingo Santana, and mother, Enancia Santana, emigrated from Puerto Rico
in 1901 to work on sugar plantations. In 1928, the family moved to Kona
and took on contracts as coffee pickers. Later, John Santana worked as a road
worker, night watchman, school custodian, and school bus driver. In 1945,
Santana began his own coffee farm on leased land in Kahalu'u, Kona. He
married Mary Rivera in 1937, and the couple raised nine children, a niece,
and an adopted grandson. Santana died in 2003.

COH's Warren Nishimoto interviewed John Santana in 1980 for *A Social History of Kona.* Santana's story begins with his father Domingo's emigra-
tion from Puerto Rico. Domingo's life history is similar to that of many immigrants who found Kona, with its rich, abundant agricultural lands, to be a
haven for former plantation workers seeking greater economic independence,
lifestyle diversity, and working conditions similar to what they left behind in
their homelands.

KOHALA

He [Domingo Santana] came from Puerto Rico. He came to Hawai'i in the
year 1901. Of course, there came many Puerto Ricans, but some they ship
to Kaua'i, some to Maui, some to the Big Island. He used to work in the

[sugar]cane fields; that's what people used to do at that time, mostly, work in the cane fields.

She [Enancia Santana] was a housewife. She only take care the house, the cooking, wash clothes. And she used to do a little sewing, too, for people, a little tailor[ing], yeah.

I was born 1906 at Kohala Plantation, Kohala Mill. I remember I was about seven years or eight years old, my father used to take me to the cane fields to teach me how to work. Weeding, hō hana, we call it.

Of course it wasn't every day, but at least two days a week I used to go with my father to work in the cane fields. This was during school vacation and I remember my salary was about fifteen cents a day.

At that time their [parents'] salary was very cheap, I think it was about eighteen dollars or twenty dollars a month. And people had to work about ten hours a day.

Sometimes we used to go down fishing, too. We used to walk down from the camp, we used to walk right down to the sea. Sometimes we catch poʻo-paʻa. And nighttime, sometimes we catch lobsters, we catch mū. Mū, that kind of big fish, get that teeth, more like human teeth. With our bamboo, sometimes we catch menpachi. We take them home, eat them.

MALIʻO

Then after that, well, we moved from Kohala Mill to Hāwī. And we went to live at one place they call Maliʻo. There was a big Puerto Rican camp over there; they had about twelve houses over there. And they had a store over there.

So, we had two-bedroom house, one bedroom for me and one for my father and mother. Then we had the parlor and we had the kitchen. No more water pipe going inside the house. We had outside toilet.

Maliʻo, I used to work in the cane field, too, once in a while, but most time I stayed at home. My father had the cow—he bought one cow—and I used to cut grass for the cow and keep a good supply of wood at home for cooking.

Food, well, rice, potatoes, those kind of food, bananas. And there used to be some kind of wild beans in the field, you know, inside the cane fields. In Spanish they called that chicharo. Almost like lima beans but a little smaller, you know.

When I used to go to school, there were other boys, you know, Hawaiian boys, Japanese boys, Portuguese boys, and we all played together. But when we come home, why, only Puerto Rican boys were there. We played marbles (chuckles), those kind of games.

MAUI

You see, my mother had a sister over there in Wailuku. She always advised my father to move to Wailuku because they were close.

So when we moved to Maui [in 1916], well, my father never put me to school, he put me into that cane field to work. So, there in the cane field [of Wailuku Sugar Company], since I was a young boy, they used to give me a ukupau, about nine short lines. Watercourse lines, they call them. Weeding, hō hana, then from there they put me as a flagboy.

Water used to bring the cane down through the flume, take it down the chute. Then they had the wagons underneath the chute, see. When all those wagons were full, then the train come and take all those wagons to the mill.

If the flume got stuck by my place then I would put the flag down, I shake it. Then they stop throwing cane on the flume until everything is unplugged. Like us, we the flagboy, we the ones who unplug, throw the cane out. When everything was unplugged, then we would put the flag up and then they start putting cane on the flume again, see.

So I worked on that flume until the cane season was over, then they transferred me to the mill. In the mill had one tool room, then they put me in the tool room to take care of the tools. Had all kinds of tools over there, had wrenches and stops and bolts and screws and washers, and all kinds of things, see.

Then the mill engineer transferred me to the fireroom in the mill. They had like a little chute where all the trash [i.e., cane leaves, tops, and spoiled cane] used to come. And over here, we had like a little flume and the trash used to run right into the fireplace.

So there was a hole that I used to look through, and when I see there's no trash inside the fireplace, I used to pull the chain, then the trash run right into the fireplace. I want to make sure that the steam was high all the time, I no can let it go down because otherwise the rollers [which pressed the cane and extracted the juice] couldn't go over there on the other side.

The pay was kind of little bad, [but] more than outside in the cane fields. At that time if you worked over twenty three days a month, they give you a little bonus on top, you see.

I was kind of young, but I was kind of tall, see, so maybe that's why they give me that kind of work. (Laughs.) Oh, I worked there for about two years then I quit there—was kind of a little too hard—and I wen work in the carpenter shop.

So in the carpenter shop there had one other Puerto Rican boy and he used to deliver the lumber, take the lumber here and there. Then I used to go with him, help him with the lumber on the truck.

When we went from Mali'o—from Hāwī to Maui—we went to live at a place they called Pu'uohala. We lived there for a while, then my aunty wen move to the Mainland so my mother didn't want to stay in the camp any longer. So my father moved to a place they called Green Camp in Wailuku. Green Camp was nearly all Puerto Ricans, Portuguese.

Hāwī no had town, but Wailuku used to have town. I used to go to the movies with the other boys, we used to get fun. We used to go to a place where they sell ice cream. I used to eat a lot of banana specials they call, ice cream and bananas, and, oh, it was good.

KOHALA

From Maui we moved [back] to Hāwī. My father stayed in Hāwī, but I moved to Union Mill. That's where I started working as a blacksmith helper.

I used to handle the hammer the whole day through, you see, for a while. [Also] blowtorch, yeah. Cut iron, that was my job. Flat irons was for fix those cane wagons, see.

But after, when the cane season came on, well, they moved me to the mill. I learned how to dry the sugar, run that little machine. Then, I worked there until the cane season were over then they put me outside [in] the field, go make lines, furrows, with the big farm plow for plant cane.

KONA

My father wanted to move to Kona because while he was in Puerto Rico, he used to like to pick coffee when he was a young boy and he wanted to try the coffee fields again.

And some friends of his from Mali'o, they had moved to Kona, see. They told him that he could pick coffee and it was much easier than working in the fields. In the cane field he had the foreman on him all the time to make him work, you see. No more chance to [stop and] stand up, like that, in the cane field.

And here in Kona, well, if you had a little money you had a chance to build up something. Maybe you like build a piggery, raise pigs, or maybe if you get money you can lease a piece of land and raise your own cattle like that.

So I rather work in the coffee land, take contracts, you're your own boss. If you want to work hard, you work hard. If you want to work slow or whatever, you're your own boss, nobody boss you.

So when I came from Union Mill, Kohala side, to Kona, I started to pick coffee. Hundred-pound bag, fifty cents.

Coffee farmer rakes coffee on drying platform, Kona, 1980. The movable iron roof protects the coffee from rain (Center for Oral History photo).

Lower elevation, well, the coffee ripe plenty all one time, you can just scrape [coffee off the branches]. If you're a fast picker maybe you can pick two bags, three bags. [But] on the low elevation, the coffee ripens much faster, so that much faster the coffee finish, you see, pau.

So we used to go look for high elevations where there was more coffee and we would pick there. Like Captain Cook side, way up on the hill, the coffee sometimes last the whole year through because high elevation.

Some farmers they get their own mahina men. Workers. But mahina men couldn't take care of all the coffee, you see, so they hire outside people. But the mahina men they get their own houses from the coffee farmer. Like us, we have to rent, pay our own rent.

When the coffee season was over we used to take contracts. At that time never have poison for spray the grass. All was [weeding] with the hoe, you see. So we used to take contracts to hoe, clean the coffee land.

I think it was for about two months or three months I worked in the cotton fields. From Kuakini Highway, mauka side, was cotton. I picked a little cotton and cleaned, hō hana this cotton, too, you see.

LĀNA'I

Somebody came from Lāna'i and said there was a job over there, and that working in the pineapple field was easy. So I figure I'm going to take a chance, so I went with one friend of mine to Lāna'i, see. So it happened that when I reached there, they put me right on the road job, you see, construction job.

That's the first time I work on the road, you see, when I went over there. So after we got through there, well, already I knew how to work with rock.

Then after the road finished, they put me as a truck swamper. Yeah, the men working alongside the truck and they used to throw the pineapple boxes on top the trailer. But if you go too fast, well, they no could keep up with the truck, see. I go out with the driver in the pineapple fields with a trailer, then I stay right on top the truck with a whistle. Maybe I whistle one time it means go a little faster. Maybe if I whistle two times, slow down.

Then when the trailer was full we go take 'em down the pier where the barge come and take all the pineapple to Honolulu.

There was some other guys living in the same house, you see, single men. But me and two more other boys, we had our own room. The same guy that went with me to Lānaʻi, I used to go and eat in his house, you see, board in his house.

MAUI

I had a friend up Maui that lived in Kaupakulua and I went and I stayed with him over there. Then, in Kaupakulua I worked with some Portuguese, the Santos, they called them. They got cane fields and pineapple fields.

While I was working for them I had a job in Kula—road wen open. So, I wen ask for job over there and I got job over there. They made a camp up there and I stayed up in the camp, you see. From there we go work up on the road. It wasn't hard, the only thing was hard was the cold up there.

KONA

At that time the job ended over there in Maui, then I came back to Kona. At that time my mother was sick, she had cancer, and that very same year she died. That was on July 30, I remember, 1930, she died.

Then, from then on, I got me a job with Medeiros who was a contractor and I worked for him for about six months.

Then again in 1931, I began to work on small jobs, coffee jobs. You see, when the job ended over there I came back and started working jobs here and there: contract jobs, weeding coffee, and making walls, like that, pulling lantana.

And 1935 I worked for the WPA [Works Progress Administration]. At that time, loading trucks, all manpower. And I used to grade rock on the road, you know, level rock, and work like that.

And when I got married in 1937 I still was working for the WPA. Then that's when I was working for Frank Greenwell, in 1937. Well, pasture land, go pull guava inside here and there in the pasture. Sometimes make [stone] walls like that in the pasture land.

The house that I used to live was Frank Greenwell's house, too. So, I paid one dollar fifty cents a month, and Frank Greenwell used to pay me one dollar a day.

Then I came back again, I started working for WPA again, see. All these roads around here, I worked.

In 1942 I wen work at the airport, Hilo Airport. At that time they were enlarging the airport, making it bigger. And they were making some holes in the ground to put some bumps or I don't know what. That was during the war, you see.

HONOLULU

My brother-in-law helped me get a job at Hawaiian Electric Company.

I saw the big city there and lot of people and a lot of cars and a lot of traffic. Something new to me, so I liked it.

The job that I was working on ended because we was putting a new boiler, and making the trenches, and other little jobs. I couldn't find any job so I came back to Kona.

KONA

I bought this land here. I bought it from a Japanese man here, Yanagi. He still had about ten or twelve years left to go on the lease and I gave him $300 for the lease. Three-and-one-half acres. Small land but good enough for me and my wife to take care. Sometimes the kids help, too, but they were small and we couldn't expect much from them.

At that time we used to grind our own coffee, you see, we used to dry our own coffee. When you grind coffee, in the morning you have to go inside the tub and you wash the coffee, then you throw it on top the screen to drain, then you have to go and spread it on top the platform. From then on, every little while you have to go and [rake] it, so that it dries all even.

Onaka had a coffee mill up Hōlualoa and he used to buy our coffee.

Those who had big farms, they don't have to depend on the other jobs, they can get along with their own coffee fields. But those who get small land like me, well, that coffee, it's not enough to keep you going the whole year, whatever you make from the coffee land.

Like in my case, too, sometimes I had to apply for welfare help, you see. And sometimes, when I do a little job and the job wasn't enough for me to get along, welfare used to make up the difference.

I worked nighttime as a security guard [in 1951 during a strike at Kona Inn]. Spin around the hotel, keep on going the whole night like that until six o'clock in the morning.

But I didn't know the score, you see. So, when I was working there someone told me the reason that [previous] watchman quit the job was that somebody gave him good licking because he was in the union and he wasn't supposed to work.

I used to go around and I figure maybe somebody watching. (Laughs.) Somebody might shoot you or hit you with stones or something like that. The policeman used to stay over there in the Inn with me. Because the strikers, you can never tell.

I wanted more money, and if you go work construction you get more money, you see. That's how I went to work for Honolulu Builders [in Kona]. When the job got finished over here, I went to Waimea. At that time they were going to build a new school. Well, all that yard over there, we leveled that ground there, you see.

I couldn't stand that cold, so I worked there, I think, three or four months. Then I came back home.

I went to work [as a janitor] at Punahulu School, quite a ways from here, about ten or eleven miles, I guess. I only worked a day a week. Then from there they transferred me to Kalaoa School, then I think at Kalaoa School I worked for about three days a week.

Then at that time the [county] chairman, there was a woman chairman, I forget even her name [Helene Hale]. I supported her during the election time so she told me to go apply for driver, bus driving. So that's how from then on I worked full-time, you see.

Well, I had two buses, one for small kids—preschool kids—and the other one for the big kids. So in the morning I go pick up the preschool kids and then after that I go pick up the big ones. In the afternoon, the preschool kids pau school first and I go pick them up, take them home. After that I go get the bigger ones.

So my wife took over the coffee with the kids, or maybe I find somebody to help my wife—you know, help pick. And I had to pay him.

Then as time went on they raised me up to three dollars fifty cents an hour, bus driving. And I worked until around 1969, if I'm not mistaken. Then I retired.

Well, when I think about all those things that I went through, well, sometimes I think that it was kind of hard. The bad times that we had before: how we didn't have any jobs and sometimes we ran short of food and we have to go down to the beach and pass all of our time down there fishing, trying to get some puhis, long eels, and dry them up so that we could eat it with rice or something like that because no more money to buy food in the store.

Before, we had to depend on welfare for help, so I don't depend too much on welfare now, pau. When you stay under the welfare, too much humbug, every time you have to go and report. You're limited [in income], you see, you cannot go over what is required.

Well, so far, I feel good, I feel strong and I can still work, but when I cannot work, somebody gotta take over. Well, that's my youngest boy. He have to take over I guess. (Laughs.) I hope by that time I get the lease. This [land] belongs to the Bishop Estate. If not, well, we gotta go rent one house.

GLOSSARY

hō hana	weeding with hoe
mahina	farm
mauka	inland
menpachi	squirrel fish
mū	bigeye emperor fish
po'opa'a	hawkfish
pau	over, finished
puhi	eel
ukupau	piece work
wen	auxiliay verb designating past tense

ETSUO SAYAMA

CIVILIAN IN WARTIME HAWAI'I

I used to be a pitcher, so we used to play ball with the army guys. Lot of the engineers, they not the type that play ball. Only all rough guys like us got the skill to play ball, see. Each area [U.S. Engineer Department sites] had their own teams. And then within Punahou, survey mapping, we had our team. And the [Hawaiian] Constructors, too, the contractors.

Etsuo Sayama was born in Nu'uanu, near Downtown Honolulu, in 1915 to Shosuke and Etsuyo Sayama, emigrants from Yamaguchi prefecture, Japan. After Shosuke Sayama died of influenza in 1922, Etsuyo Sayama and her three children returned to Japan.

With the 1924 Asian Exclusion Act about to take effect, she brought Etsuo back to Hawai'i in 1923. His sister, who died the following year, and brother remained in Japan. Sayama's mother married Matsuki Tamura in 1929.

Etsuo Sayama's formal education, except for first grade in Japan, took place in Hawai'i at Kauluwela, Kawānanakoa, Central Intermediate, and McKinley High Schools, and the University of Hawai'i. He attended UH on a scholarship and majored in sugar technology, graduating in 1937.

Sayama got a job as an assistant agriculturalist at Waialua Agricultural Company. In 1938 he left sugar plantation work to enter federal civil service as an engineers' aide for the U.S. Army Air Corps Quartermaster Department at Hickam Field.

On December 7, 1941, Sayama heard a U.S. anti-aircraft shell explode as it fell on the Cherry Blossom restaurant in Nu'uanu. Twelve people were killed in the blast.

With the start of World War II, the U.S. Engineer Department (later called the US Army Corps of Engineers) established the headquarters of the Honolulu Engineer District and the Hawaiian Constructors, a subcontractor, on the grounds of Punahou School. Sayama worked there throughout the war as a draftsman for the U.S. Engineer Department.

Most of Sayama's postwar work involved engineering jobs with the federal government, including two tours of duty in Japan.

Sayama married Yaeko Iwamoto in 1942. The couple had four daughters and a son. Sayama officially retired in 1973 but continued to work in Japan until 1975. He was widowed that same year. He died in 2007. His lifelong hobby was collecting and producing commemorative postal covers—stamped envelopes featuring commemorative designs (cachets) and significant cancellation dates.

Warren Nishimoto interviewed Etsuo Sayama in 1992 for *An Era of Change: Oral Histories of Civilians in World War II Hawai'i* (COH, 1994), a project funded by the National Park Service. This edited narrative is a condensation of Sayama's three-session oral history interview.

SURPLUS KIND OF KIDS

I had a poor start in life. All my classmates and friends, they had both parents. Like me, I'm just going back and forth all kind of place, no place to live. Because my father died [in 1922].

My father was a barber. That's the extent that I know about him because he died when I was so young. Not only him, see, lot of people died, you know. That [influenza] epidemic from World War I went around the world.

Last weekend I went to my box out here. You know, I move so often, all my stuff is boxed. So I took out [his photo] just to see, get a perspective of the history. My only image of him is the picture.

My mother was a housewife at home, because three children, yeah. With the income gone, she figured she cannot support three kids. And of course, her parents were concerned, too. So [we] went back [to Japan].

[I remember] only a smattering. When you are singing, they call 'em shō-ka. Music class. And then one more thing was the math. They really drilled you in math. And then another thing they had is what they call shūshin. They really stress that, see. So those three things really stuck with me as far as Japanese education is concerned.

They were going to come out with an [Asian] exclusion law [in 1924]. She [my mother] said, well, she'd take me over [to Hawai'i in 1923], and then left the two kids with her [parents]. Naturally she didn't have enough money for all three kids. And the girl died the following year, I think. But my brother survived and grew up, went to school. Then he got a job with the Manchurian railroads, so he went to Manchuria until World War II broke out.

Of course, my mother, when she cared for me, did all kind of work. This is subsequent to coming back from Japan. She would go to work early in the morning and then come home in the evening. And then, for eating, the next-door lady would feed me. Or later on, I used to just feed myself [leftovers]. Nokori-mono, what they call.

She worked as a housemaid [for the Robinsons] and then she also worked at a tailor on Beretania Street, Fujii. I guess the olden days, all Japanese they learn saihō, which is seamstress, that kind of stuff, so she worked there. And then, she was pretty good cook, so she used to work at okazu-ya, you know, catering service like that. So she had a hard time, too, doing all kind until she remarried.

The Kimura family in Waikīkī was related to my mother's side. Mr. Kimura was a sort of head waiter at Moana Hotel. He said, "Oh, he's [Matsuki Tamura] a conscientious man." And so they matched them.

You know, I guess maybe hard to merge one time, yeah. They took me to Mr. Kimura's house in Waikīkī, so I lived with that family. But when I live separately like that, without my mother, my thinking came different. That was childhood, so I don't know how much it affected me. But I never can call him "Father," you know, "Otōsan."

He started working for a [telephone] cable company. They came back to Nu'uanu Street again, when I joined them. And there was a lane from Nu'uanu Street, Kukui Lane, that wound its way out to Kukui Street. So we lived on the second floor there.

When I was born and lived there [in Nu'uanu], before I went to Japan, was mostly Japanese people. When I went to the Kukui Lane [in 1930], they had big tenement houses across from where we lived. Was a mixture, all kind [of] people. But our camp [housing area] was predominantly Japanese.

After I came back [from Japan], I had to repeat school, first grade. So I had three years of first grade. And then, they let me skip—not skip grade, but only half a year each time and I made up for all the lost time, see.

Kawānanakoa School started off as an offshoot of Royal School. Royal School was the school before for the elites, yeah, the monarchy and all that. And I guess we were surplus kind of kids (chuckles), you know, come from Japan.

They borrowed a Japanese-[language] school at [Honpa] Hongwanji [Mission] on Fort Street. They don't use the building in the morning, so we went there. And that gradually became bigger and bigger, and then they built the Kawānanakoa School.

We used to go into all kind of sports, especially basketball. Lot of my activities, I got hampered by my leg. You know, one side short. So, like swimming, my kicking not so good, so you know what they make me do?

I used to be good in plunge. All you do is plunge and then the farthest you go, you the winner, see. (Laughs.)

As I grew older, I didn't want to go furo-ya too much. So Nuʻuanu Y[MCA] used to be my (chuckles) bathhouse. Nuʻuanu Y used to really serve us Oriental kids, because Central Y was haole YMCA. The membership there was more haole people.

BIGGEST MISTAKE

I guess you could have gone astray all kind of ways at McKinley High School. We collected everybody in town, go to that one high school. Didn't have Farrington, didn't have Roosevelt. And Punahou, we cannot afford. And St. Louis, well, the Chinese people used to go St. Louis.

[But] I had good environment of friends that wouldn't lead me astray. Like McKinley—MCC, they call 'em, McKinley Citizenship Club. And I was in the chemistry club 'cause I like science. And then of course, National Honor Society, I was a member, too.

She [Kawānanakoa teacher Kathryn Beveridge] told me to go to law school. So that was my first ambition. If UH had a law school, I would have gone there. But when I went McKinley [High School], no more law school in Hawaiʻi. And to go over to Mainland is out of the picture.

So I did the next best thing. I thought, well, living in Hawaiʻi, you can't go wrong with sugar industry. So I took sugar technology [major at University of Hawaiʻi], which was my biggest mistake.

There were fifteen of us [graduates]. Ten Orientals, five haole boys. The five haole boys all were given student-in-training at HSPA [Hawaiʻi Sugar Planters' Association] experiment station. Among ten of us Orientals, I was the only one that got a position.

Well, my mother's cousin was a cook [for the Robinsons]. And Mr. [Mark] Robinson had plenty land in Oʻahu Sugar [Company]. So he had connections. That, too, was a plus for me, see.

But I think the most important thing was, for some reason, the agriculturalist there [at Waialua Agricultural Company] was a Japanese. That was the only [plantation] I noticed that the head agriculturalist was a nisei, Sam Kawahara. Later on I found out he was a protégé of the Atherton family. So I said, "If he's gonna be my boss, I will have a chance."

The Mainland haoles come, they won't hire 'em for sugar, they hire 'em for diversified agriculture, see. I was made partner with a guy from Mainland. His specialty was potato.

He was working for Castle & Cooke Downtown, but all the people that work good-level position Downtown, they had to go to plantation and go through exposure starting with hō hana. And drive mule, spray poison, and you cut cane, and you hāpai kō to the train. We had to do all that. 'Cause schoolwork doesn't mean anything to them, as [much as] practical work and the appreciation of what the other laborers are doing.

That guy who had education in potato was getting his monthly salary from Castle & Cooke. Me, I was getting piecemeal pay. They used to pay us by how many lines, rows, you finished, see. And because I was living in the dormitory, I can't even barely make dormitory money. So I get nothing to take home to my parents.

I was in the dormitory, so the lady would prepare for us kaukau tin. Spam in all kind of shape, not only fried Spam. When you see the same thing over and over, you get disgusted. So I would exchange lunch with the fellows. Those fellows are glad because at home they get nishime and all kind of Japanese kind of okazu. And they like Spam because maybe the family couldn't afford to buy Spam.

And another thing was the social life. I got no social life out there, I don't know anybody. I call it social life, but actually I guess I missed my girlfriend [Yaeko Iwamoto], next-door girl, who eventually became my wife.

So all those things, you know, the working condition, the unfair wage system, and as I said, the isolation from the city that I was used to.

I went to see [the manager] Mr. [John] Midkiff, and I said, "You know, I'm thinking of leaving."

And I'll never forget this, but he told me, in a benevolent way, "Mr. Sayama, I know you having a hard time getting adjusted, but both Mr. Kawahara and we like your work so far, and we'd like to see you keep on."

He was fair-minded to have even hired Mr. Kawahara at such a high position. But I said I didn't think there was a future for me.

And he said, "Well, you know, I'll tell you this confidentially, but if you quit here, you gonna be blacklisted, and you will never work on a plantation system."

HICKAM FIELD

I quit Waialua [Agricultural Company], so I gotta start over, what to do, you know. Before I went Waialua, I worked [at Nuʻuanu YMCA] as a janitor. During the time I was working Nuʻuanu Y, I took civil service exam.

And I got a call from Hickam Field. They were looking for surveyors. When they look in the transit, and you see somebody holding the pole, I was the guy. And then we needed high pole—you see, from Hickam Field to Fort Kam[ehameha] to our airport was cane field, those days.

When Hickam Field was started, we were working for the [U.S. Army Air] Corps Quartermaster [Department]. But later on, after working couple of years at Hickam Field, they said corps of engineers gonna take over construction of Hickam Field. And I was moved to [Fort] Shafter. And the construction we were doing was primarily building warehouses so the quartermaster can keep their supply.

They hurried it up to build that Hickam Field, because war was imminent. And sure enough, before we can even prepare ourselves, bang, they hit us on December 7. And so, few days after that, us guys down Shafter (chuckles), we were transferred to corps of engineers.

DECEMBER 7, 1941

Early, when that excitement came up, I think I was listening to the radio to find out what the hell's going on, because you hear all that bombing noise and all that, but you don't know what's happening. I forgot his name [Webley Edwards], he said that this is the real McCoy, or whatever.

That thing [a U.S. anti-aircraft projectile] fell, and of course, we ran right to the window, living on the second floor, and I saw bodies on the sidewalk. I guess they got blown out, when, you know, the explosion. And then the ambulance started to come, see.

On Nu'uanu Street, where Foster [Botanical] Garden is now, used to be a [Hawai'i] Chūō Gakuin, Japanese-[language] school. And my neighbors—you know, my future wife had three younger sisters—I think some of them were going Sunday school. And they came home and said, oh, some of their friends got hurt and were taken to hospital.

Oh, I thought Japan was gonna start bombing the whole place up. Although later on, we read in the paper, it was our own [U.S.] unexploded projectile that came down all over the city.

I told my parents, "We better go someplace." We didn't have car or anything. My mother used to work for the Robinson family up Nu'uanu, and her cousin was the cook. And she had a domestic help's quarters, away from the main building. So she [my mother] said, "Oh, let's go there."

I don't even know if we talked to the Robinson family. Because Japanese and haoles, yeah, you know what I mean? You don't feel right, too, when they tell you Japan is attacking. Because I know my parents them used to collect the silvery [foil] paper wrapped around the pack of cigarettes like that. They used to send Japan [for metal recycling], because our parents are from Japan. They didn't know they were gonna fight America.

We just stayed put in the house. And listened to the radio. And the following morning, got up. They said, oh, they were calling all civil service and federal workers, report to your post. Prior to that, they [the army] had given us identification cards and whatnot already. So I had the ID card, and I went.

You know the [Royal] Mausoleum? And then, Robinson family, and came the [O'ahu] Cemetery. And right there, by that cemetery, there's a bus stop.

There were several people, official-looking people, they said, "Where are you going?" I said, "I'm going to work." "Where?" "Fort Shafter." They were stopping people and checking up, where you going and what you gonna do, and all that.

When I went on the bus, either from the bus or outside, I noticed plenty people working in the cemetery. And I think they had a trench digger or something, anyway, equipment. And they needed plenty people to dig trenches. Bodies were being brought to that area.

When I got to that [Fort Shafter] gate, I showed my pass, but he [the sentry] said, "If I were you, go home." And I said, "For what?" He said, "Change clothes."

And I had [on] blue. He said they got rumors that Japanese parachuters in blue were coming down on St. Louis Heights and they didn't know where [else], but that was the rumor. Said, "Our soldiers might get trigger-happy, you walk around in Fort Shafter."

So I went home, changed clothes, and went back to work.

MARTIAL LAW AND BLACKOUT

With martial law on, whatever law the military is giving, they give it to the radio station. And they would, in turn, give it to us.

I don't know if my parents had shortwave or what, but I know lot of the older Japanese used to listen to shortwave to find out if Japan was broadcasting anything. But soon thereafter, they made everybody, aliens anyway, turn in their [shortwave] radio.

Right off the bat, you had the blackout. So all you did was go to work and come home, and stay home. If you use the light, you gotta make sure nothing leaked out. You were really confined.

I had a window fronting Nu'uanu Street. [One night there was] knocking at the door. Open the door, I look at the guy, policeman. He said, "You know over there, the light is coming out strong." So I went in, I said, "Oh yeah, I forgot to push it all the way up." We had this black cloth on the window, and when you pull it up, then it automatically sealed off.

Then I look at him. I said, "Ey, you Moke, yeah?" He said, "How come you know me?" I said, "University, you used to play basketball." He let me go. But if I didn't know the guy, I think I would have been thrown in the slammer or at least be fined.

MARRIAGE IN WARTIME

Plenty people got married during the wartime, my age anyway. I guess, you figure,. you don't know what's gonna happen, so might as well. My wife's parents had somebody [a go-between] say that this guy was interested in my wife-[to-be]. So they sort of put us in a spot, see. So I guess we figured, we living next door to each other, might as well get married. She only going move one door away.

I call up one of the justice of peace. And, "Could you get us married?" He said, "Oh, come over in the morning."

We didn't want to get too many people involved, so I had my best man, and my wife had her bridesmaid. And two Japan people that was getting married, too. If you have more than so many people congregating, you have to have permit. So rather than go through all that, hardly anybody knew we got married even.

My best man had a station wagon. He took us out to Kokokahi, YWCA camp, you know, Kāne'ohe Bay. And there's a bungalow there. And we spent our honeymoon there.

There's a long pier. And during the day I caught some 'ōpae. Put 'em in the net, and then I tied string, and I put 'em underneath the pier. Pāpio is good fishing early in the morning, depend on the tide. So I told my wife, "Ey, let's go wake up early, go." "Okay."

Etsuo Sayama works at his drafting table in the Honolulu Engineer District survey mapping section, Old School Hall, Punahou School, Honolulu, ca. 1943 (photo courtesy of Etsuo Sayama).

I was underneath the pier, untying that 'ōpae, the bait. And here comes the sentry with a gun. He say, "What you doing under there?" "Oh, I'm getting this bait." So I brought it up and show it to him.

Good thing my wife was there, too. She said, "We just came out on our honeymoon, and get no place to go, so we going fishing."

"Okay, then. But don't do suspicious thing as going underneath da kine pier, like that. We thought you might be putting, you know, detonator, or something."

Later on, that morning, Waimānalo, somebody was shot at. I don't know if he was injured or what, but similar situation. Maybe the guy went out fishing too early (chuckles).

After we got married in July of '42, she was in the hospital until '43. She wasn't with us for one year. Those days, Lē'ahi Hospital, the Japanese looked upon it as like sort of a—not disgrace but ostracized kind [of] place. Because that was consumption, yeah, TB [tuberculosis]. But I'm glad she went there, because otherwise her life would have been really shortened.

U.S. ENGINEER DEPARTMENT

I'm the only breadwinner in the family, under that wartime conditions. My stepfather was an alien, so he was [fired]. He didn't have the job with the cable company anymore. In fact, my stepbrother—I forgot what grade he was—but I was sending 'em to school.

When the war broke out, I was moved to Young Hotel [partly occupied by the U.S. Engineer Department]. And [their move] from Young Hotel to Punahou [School], oh, was practically immediate.

At Dillingham Hall, where they had the two stories of work there, the engineers had their own draftsmen to do electrical, or plumbing, or structural, all the different civil categories. And we were next to that, see. I was in the old schoolhouse [Old School Hall]. Our building, the second floor, where we stayed, was the drafting room. The first floor was for equipment for surveyors like that.

The engineers would draw plans. We would do the tracing. Mostly we were concerned with the not-too-complicated drawings, at my level anyway.

But lot of these projects were all outlying areas where they had no preliminary plans, you know, the survey data. So you start from scratch. You send the crew out to survey and then you drew the plans and control points, and the contours, so that the engineers can site whatever needed to be sited. If the tree is in the way, you cut down the trees and all that.

We got along fine [with the Mainland workers]. Liquor was rationed, so [you needed a] liquor permit. I don't drink, but I buy liquor for them

Headquarters of the U.S. Engineer Department, Punahou School, ca. 1943. Left, Dillingham Hall; right, Old School Hall (U.S. Army Corps of Engineers photo, Punahou School Archives, reproduced by courtesy of Punahou School).

(chuckles). When you in the same boat, you get more friendly. Not like before the war when we were on separate strata, so to speak.

And then, lot of the army people were assigned to us, too. Like for engineering or surveying like that. So we get to know the army guys.

I used to be a pitcher, so we used to play ball with the army guys. Lot of the engineers, they not the type that play ball. Only all rough guys like us got the skill to play ball, see. Each area [U.S. Engineer Department sites] had their own teams. And then within Punahou, survey mapping, we had our team. And the [Hawaiian] Constructors, too, the contractors.

The troops would go and watch. Only thing, I don't know how much I look like Emperor Hirohito, [but] I [was] razzed when I'm pitching. "Hey, Hirohito!" (Laughs.)

Wherever you want to go work, you have to think of two things: [job security and] to get away from the draft. Lot of us had our name on that register already. And so, as the war progressed, they picked you one by one. And the other thing was if you work for the federal [government], then at least for the duration [of the war], you set.

Lot of niseis were going in the post office work, see. Because no discrimination, you know, postal clerk. And in fact, during the war, when I

TOP: Baseball game, Punahou School, ca. 1943; BOTTOM: Drafting Section baseball team, Punahou School, ca. 1943 (photos courtesy of Etsuo Sayama).

was working Punahou, I got a call. So I said, "I think I go work post office." Because [collecting] stamps was my hobby already.

The big boss said, "If you want to, I can release you." But he said, "You're deferred because you were in war[-related] work. If you go to the post office, I don't think the post office can give you that same deferment." So I said, "Oh, I'll stick with you." (Laughs.)

INTERROGATION

I couldn't go visit my wife in the hospital because no more bus system after working hours—blackout, you know, unless you have your own car. But my boss was good. He told me, "Oh, go work certain time and then either get comp time, or take annual leave." Wednesday afternoon used to be my visiting hour. And then Sundays. Because Saturdays, I think, we used to work.

I can't even visit her [at night]. So, what you going to do? You stay home, you put a dark screen right around the window, so light won't go out. All you can do is listen to the radio, read. So I started to think of making covers.

A cover is an envelope with certain stamp and certain cachet—cachet is the picture—commemorating the event. And this was my first cover. The first anniversary of Pearl Harbor.

George Cuevas was the one that did lot of designing for me for my covers. He sketched it out. Being a draftsman, I improved on it. And then, brought it down to the printers and they would photographically reduce it to this size.

Later on, I got called in by military intelligence. They were headquartered at the Dillingham Building on Bishop Street. The guy [the interrogator], he had a dossier on me, because he knew I had a brother in Japan. 'Cause he asked me, if my brother came on the submarine, "What would you do to help him?"

I said, "First of all, I don't know how my brother look." I said, "We were separated when we were kids. And the last I heard, he was in Manchuria."

Then, oh, they ask all kind of questions, though. [I was] more scared than anything else, yeah. Because by then, I had heard of internment and all that. So, I didn't want to go Mainland, you know, be interned.

[They] said, "You've been corresponding with lot of military people, and sending out covers, and asking for APO and navy cancellations. Why do you need that for? Unless you trying to get spy data."

I said, "Oh, that's our hobby." And I said, "Look, the first anniversary of Pearl Harbor, I made one in honor of all our men that died." And I told 'em I been doing that ever since.

I had plenty 442[nd Regimental Combat Team] friends—100th [Battalion] and 442—in Italy. And since I was connected with YMCA, I used to send 'em YMCA newspapers. They also was lacking in stationery to correspond.

And I think the part that they really came after me [for] was I tried to send a bunch of envelopes [printed with the 442nd photo and slogan] for the 442nd to send back to me. I had a space left over on top [of the envelope], so they could write their signature, and outfit they belong to. And I get censorship stamp [on the returned covers], too, yeah. And later on, those covers sold pretty good. Because the Mainland guys, they couldn't get that kind.

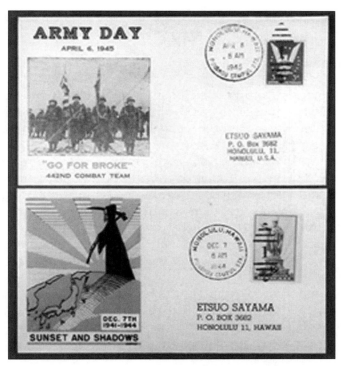

Etsuo Sayama's covers commemorate the 442nd Regimental Combat Team (the Army Day text was added later) and the third anniversary of the December 7, 1941 attack on Pearl Harbor (Center for Oral History photo).

But at that time, I was sending too many of the 442, I think. So that brought it to a climax, I think, for them to investigate me.

I was the only one in Hawai'i that made patriotic covers. On the Mainland they had all kind of what they call cachet makers. The patriotic covers became famous during the Civil War. Those things became real valuable. So when World War II started, they started to make patriotic covers.

I couldn't get 'em [cancelled] on December 7, '41, but all these [others] are dates that [are] the actual date of happening. And this was easy for me because I [went to the] Punahou campus station [post office], see.

The December 7, '43, December 7, '44 [anniversary covers], it's all George Cuevas's design. And this [1944] was considered one of the best designs concerning December 7, nationally. In fact, I got write-up by from a professor at New York University. He said he considered this the most outstanding patriotic cover of the war.

I explained we were winning and we were going towards Japan already. And using the Japan flag [and] grim reaper, [we] called it "sunset and shadows." That guy [Cuevas] get really good ideas.

And then December 7, '45, the war ended already, he had gone back [to the Mainland], so I had to make my own. (Laughs.)

AFTER THE WAR

Of course, when they dropped the bomb [on Hiroshima and Nagasaki], it was pau. Before the thing actually ended, I think there was pressure from Punahou School, too. They want the school back, see. Then we moved there [to Fort Armstrong].

I went to work for this Ben Hayashi [in 1947]. He's a private contractor. And I stayed there for a couple of years [until 1950]. I came back to Fort Armstrong again as area engineer. I used to go on inspection tours to Okinawa, Korea, and Japan. And then eventually I transferred there [to Japan] because the family wanted to go there, too.

I retired [in 1973]. When I got out, I was GS-13 engineer. And then came back [to Hawai'i] in '75 because my wife got sick. And then she died six months later.

I carried on my wife's wishes. For my children, kodomo no tame ni [for the sake of the children]. I got them all through college. I think I did pretty well. I didn't come out to be a name, personality, in our community, but I think I did my share. For my family, anyway.

GLOSSARY

da kine	unspecified referent
furo-ya	bathhouse
haole	Caucasian
hāpai kō	to load harvested sugar cane bundles
hō hana	weeding with a hoe
kaukau tin	lunch pail
nisei	second-generation Japanese American
nishime	vegetable dish
nokori-mono	leftovers
okazu	side dish
okazu-ya	Japanese delicatessen
'ōpae	shrimp
otōsan	father
pāpio	young jack fish
pau	over, finished
saihō	sewing
shōka	singing
shūshin	morals, ethics

WILLIE THOMPSON

WORKING COWBOY

Before you can be a cowboy, you got to get a degree, a "Ph.D." I got mine when I was twelve years old. First thing we do, we go work on the fence. Like today, you got a steel post, you just pound 'em down, eh? Those days, all with the hole digger, see? So, that's "Ph.D.," eh, "post hole digger."

William "Willie" Thompson, third of eleven children, was born in Kula, Maui in 1902. His father, Charles Thompson, was German; his mother, Annie Ah Quin, was Hawaiian-Chinese. On his family's ranch, Willie Thompson farmed vegetables, milked cows, and trained horses. At age eighteen, he left for Honolulu, where he groomed and exercised polo ponies for the O'ahu Polo Club. He later became a cowboy for Kona's McCandless Ranch. Beginning in 1924, Thompson worked in construction, first for a private contractor, then for Hawai'i County. Initially elected to the Hawai'i County Board of Supervisors in 1942, he served intermittently until 1968. Thompson ranched on leased land in Hōnaunau, South Kona, until his death in 1996.

Warren Nishimoto, who interviewed Thompson in 1981 for COH's Kona project, remembers a genial, gravelly-voiced man who always wore a cowboy hat. The interview took place at Thompson's ranch house where, Nishimoto noticed, on one wall hung a "cowboy Ph.D." diploma. The complete interview transcript, from which the following narrative has been edited, is found in *A Social History of Kona.*

* * * * *

My father was a rancher. We had some cattle, but actually, we have more the milking stock. They [the stock] were about half mile from the house. Maybe not quite a half mile, but quite a ways down, where they go out, daytime, in the pasture. Mostly all cactus down in that place. Then, in the evening, bring 'em home right in the little paddock right next to the milking pen. In the morning, we get up, well, the cows right there. We never had no barn to milk cows in. You milk 'em right outside.

We sold milk to the Kula Sanatorium. When we deliver milk, we ride our horse, or mule, jackass, like that, hanging on to the milk cans. Just about a mile. I had to deliver milk and go to school. The sanatorium [was] up on the hill, and the school right below, you see.

After school, [we] come home, we have to go and plow the field up. We plow, plant corn, or plant whatever. Then, down in that lower land, where I said there's cactus, we raise pigs down there. They live on cactus. Once a day, you feed 'em corn, too.

We [also] had chickens. Of course, chickens, we had a chicken coop, where you keep the chickens in. Some run loose, but most of 'em all penned up. My sisters and all, they handled the chicken part. We boys would get out in the field.

There was another ranch right next to us—Kamaole Ranch. They had horses, but nobody [to] train 'em. So we trained these horses. We take couple of horses and stick 'em out up at our place. Horse, we get five dollars a head, and the mules, ten bucks. (Chuckles.) Mules were harder to train.

First you catch 'em, tie 'em up, put a halter on 'em. We all try to treat 'em gently. Make the horse understand that you're not going to hurt 'em, eh. You see, we have plenty grain, so we feed our horses cracked corn. They get to come to you. You pet 'em, brush 'em down, and all that. They get tame.

When we get spare time, we want to hunt and go up Haleakalā. You can't take your work horse up there, so we get this half-broken horse and go up. Those days, we used to do that when this people [visitors] come from away; they want to get up the mountain. Then we make ten dollars, take 'em up.

After the horse is real tame, then they [the owners] go out and take 'em to the plantation. They sell 'em, eh? If they can get $150, that's good money. But around $50 was about the regular price for a horse.

Those days, over in Maui, they had a Maui High [School], but only haoles go there. The Chinese, most of 'em went to St. Louis College [in Honolulu]. Hawaiians, they had this Lahainaluna on Maui. Then, the girls, they had that Mauna Olu Seminary. My sisters went there. But I never had a chance to go to [high] school.

See, my mother died when we were young. I had to work. Just drive a [telephone company] truck. And that was considered a good job, because [while] I was driving truck, the other guys climbing pole and all that. But I didn't last too long. Maybe three months I worked. From there, then I went to Honolulu. I rather be on a horse.

They had the Oʻahu Polo Club, owned by Dillinghams—I guess the hui, whatever. The only people they had down there working with 'em, they had this colored boys, Puerto Ricans, and something like that.

Then, a friend of mine, he knows this Dillinghams and whoever the manager running the stable. He come to me and he says, "Say, you want to go to [U.S.] Mainland?"

I said, "Sure." Gosh, when you say going to the Mainland, why, that's something—no poor kid can go up there, you know. Those days, no plane, you have to go on a boat.

He said, "There's a job down Honolulu. And around two months' time—two, three months—they're going to take this team up. They have to take their own horses, see? If you go down there and learn what they want, you can go, because they can't [bring] these colored boys up there." Those days, they have segregation, eh?

They're down at Kapiʻolani Park. Right in the kiawe, that's where the stables were. I got along fine with the boys that working there. Oh, they had plenty of horses there. They had Parker Ranch horses; and the army, they had horses there.

They gave me this certain string of horses to handle. That's my job. I feed 'em, and I brush 'em down, and I take care of that. Every morning, we go out and exercise 'em. Ride 'em around.

I learned quite a lot there, too. We have a different method training cowboy horses. Cowboy horse, you want to go straight. You teach them how to follow a cow, and their mind is on that cow. It's very seldom that you make a sharp circle and turn around. The polo horse, you have to turn in a circle right away. With a polo horse, the ball coming this way, well, you see that ball and all of a sudden that ball ricochet and go the other way, that horse have to be there and block the other guy up. They got to be quick.

Before, each polo player, he's got at least five horses out there ready. That horse not responding right, he ride back. He's got his man trained there. He give you the signal. You right there with [another] horse—[it's] ready, saddled up, and everything. Three minutes, they ride 'em maybe. Out they go. The next horse come in. [And] those guys, they bet money, you know. That's not this kind [of] ten-cents game.

The week we were supposed to go the Mainland, the damn stable burned down in the Mainland. It was sad thing, you know. When the [Mainland] stable burned, the horses all were burned; some killed. So, no polo game.

Then, one morning, I made up my mind. I said, "I think I want to go [quit]. I not going stick around this stable here just brushing horses. I'm not brought up that way."

So, I wrote a letter to this [Samuel] Dowsett [of McCandless Ranch]. He and my dad were good friends. I thought if he take me up here in Kona, I come up here and see if he had a job for me. He said, "You can go up with me if you want to work up there, all right." But he said, "Kona not like here. Over there, rain all the time."

I said, "I don't care. I rather be outside."

The boats used to come in every ten days. You come over, you're on five-dollar steerage. I tell you, the first couple of weeks, I was ready to go somewhere [else]. It rained, rained, rained every day. This was all forest in there. No more paved roads. No water line. Telephone, two wires running right through and everybody on that line.

I said, "Where's all the horses? I came here to train horse."

"Oh, they're all up in the mountain." Then we went up the mountain. It was cold like a son of a gun. (Chuckles.) And they had these damn old shacks, you know [made with] the damn one-by-twelve [foot boards]. They have crack in [between them], and the wind blowing.

We trained a few [horses] up there. We kind of halter break 'em little bit. But up there rain all the time. You know, rain, the horses' hoof get soft, eh? All rocks up there. Well, you can't ride 'em. So, I took the horses to Nāpō'o-po'o. I took sixteen [horses] and a mule down. Drive 'em down. That used to be all sand beach there. We saddle 'em up in the pen, and then take 'em out, let 'em go on the sand. They scared the water, eh? Then they get used to it. Down there, strange place, they get tame quick. That was a big time, but after that, I trained the rest up the mountain. Only few at a time.

In 1922—I'll never forget that—February 22. They said they were going to have this rodeo, and anybody who can ride those horses would get $300 prize. The boss said, "Any of you boys"—was half a dozen of us—"any of you boys want to go down, the ranch pay all your expense go down."

Well, right off, I said, "I go down."

"Any other boys want to go?" Nobody want to go.

So, I went down. I watched the first night. They had one Indian guy. I'll never forget him. His name was Grady Smith. Well, he come down and he ride a horse. Straight bucking. Oh, what a champion! Then, they had a girl there. She rides one little pony there. She ride the horse—a few jumps. Well, that's great thing. Then, these Parker Ranch cowboys. All the ranches, all the big ranches from Maui and all over, [were] all down there. And not one of 'em [cowboys] stayed on [the bucking horses].

Anyway, when it came to my night, I went there and I went [to] register, see. I never go there with the way they dress with all chaps and every damn thing, you know. I just had a khaki pants, khaki shirt on. Well, I had a kind of cheap cowboy hat. (Chuckles.) Then, put a red neckerchief on. Those twenty-cents neckerchiefs.

They look at me and, "You cowboy?"

I said, "Well, I ride a little bit."

The guy look at me, "Well, we try you out."

Then, this guy, Eben Low. He was a oldtime cowboy. He was working on Maui. Well, he was one of the judges. When he heard the name, he said, "Well, you Charlie's son?"

I said, "Yeah."

Then, he talked to me in Hawaiian. He said, "You squeeze your knees up, get 'em all up tight, you know. These damn horses buck. They not like our kind of Hawaiian horses here." Well, he gave me a little encouragement, you see.

I had my own saddle. You see, the guys, if they saddle the horse, they going put the saddle way behind, eh? Well, that horse going to fly you off either backwards or frontwards. But [if] you saddle 'em right up on his withers, almost on the neck, way up there, well, the kick is all behind [you].

Meantime, this guy [rodeo handler], he's got his spurs on that horse's neck. I jump on the horse. There's a rope, just a rope around the neck there. The head is free. When they let that horse go, well, naturally, that horse, from that backing up, he's still going back more. He go and he get right down on his haunches. When he came up, look out. You either drop behind or you going fly. [But] I stayed on the horse. And you want to see the crowd roar and roar. These guys from Maui, all the big ranches there, "He's Maui boy." [The] *Mauna Loa* sailors, well, they know me because we used to ship cattle down here [in Kona]. They see me down the wharf. "Oh, Kona boy, Kona boy."

So, now, they gave me Honest John. Honest John, he's the one that nobody ever stay on that son of a gun. And I went there; I rode this one. And I stayed on. I stayed on two horses now.

So the third night, they had White Lightning. He wasn't too wide, but tall son of a gun. Well, I don't think that bugger been in a harness. I put the saddle—put way as far forward as possible. I got on. Well, that horse buck till he couldn't buck no more.

The boss of that show, he said, "You come down in the morning and you'll get your payoff." Son of a gun, they gave me 300 bucks and a saddle. This guy [rodeo boss] wanted me work for him. I said, "No, no. I get a job in Kona. I going back up there."

I [be]came boss of the cowboys—head cowboy. That [McCandless] Ranch had mostly all wild cattle. Mostly all this old Mexican longhorn cattle. And that was all raw land—all forest. In the summertime, they had sheep grass, they call [it]. But when it came the winter, you get trouble because no more grass outside. Too cold. Then, you push 'em [cattle] down [into] the forest. The cattle, actually, were living on fern. And that vine that grows— 'iwa'iwa vine, they live on that.

Those days, you got to ship all the cattle [to] Honolulu. We drive 'em down [to Nāpō'opo'o]. The [cattle] leaders, they follow you, then the rest follow behind. But when you get out in the real open place, oh, gosh, [if] they ever break loose, the whole bunch go. You down [by] the fence, and they start breaking all over. Drove 'em around, herd 'em back again. Oh, that was no fun, boy.

Cattle, they shipped 'em. You got to swim 'em out, though, with the horse. One of those rowboats come in, and they anchor there. As soon as they [the cattle] float, you toss your rope, you throw it to the boat. Then they put, let's see, I think maybe about four or five, six [cattle] on each side [of the row-boat]. Then they take 'em to the mother ship. They have a net sling. Put 'em under their [the cattle's] belly, and they hoist 'em up. It was quite a sight.

In 1923 I got married. And they promised they going to give me a raise. They say, "Well, maybe we give you a hundred dollars." So, I figure, a hundred dollars [a month], I can feed the family. But they never did give me any

Cattle boat with lines, Kona, Hawai'i, 1916 (photo reproduced by courtesy of the Lyman Museum).

Cattle shipping, Kona, Hawai'i, 1920s (photo reproduced by courtesy of the Lyman Museum).

raise. In 1924, my first child was born. Fifty dollars can't take care a wife and one child, eh? I just quit.

I built [a] house when I was still with the ranch. This contractor [Jim Lewis], he lives right across the street from where I live. I was digging up some guava stumps. He saw me there. He said, "Good morning, boy!" You know, he kind of hard of hearing guy, so he talk loud. He said, "What you doing there?"

So I said, "Well, I just kind of digging up some stumps around here."

He says, "Well, you let the guava grow. You come work for me." Just like that. When I was working with Jim Lewis, he had this contract. He had some repair work, gutters, and all that stuff. Mostly all these county built school cottages and all that. School buildings. I [was] just holding this, putting the thing up, go get this. Well, I started from that. Then, by and by, I got to be pretty good carpenter.

Then [Lewis] moved to Hilo. He wanted me to go to Hilo, but I didn't want to go. I got married and had two kids, so I didn't want to go out of the district. When I worked with Jim Lewis, Julian Yates was a [county] supervisor. They let out all these contracts, so that's how we got kind of acquainted. He comes around the job sometimes. Those days, the supervisor, he's all around. You know, cow on the road. They don't call the owner, they call the supervisor. (Chuckles.)

Well, when he knew I was pau from Jim Lewis, he [Yates] called me up and say, "You better come work with us." You see, I married a sheriff's granddaughter down here. The old sheriff, he was kinda powerful in politics, too. Because the high sheriffs used to get elected by the people around the island. He was kind of a religious old guy, so the Hawaiians kind of leaned towards him. Of course, my wife [Juliet Thompson], she was quite a politician, too. That's why the county, I think, they figured they'd pick me up.

I [also] did a little politics. When Julian went away, they got Jack Greenwell to fill his unexpired term. He served the unexpired term, then he ran one term. Jack served about two and a half years. Then we heard he wasn't running for reelection. That's when all these farmers here, they came and see me. They want me to run. I figured I wasn't the man for that job. Not my line. But I couldn't [help] it. They went out to circle [circulate] my nomination papers. All they asked me, to put my signature on it. I went to Parker Ranch to see the people there. And then, I went to Kohala, and I went to Ka'ū. Anybody connected with the school[s], they know me. So, I got the votes. I got elected outright.

I got around and kind of learned what they [i.e., supervisors] have to do, all the procedures and all that, but didn't take me long. When I want something for my district, I go to the mayor. I say, "We want this road done," or something like that.

"Well, you go see [Thomas] Cunningham. He's the finance chairman."

So I go to Cunningham and I tell him. He said, "Why, sure. We'll give you some money for that. You go talk with the auditor."

Those days, the auditor, he's the guy that, if have money, he know where the money going to come from and all that. Well, I made friends with those guys. So I never had no trouble at all whenever we need some money here. We had our little difference there, but after you get outside and all go eat lunch together, what the hell? You don't have to be fighting one another. (Laughs.) The main thing is to get money for your district, see?

Long before water came in, I used to campaign. I said, "One thing, I'm going to see that you get water here." No rain, no water. The farmers, they don't have too many [water] tanks. As they increase the farm, they don't increase their water supply. Then, [too], they get more kids in the family and use more water. They go all the way to Waimea, go to Ka'ū, buy 5,000 gallons of water. It was sixty dollars a load to bring 'em in.

When I was with McCandless, we dug wells there. It's brackish [water], but it's all right. [Governor William Quinn] sent his man up here. I said,

"Now, you look here. We're miles away from the ocean. But the land low. I went [down] forty-four feet, and I got fresh water—almost fresh. You dig here, and this vein, it goes straight down to where have two wells down below. And both wells are good water. We drink the water and [use it] for the cattle." And by gosh, they took my word and they dug that well. This was the first well, Ke'ei, down here. So, that's how they got water in Kona.

You see [now] the people have a better standard of living, too. They get water. The households there, they buy washing machines. They have patent [flush] toilets. They have a vegetable garden right around their house there. And some of them have a lawn.

The supervisor, that's sort of part-time [job]. I worked for the McCandless Ranch from '42 up to 1950, I think. By that time [ca. 1950], I started my own [ranch], too, eh? I don't have pasture land of my own. All lease. Get government land and Bishop Estate [land].

I like cowboying. Six o'clock, I'm up every morning. Every day you get something in mind you have to do. I run about 300 head [of cattle]. Even at my age, I still go out rope 'em. I don't say I'm the best, but I can catch 'em.

GLOSSARY

haole	Caucasian
hui	organization
'iwa'iwa	maidenhair fern
kiawe	algaroba tree
pau	over, finished

KAZUE IWAHARA UYEDA

THE STORE THAT CARRIED EVERYTHING

Those days, businesses weren't self-service. When we had a customer, we would greet him courteously and ask what he needed. Then after showing him the selections and the customer's decision was made, we would wrap the merchandise using wrapping paper that came in large rolls. Then the package would be tied carefully with twine and given to the customer.

Taketo Iwahara and Ryo Shishido Iwahara immigrated to Hawai'i from Hiroshima, Japan. Iwahara Shōten, the family store, was located at King and Iwilei Streets in the 'A'ala district of Honolulu.

Born in 1917, Kazue Uyeda is the oldest of four children. After graduating from Central Intermediate in 1932, she studied in Japan. She returned in 1937 and married in 1943. When her father was interned in World War II, Uyeda and her brother operated the store until the government closed it in 1944.

Michi Kodama-Nishimoto interviewed Kazue Uyeda at the family-run Uyeda Shoe Store in 1993. This edited narrative is taken from her interview.

IWAHARA FAMILY

I guess my grandfather, Kurataro [Iwahara], came here with some capital that his father had given him to do business; whereas, most families were just brought in as plantation workers. So, in that sense, my grandfather was very fortunate that he was able to bring some capital to start off the business.

He had, more or less, a general store. They used to sell not only hardware but had provisions for everyday supply, like miso, shōyu, and other groceries. So the people would come in to buy all those supplies, and then board the train and go back to their homes. Plantations were in Waipahu and 'Aiea

Iwahara Shōten (corner store), early 1900s (photo courtesy of Kazue Uyeda)

and all those areas. And the only means of transportation was by train those days.

Their store was, as you know, right in front of that Oʻahu Railway [and Land Co.] station, and the last train would leave the station at twelve midnight. And so when they heard the whistle blow, they would say, "Oh, it's time to close shop."

My mother was born in Koi, Hiroshima-ken. My mother went to Yamanaka Koto Jogakkō in Hiroshima. But while she was at Yamanaka Jogakkō, her father was transferred to Taiwan for some kind of diplomatic job. So he moved the family there. My grandfather on Iwahara side came for her as soon as she graduated jogakkō, and brought her to Hawaiʻi. What I've been told is that her father and my father's mother were brother and sister. In other words, they were first cousins. So I guess their marriage must have been arranged, yeah? (Chuckles.)

Wedding portrait of Kazue Uyeda's parents, 1911 (photo courtesy of Kazue Uyeda).

[Father] was also born in Koi-machi, Hiroshima. The Iwahara and the Shishido families were all living in Koi-machi, Koi village, in those days. I think he graduated chūgakkō, and as soon as he did, he came here.

I guess they decided on getting a house and built a home in Kuakini. So my parents and my uncle and aunt lived together in Kuakini for several years. And that house is still standing in Huli Lane. Well, considering those days, it was a pretty nice home. It had a nice veranda and a yard, plants and trees. (Chuckles.)

When they were open until twelve o'clock, it must have been way before the time I was born. [Our store hours were] from seven to nine. After they closed the shop, they would pack all of us in the car and take us back home. Do you know what I remember? On our way home, we would stop by that Darumaya [Fruit and Fountain] and pick up fruits or whatever and then go back home to Kuakini. And early the following morning while we were still sleepy, they would wrap us in warm—we used to call that tanzen, you know, those wataire warm jacketlike clothing as it was rather chilly in the early morning. They would then pack us in the car and go to 'A'ala to open shop bright and early at seven o'clock.

STORES OF 'A'ALA

When I was a child, the next-door neighbor was this Sun Loy [Dry Goods]. Oh, they had a big variety of men's clothing. Ties and handkerchiefs. Jackets and whatnot. Mrs. Chang used to run this business. Mrs. Chang was the sister of Mr. Ah Wah Wong, who was known as the mayor of Chinatown.

A lot of Filipinos used to patronize them. I've heard that Filipino young men liked to dress up, but with their meager earnings one man alone couldn't afford a suit of his own. So they pooled together to buy one outfit and shared with friends, taking turns and then went dating (laughs). And because there was a big Filipino community in Iwilei area near the Dole cannery, Sun Loy must have had a lot of Filipino trade.

And next was a Chinese[-owned] restaurant. I can't remember the name, but it was a very busy restaurant because there weren't too many restaurants around that area. They served the regular kind of Western food.

And next was Kawano's Aloha Curio. Mr. and Mrs. Isomatsu Kawano were the owners there. They carried a lot of those coconut ashtrays and tie hangers and also craft work made out of koa. The sailors and all those military people would come around and buy curios for souvenirs.

Mrs. Kawano and her sister, Mrs. Ohta, who happens to be the 'ukulele player Ohta-san's mother, and Chiyono-san, the shop saleslady, and another helper, Yano-san, worked all day making silk leis. They had bolts and bolts of that material piled up and they would cut them into strips for lei making. In those days for graduation, it was customary for friends and relatives to send baskets of flowers and not only flower leis but silk leis to the graduates.

They had a fountain, you see, on one side of the store. They served the best banana split. The kids around there, including me, would go in there to scribble on the [condensation on the] stainless steel counter. And then, Mrs. Ohta and Chiyono-san would say, "Ey, you kids! Get out!" (Laughs.)

And next was Awamura's Heiwa-Do. The Awamuras came from Maui when I was in the fifth grade, I think. They would repair watches and clocks. They sold diamonds and rings and other jewelry, brooches and whatnot.

And next was another Chinese men's shop. I think they sold men's clothing. Just like Sun Loy. Mr. Chow—I don't remember the [first] name, but Mr. [Richard] Chow, the son of that owner, has become quite a well-known businessman. He used to come around to my shop [Uyeda Shoe Store] to sell us shoes.

They carried a lot of trousers, I remember. Do you know how they were arranged? They had rows and rows of bars and they would hang the pants over the bars. There was a little space in between and being kids, we would play hide-and-seek. (Laughs.)

After Chow's dry goods store, there was a big pathway where people could walk through there, going to the fish market in the back.

Then came the Chinese candy store. Oh, it was a big candy store, probably the biggest candy store in downtown Honolulu, because they were selling all kinds of varieties. Some of them were manufactured upstairs, you know. They had the hard red coconut candy that were wrapped individually. They had lemon drops and many other varieties of drops. And they also carried crack seed and all kinds of cookies. And they had chocolates, too. Hershey's chocolates. Oh, they were our favorites.

Next was a tailor shop. Later on, it was taken over by Okazaki. After the Okazakis retired, Mr. Morikubo came in. Pacific Woolen. But when I was a child, that tailor shop was run by a Chinese woman. I wouldn't know her name.

[M. Kobayashi Shōten] carried mainly women's material for dresses and whatnot. They carried everything from thread to buttons and all sorts of accessories. Mrs. Kobayashi, who happened to be an instructor at Keister Sewing School, operated Keister Sewing School way up on Liliha Street together with Mrs. R. Murata for many years. I went to Keister Sewing School for two summers during summer vacation.

[Next was Sato Clothiers.] By the time Satos came in, I think the one that was next to Kobayashi quit and Okazaki Tailor came in.

They [the Miyakes, Lion Shoe Store owners,] were from Okayama. My mother used to say Kawano no oba-san and Mrs. Miyake were very close. They may have been in business for ten years or more and may have gone back to Japan around 1933.

Mr. Fukuda's name was Zenichi. They [Hawai'i Importing Company] were [Kobayashis'] competitors. And Mr. Noboru Hino, later owner of Fashions by Hino of Ala Moana Center, was working for the Fukudas at that time and for the Okamoto family, who operated Hawai'i Importing Company [after the Fukudas left].

Akahoshi [Drug Store] used to have a fountain, and so on Saturday evenings after we closed shop, my mother would call Akahoshi and order ice cream to serve the clerks as refreshment. The big scoop of ice cream came in a serving dish with all varieties of flavor poured on top and they cost only ten cents per cup.

Mr. [Kanji] Okahiro [of Okahiro Cyclery on the Iwilei Road side] was from Yamaguchi-ken. Mr. Okahiro was a very nice person but always [covered in] black! You know why? Because he used to handle motorcycles. He would service them. A lot of policemen used to come there because they used to drive Harley-Davidson motorcycles. And he also had bicycles, naturally. People were riding a lot of bicycles those days.

[The next-door restaurant] was operated by a Chinese family. They served meals, American-type of meals. They had a counter there, I remember, and people would come in for a cup of coffee and a piece of pie or something. They sold the best custard pies, those days. So, once in a while, my mom would treat us. And the whole pie used to cost only forty cents. I still remember that. (Chuckles.)

Way back when I was a youngster, I remember Hawai'i Woolen was in operation there [next to the restaurant]. They were run by the Matsuuemon Tanimuras. They carried woolen materials. There were no such things as nylons or all those mixtures, you know.

In those days, until Sato Clothiers came into business, everybody had to have their suits made to order, and so, those days, there were a lot of tailors, Japanese tailors. In those days, they all had trousers and a vest to match and a coat. Three-piece suits. (Chuckles.) The only thing that I could remember was riding a tricycle and when I went into the store, they would scold and say, "Get the hell out." (Laughs.)

[Then] there was a barbershop. Mr. Honda was a longtime *Hawai'i Hochi* newspaper writer. The wife used to be the barber, and her son was my classmate, Takao Honda.

[Next door] this Filipino guy used to run that [tattoo] place. [He] had lots of samples, pictures that the customers could choose and he would use that pattern to work on the person. I think tattoo seemed to be quite popular those days and a lot of sailors used to come around.

The Komeiji family [of Asahi Furniture Company] and our family were real good friends as we were neighbors for a great many years. The [Risuke] Komeijis had eight children. I used to see Mrs. Komeiji in the warehouse sewing draperies and couch covers, so I asked one of the daughters how her mother ever found time to do all the laundry aside from raising the family. The answer was, "Oh, my mom used to wake up at three o'clock every single morning to do the washing until we grew up!"

Their store space was the largest in this area. I think at least two stores' spaces. And they had a mezzanine, where they could store or display their furniture, too. They carried beds, and couches, and dinner tables, and everything that you need to furnish a home. American-style, strictly.

'A'ala Rengō was considered a shopping center, those days. Before Ala Moana Center came into existence, this was one of the larger shopping areas in town. So as you can see, we had all sorts of merchants carrying different types of merchandise.

You may not believe it, but, I think, 'A'ala Rengō was the first organization that had started illuminating their building [for Christmas], and even lighted up the monkey pod trees in 'A'ala Park. It was really a big thing.

Occasionally when 'A'ala Rengō had a sale for school opening or at Christmastime, they would have a large combined ad published in the newspaper. And also once in a while in certain types of promotions or magazines.

Christmas illumination of 'A'ala Rengō, ca. 1940 (photo courtesy of Jane Komeiji).

IWAHARA SHŌTEN

Iwahara Shōten's logo was "Nandemo aru mise, yasui mise"—the store that carried everything, the inexpensive store. We had everything from needles and pins to toothbrushes, toothpaste, and shoe polishes, shoe strings, (laughs) and the larger tools. We had paints, stepladders, and even the carpenter's overalls—you know those outfits that carpenters used to wear. We even carried shirts and canvas shoes for the carpenters. We had tubs and buckets, and the Japanese zaru, or bamboo colanders. Nails by the tons, you know, of all different sizes.

We had large show windows. On the King Street side we had several showcases lined up with displays of curios, flower vases, trays, and many other items. And on the extreme left side of the wall there were glass cupboard shelves where stationery and all sorts of paper goods were kept. The kitchenwares and other housewares like toasters and coffee makers were stored way inside of the store.

On the Iwilei side we had more carpenter's tools. The tools were displayed on a large vertical glass case from where customers could make selections. We also carried about the largest selections of knives and scissors—from tiny manicuring scissors to the huge fourteen-inch tailor's scissors and also those buttonhole scissors that we can hardly find these days. Concerning knives, we had all sorts of kitchen knives made in U.S., Germany, and Japan, and cane knives used by plantation workers. We even carried Parker pens, harmonicas, and expensive French-made binoculars.

Iwilei Street entrance to Iwahara Shōten. Left to right, Ryo Iwahara, Takao Tsuda, Minoru Tarui, Yoshito Baba, and Jukichi Nobuhara, 1940 (photo courtesy of Kazue Uyeda).

Mainly the tools came directly from the Mainland. But the wholesalers for tools at that time were American Factors—they call that Amfac now—and Lewers & Cooke. They were the two main wholesalers that we dealt with. And paper goods were ordered through Honolulu Paper, you know, Hopaco.

A lot of Japanese goods were sent directly from Japan because my grandfather was still very active. In other words, my grandfather was in charge of the wholesaling in Japan and would send the merchandise directly to Iwahara Shōten.

A lot of merchandise was stacked on the first floor. We had two mezzanine-type floors. And then we had the upstairs, which was like a warehouse. Our living quarters were only in the front section. Plus we had an attic. The attic was stored with children's bicycles and toys, and whatnot. Then we had a separate warehouse in the back of 'A'ala Market. [Later] we bought out Sun Loy, a men's clothing store that I had told you about, and we enlarged the store.

There were constantly at least six or seven men clerks. Later on we hired a lady clerk, Miss Isono. Those days, businesses weren't self-service. When we had a customer, we would greet him courteously and ask what he needed. Then after showing him the selections and the customer's decision was made, we would wrap the merchandise using wrapping paper that came in large rolls. Then the package would be tied carefully with twine and given to the customer.

Oh, my mother used to help as a salesperson, too. Of course, she had to take care of her family first, but whenever she found time, she would come down to help. You know it was a dusty place, that 'A'ala Park (laughs). So every day it was a chore to wipe around the glass counters and keep things in order and then at the same time make sales.

From my childhood days, we had three or four oba-san that came and worked for us for a number of years. And the oba-san took care of the household chores upstairs. Some of them had to go back to Japan, but the last one, Mrs. Otoide, stayed with our family for about fifteen years.

Before seven o'clock, they [the employees] were already at the store and then had their breakfast. They had three meals at the store, so Oba-san would cook the three meals for them. We ate in two shifts. My father and Nobuhara-san, the o-jii-san, and then the other Nobuhara-san and Tsuda-san, plus my brother and my sisters would eat in the first shift. Then the second shift was the rest of the employees, plus my mother and Oba-san, and I.

They worked all day and I think they hardly had any days off, only perhaps on Sunday and on a few big holidays. But you know, even on Sundays I remember my father had the store opened till noon. So half of the employees would come this Sunday and then the other half would come the following Sunday.

That's why my mother had to do the cooking on Sunday because it was a day off for Oba-san. She really made some exotic dishes as she used to like to cook and made lots of gochisō to compensate for the hard work they did on Sunday. She used to make yakiniku, or barbeque meat on the hibachi.

Then after they went home, my parents would take it easy, and took naps in the afternoon. Then in the evening, the family would usually go to the movies to either Nihon Gekijo or Honolulu-za to enjoy the show. That was how we spent our day on Sundays.

Christmas and New Year's Eve were very, very busy. We had to hire extra help. Like Tsuda-san's brother and a few other temporary clerks. Housewares and kitchenwares and also lacquered ware like trays and soup bowls were popular gift items. And toys, oh, we used to sell a lot of them. Mama dolls. We had children's bicycles and tricycles, and toy cars for the little boys. They were all lined up outside on the sidewalk and we had to chain them.

[For New Year's] customers used to come to buy kamidana, or a miniature Shinto shrine; sanbō, or a wooden elevated tray, to place the kagami-mochi, saiwai-gami, and beautifully decorated hagoita, and other articles needed for New Year's festival. On New Year's Day all of the employees would come to exchange greeting and then would sit down to enjoy the gochisō spread on the table. That's how we celebrated our O-shōgatsu.

We used to sell a lot of o-ningyo because it was a custom those days to help celebrate a friend's baby girl on Hina-zekku or Girls' Day, and the same to a friend's baby boy on Tango-no-sekku, or Boys' Day on May the fifth. Of course they all came in boxes, but I remember they had to assemble certain parts of the doll and then they were stacked on the shelves for display.

SCHOOLING IN HONOLULU

Only at Christmastime when it was very busy I remember helping at the store. I was much too young to stay in the store as I was still going to school. By the time I returned from Japanese-language school it was already about 5:30 p.m. So I just had dinner that Oba-san had prepared and perhaps played around a little and did my studies.

I attended Royal Annex School on Fort Street when I was in the first and second grade and then transferred to Kauluwela Elementary in the third, as my family lived in the Kuakini area at that time. Then after my third grade my parents decided on living in town, upstairs of the store, and therefore had to be transferred again to Ka'iulani School for my fourth, fifth, and sixth grades. After elementary I attended Central Junior High School and graduated in 1932.

SCHOOLING IN JAPAN

My mother said, "Would you care to go to Japan and go to a school in Japan?" In those days we were more tomboyish and ran around. So she figured that it might be a good idea to send me to Japan to learn some manners and become a little more ladylike and also further my education. I thought, well, it's a pretty good idea (laughs).

In those times the majority of our parents hardly spoke English so we had to speak Japanese at home. And the textbooks that we had at Hongwanji Japanese-language school were of pretty high standard, and so after I went to Japan I found out that the textbooks that we were using in Hawai'i and in Japan were almost about the same and not much difference. Of course, I had to take an exam and then they admitted me into the third grade [of high school] from the second semester.

But from that semester the Japanese literature started with bungo-tai or the literary style and was it difficult and hard to comprehend! But fortunately our teacher was very conscientious and nice to help those like me and some others.

[It was a] a Methodist school [Hiroshima Jogakuin]. We were never forced to be baptized. It was all up to each individual. But we did have chapel every morning. And, I think, it was good influence for me as I learned a lot.

I stayed with my great aunt who lived in Hiroshima City. She was like a grandmother to me, really caring. I had to catch the streetcar every day to

'A'ala Rengō neighbors see Mrs. Hanayo Kawano off to Japan aboard the *Asama Maru,* August 6, 1935 (photo courtesy of Kazue Uyeda).

go to school and on the way passed the Hiroshima Exhibition Hall, which is now a memorial of the atom bomb—called Atomic Dome.

Oh, my mother used to write me practically every week. When it got delayed, I felt so lonesome. (Laughs.) I really used to look forward to her letters to be informed on what was going on in Hawai'i.

That flood in 1934 was just awful. My mother told me that the water that suddenly started gushing inside the store became so high that they all had to scramble upstairs. The reason for this unusual flooding was due to the trash and debris that got piled up on the Beretania [Street] Bridge causing the water to flow over into 'A'ala Park and then gushing into the 'A'ala Rengō Building.

According to what my mother told me, they had to be closed for over a month. Because the damage was so great and our merchandise being mainly hardware, [it] had to be washed and cleaned and then oiled to prevent rusting. Oh, it was such a big job. Normally my father was a cheerful person. But my mom said she never did see him smile for one whole month (laughs).

I think I heard my father saying they had experienced some [effects of the] depression, but fortunately, after I came back, the U.S. government started putting in more effort into the defense jobs and so that's when we started picking up more business. We started getting busy from about 1937. The majority of the defense workers were employed at Pearl Harbor. So when they returned from work on the train from Pearl Harbor they would just cross the street and come into our store to buy tools.

Iwahara family (minus Kazue), Hilo Japanese Garden, 1936 (photo courtesy Kazue Uyeda).

[In Japan] everything seemed quite peaceful then. But after I returned to Hawai'i in May 1937 there was an incident [Marco Polo Bridge Incident] in July [7, 1937] between China and Japan which later developed into a war. From then on I think relations between Japan and the U.S. gradually started getting bad.

WORLD WAR II AND AFTER

[When Mother died in 1940] my brother was nineteen, and sister below him was sixteen, and the youngest sister was twelve years old. For me it was really a big blow and it felt as though the end of the world had come. But fortunately I had [Otoide] Oba-san to support me and I felt like she was a second mother.

It was on Sunday and on that day [December 7, 1941], we had all the employees come over to make preparations for Christmas. Then suddenly we started hearing news of the attack at Pearl Harbor and you can imagine the commotion that followed. But we kept calm and worked till about 3:00 p.m. and after serving an early supper, we sent them home. Then at about 4:30 p.m. a police officer and another person came to ask for my father, saying that they needed him for some interrogation and to bring his coat with shoes as he may not be able to return for a few days.

It was in February [1942] that we got the official word informing us that all internees would be shipped to the Mainland and so to get all necessary clothing and other articles packed and deliver them to the immigration station. Then after a few months later we received a letter from the internees' camp [in Montana].

Left to right, Kazue Iwahara, Maude Okamoto, Ayako Awamura, and Jane Okamoto at corner of River and King Streets, 1941 (photo courtesy of Kazue Uyeda).

Taketo Iwahara (third row, with cane), Taichi Sato of Sato Clothiers (third row, fourth from left), and other Japanese internees, Montana, ca. 1942 (photo courtesy of Kazue Uyeda).

You know, our business was special because the government considered our business as an essential one. And so we were treated a little differently from other businesses and allowed to operate under government supervision. But we had to make a report every week regarding the sales and the purchases.

In the meantime, I got married in 1943. I really wouldn't know exactly how it came about, but it seems that Mrs. Okamoto and Mrs. Kawano, being our neighbors, casually started discussing about my marriage and decided arranging one. So I had to get in touch with my father, who wrote me saying that he had to make some inquiries concerning the family background first, you know, even in the internment camp. So then my father consented and said, "I guess it's okay." (Laughs.)

Well, the condition was that I would need consent from my in-laws to have me go freely to oversee our family's business and also to check with things concerning the younger members of my family since my father was interned and away from home. My brother Akito was old enough already to run the business, so he and the manager, Nobuhara-san, ran the store. And, everybody cooperated with each other.

You know, during those war years for security reasons, we all used to buy things excessively; in other words, we did a lot of hoarding, especially canned foodstuff. Fish was very scarce, but we knew when fish came in because we would see people from all over come running to the fish market. That's when

Oba-san would run to the market to join the crowd waving their money to buy fish.

There was a martial law that anyone could not keep more than $200 [in cash]. So everybody went crazy and bought jewelry. Even the washerwoman would have a big diamond on her finger because she had lots of savings, and the only thing that she could buy were diamonds. They all went to [H. F.] Wichman [and Co.] or to Detor Jewelers. Heiwa-Do was busy, too, but they didn't carry much precious stone.

The store [Iwahara Shōten] was closed in April '44. Personnel from the office of the Alien Property Custodian came and closed it. Soon after being vested, the property was then made public for bids. My brother tried but lost the bid, which I think was a blessing in disguise as the stress would have been much too unbearable for him. After losing the bid, my brother Akito started working for the purchasing department at Dole Pineapple Company [known as Hawaiian Pineapple Company until 1960]. And the rest all had to—each had to find a new job. Most of them went to hardware stores. I felt so sad. But what could I do.

My father was already in Japan when the store was taken over. He was shipped back to Japan on the prisoner exchange ship called *Gripsholm* which carried internees and prisoners of war back and forth between U.S. and Japan. My father was shipped on the second voyage in September 1943 from New York which took almost three months to reach Japan. My grandmother was still living then, so father looked after her and spent an ordinary life back there.

In the meantime the relatives felt that Father should remarry because he was gradually getting old and needed someone to care for him. My father spent several peaceful and happy years with our second mother and in 1967 we were finally able to persuade him and Mother to come and visit us here in Hawai'i. I'm really glad that both of them had come to meet with all of us children and grandchildren and also his old acquaintances of 'A'ala Rengō. The 'A'ala Rengō neighbors hosted a reunion in honor of Father when Mrs. Okamoto and Mr. Hino were all still active.

After enjoying being with the family for about three months, they returned to Hiroshima, but no sooner had they returned his health started declining and in February the following year of 1968 he passed away with stomach cancer.

After my father's passing my mother took care of all the aftermath but then in 1975 she asked for Brother to come back to Hiroshima to help her with managing Father's estate. Brother Akito and family have since been living there and come visit once in a great while.

I noticed that trends were changing as time went on with shoppers gradually shifting towards Ala Moana Shopping Center, which seemed to affect the majority of businesses in downtown Honolulu. But really 'A'ala Rengō had its heyday and flourished for many decades, I must say.

GLOSSARY

bungo-tai	literary style
chūgakkō	junior high school
crack seed	Chinese-style preserved fruit and seeds
gekijo	theater
gochisō	feast; good things to eat
hagoita	battledore
hibachi	charcoal brazier
Hina-zekku	Girls' Day Festival, March 3rd
jogakkō	girls' high school
kagami-mochi	round mirror-shaped rice cake
kamidana	household altar
ken	prefecture
machi	town
miso	fermented soybean paste
ningyo	doll
no	belonging to, made of
o-	honorific prefix
oba-san	auntie, middle-aged woman
o-jii-san	grandfather, old man
O-shōgatsu	New Year
saiwai-gami	decorative good-luck paper
-san	suffix attached to name; Mr., Mrs., Miss
sanbō	small wooden stand
shōyu	soy sauce
Tango-no-sekku	Boys' Day Festival, May 5th
tanzen	padded kimono
wataire	padded garment
'ukulele	small stringed instrument
yakiniku	grilled meat
-za	theater
zaru	basket

EDITH ANZAI YONENAKA

RECOLLECTIONS FROM THE WINDWARD SIDE

My mama very seldom went to town, but my father used to do his month's shopping there. Used to buy rice—and that's two 100-pound bags of rice—one big tub of miso, tubful of shōyu, and crackers. He used to buy crackers by the case. And some canned stuff, sugar and salt, I suppose. I remember the good things, like the can of cookies that he used to buy once in a while.

Edith Anzai Yonenaka, the fourth of ten children, was born in Kahana Valley, Oʻahu, in 1919. Her father, a sugarcane farmer, and her mother, a homemaker, were emigrants from Fukushima, Japan. The Anzais lived in a housing area called Tanaka Camp.

In August 1941, Yonenaka and members of her family started the Kaʻaʻawa Vegetable Stand, later renamed Kaʻaʻawa Store, which prospered with the patronage of military personnel during World War II.

She married Harold Yonenaka in 1952. That same year, she began a twenty-eight-year career as Kaʻaʻawa's postmistress. Retired in 1980, she spent her time helping the Kaʻaʻawa Community Association, tending her garden, and selling beauty products. Edith Yonenaka died in 1994.

Yonenaka was interviewed by Michi Kodama-Nishimoto for COH's *Five Life Histories* (1983). Kodama-Nishimoto found her to be a warm, generous woman, devoted to her family and community.

KAHANA VALLEY

[Kahana Valley] was green, with all the sugarcane. On the mountainside was a lot of guava trees, some mangoes, and mountain apple. There was a stream, just about in the middle of the valley, coming down to the ocean.

Kahana Bay and Valley, Punalu'u at right, 1931 (O. S. Picher, Hawai'i State Archives).

When you look up in the valley, [our camp] was on the left side. There was one Filipino family for a while. There was one Korean family, too, and about three or four Japanese families in the camp. The rest were all Filipino bachelors. The bachelors' homes were just long homes with rooms, and then they had another building right below that, [which] was the kitchen.

Then on the right-hand side [of the valley] there was another little village there where a lot of other people lived. They were mostly Hawaiians. They fished and had taro patches.

Down there in the bay, they used to catch a lot of akule. By the Crouching Lion [a point overlooking Kahana Bay], not way at the top but the lower part there, a Hawaiian man from inside the valley would go to look for the fish. When he saw the school of fish coming in, he'd call out. As soon as we hear his voice, we all come out from the valley.

Then all the fishermen with their boats and their nets would surround the fish. Everybody would help pull the net in. Depending on the catch, everybody [or] every family would get some fish. Then whatever was extra, they took to the market in town [Honolulu].

We used to have bridges so that we could go from one side of the valley to the other. I remember crossing that bridge near our camp. I had [a] baby on my back. I slipped and I fell in the water and it was above my head. Good thing it [the stream] wasn't too wide, so I was able to walk out to the shallow area.

The bridge was just timber, maybe ten-by-ten or twelve-by-twelve [feet]. When there's a heavy rain and the stream gets flooded, the water would wash that bridge away. The camp boss got tired of going way down the stream looking for it, so he used to tie it with pieces of wire to a tree.

TANAKA CAMP

[We lived] in Tanaka Camp. We called him [Tanaka] the camp boss. They [the Filipino bachelors] were hired actually by the camp boss. When he got through with all his work, then he would let them work for the other farmers. That's how my father used to get help from the workers there, plowing the field with the horse, and planting, and then harvesting.

[My father] leased land from the Kahuku Plantation. [At first] he grew rice [and] he had a rice patch. By the time I remember, it was all sugarcane.

I was born in Kahana Valley in the year 1919. There were ten of us; I was the fourth in the family. Ever since I was small I was the only girl, so I got used to it. My biggest job was caring for my little brothers, carrying them on my back.

This lady that used to live up there, Mrs. Nozawa, used to come and deliver all the babies. Not only on our side of the valley but on the other side, too. When my mother was giving birth, they would put this kaya, you know, the mosquito thing [i.e., netting] and hang it on the wall so that we couldn't see from the outside. When I heard the baby cry, oh, I was excited, yeah! (Laughs.)

[We had] no electricity. No running water. We had a well. It was quite deep and it was real cool down there. So my mother used to put things in a bucket and put it down in the well to preserve it. We [would] carry water from the well into the kitchen where we used to have a barrel. We had to fill up the barrel every day so Mom could use that for washing dishes.

From the well, she would get the water and put [laundry] in [another barrel], and wash [it]. [Then] she would take all the clothes in a bucket, put it on a wheelbarrow, and take it down to the river and rinse it there so she wouldn't have to keep getting the water from the well. [Kahana Valley] was such a rainy place that the clothes, the diapers, wouldn't dry fast enough. She would have to string it up inside the kitchen, right by the fire.

We had our own furo, but it was such a job for my mom and dad to get all the firewood [to heat the water], so we gave it up. [Instead], we used to go to the community furo. The camp boss would take his workers up in the mountains and chop the wood, put it in the river, and let the river bring it all the way down. [Downstream], they have a gang bringing it out of the water, stacking it right next to the furo.

TAXI TO TOWN

My father used to buy eggs, Mainland eggs, by the case. A lot of times the eggs would be rotten. Every one, we break into a bowl and make sure it's all right before we mix it in with the others. That was one of the main dishes, eggs, and that aka mame. And codfish, they'd cook it with a little bit sugar. And lots of vegetables from our garden. Every once in a while, we would have chicken that we raised.

Pig is another thing we used to raise. When one family kills [a] pig, they'd go around and sell it to the neighbors. It was really cheap. Then to preserve that, my mother used to put it in a crock. She'd melt the fat of the pork and pour that inside, so that you seal it. The only time we had beef was when somebody would come and visit us and bring us a piece. Oh, we used to look forward to people from [Honolulu] coming out to visit us.

My mama very seldom went to town, but my father used to do his month's shopping there. Used to buy rice—and that's two 100-pound bags of rice—one big tub of miso, tubful of shōyu, and crackers. He used to buy crackers by the case. And some canned stuff, sugar and salt, I suppose. I remember the good things, like the can of cookies that he used to buy once in a while.

He [would] go into town once a month on this taxi that used to run from Kahuku. There weren't very many cars. The camp boss had a car, [but] we had to depend on the taxis. Once every summer, my father used to take all of us to town. Not only our family, but the neighborhood kids, too. We'd all pile up in this car, usually the taxi he hired for the day. He'd take us to the zoo, the aquarium, and the museum. That was a treat for us!

VALLEY VISITORS

We used to mostly shop from these peddlers. You know [Ginihichi] Kaya in Punalu'u? He used to come up and bring tōfu, and vegetables, and canned stuff. Then there was Mr. Haga, he used to come from Waialua. He'd sell a lot of other things. Canned stuff, and then material for sewing clothes. About once a month, he used to come over. Lot of time, he used to spend the night at our house, because it would be [a long] way [to] Waialua.

A man used to come around and peddle Japanese medicines. He would leave us a bag full of all different kinds. He would mark it down [on] the outside of the bag. Then, the next time he come, he check to see if any of the medicines were used. He would charge us only what we used.

There was a [Buddhist] priest from that temple down in Kahuku. He used to come down to Kahana Valley, usually in the evening, and hold services at the camp, [at] the Tanakas' home. We used to go there, although we couldn't understand anything that he said. (Laughs.) We would get so sleepy, nodding our heads, and [then] waking up. Just waiting for them to start serving refreshments. (Laughs.)

This fellow from Wahiawā used to come all the way down to show movies at the Hanta Store in Ka'a'awa, right in the back of that. Japanese movies, always. It was silent, so he had to speak for them [the actors] while they're saying something. When it was time to show the movie, he'd go around the neighborhood playing [a] drum. By the boom, boom sound, everybody would know. And, oh, we'd wish we could afford to go! (Laughs.)

Sometimes when the camp boss comes down, he would bring us. That was a treat, but we couldn't come down all the time. Even the other nationalities, Hawaiians and other people, [went]. Oh, the kids used to love that! Next day in school, that's all they'd talk about, the samurai movies. (Laughs.)

KA'A'AWA SCHOOL

I think there were at least five or six of us from my family alone, walking to [Ka'a'awa] School. We used to carry umbrellas every day to school during the winter months, so we used to call it the "umbrella brigade." (Laughs.)

Some [other kids] came from Kualoa and some from Punalu'u. They all walked, too. Sometimes the taxi drivers, if they had room, would pick us up. We'd have to sit on a customer's lap or we would all have to stand on the running board. All their customers were real nice, they didn't mind. They knew what it was like, I guess, walking all that distance. So every time we see the taxi coming, we all wait and wish! (Laughs.)

[But] there was one taxi driver who catered to the haoles [Caucasians]. Oh, he would never pick us up. (Laughs.) [And] a lot of times we used to see tourists in these great big limousines coming by, all elegantly dressed people, and they'd make [i.e., wave] hello with their gloved hands to us natives. (Laughs.)

We had a flagpole right in front of the main [school] building. Every morning everybody would line up out there, pledge allegiance to the flag, sing a song, and have a prayer, too, the Lord's Prayer.

When I was in the first grade, [one] teacher taught the first grade and the fifth grade in one classroom. Then we went to the second, third and fourth grade, all in one room. And the sixth, seventh, eighth grade, that's where Mr. Looney taught us. Mr. Looney was our principal. That's how we were divided in different classrooms.

When Mrs. Richmond came, she started teaching us a lot of things besides just reading and writing. She started us in the community project. We would go out and clean the park. I remember she started us making Hawaiian quilts. Swimming was another thing she started, swimming classes.

Kualoa Ranch [Company] was owned by the Swanzy family. Mrs. [F. M.] Swanzy was a very nice woman. Every year at Christmastime, she would come. The teacher would say, "Everybody rise." And we would all rise and say, "Good morning, Mrs. Swanzy." (Laughs.) The chauffeur would bring the boxes of fruits and candies. She would hand them out individually to all of us.

When she found out about our swimming class, she asked the teacher what would be a good gift for the kids. She must have been told that towels would be good because we [had] never had those kind of big bath towels. We really cherished that. I remember I never used it for anything else except for the swimming class. (Laughs.)

I think about my Japanese[-language] schoolteacher, too. He was a very good teacher. And I'll never forget, he always taught us, "Take the good of the Japanese and be a better American citizen." Half the [grades], he would teach right after the English school. The rest of us would be playing outside. When he gets through with that, then we all come in, the next four grades.

My [younger] brothers, they had to wait for all of us. We walked home together. We'd have to walk quite a distance, and by the time we go into the valley, it would be dark. I remember I used to be so scared walking home 'cause the boys would start talking about obake stories. (Laughs.) Oh! I didn't want to be the last one in the line, so I'd run and try and stay in between, you know. And pretty soon, one person would start running and everybody would run. (Laughs.)

THE OUTSIDE WORLD

During the summer, there were a lot of mountain apple trees up there [in Kahana Valley]. They used to have a Japanese-language school in Hale'iwa. The teachers used to bring the children by bus. We [would] take them up into the valley where the children could pick the mountain apples.

This couple [from the school] needed somebody to take care of their children, so they asked my folks, and my folks agreed, so that's how I got that work.

I wanted to go to high school, but my father couldn't afford it. I think he wanted us to have a good education, and I think that hurt him more than anything, not being able to send us to school. [The younger] kids, they all had their turn of going to school, but all of us older ones, we had to go to work to help support the family.

[In Haleʻiwa], I mostly helped with the housekeeping and the cooking, laundry, and all those things. In the morning when the [teacher] was home, she would teach me how to sew. When the teacher left to go to Japanese[-language] school, I took care of the little ones.

I think it was a good experience, especially after living in Kahana [Valley]. You don't get exposed to much, way up inside there. There were times when I got a little homesick. When it was time for me to come home, just before New Year's, I would just look forward to going home in the morning (laughs) and get up early and think about it.

Every once in a while, I'd call home. [They] had those old telephones, where you put the coins in every time you make a long-distance call. [At home] we didn't have a phone, but our neighbor had a phone. She would run down and call my mom, and my mom would run to the phone.

[Then the Hagas] needed help, because the daughter-in-law was going to have another baby. She needed help taking care of the baby and help in the store, too. So that's how [Mr. Haga of Waialua] asked my father and so he sent me over there.

There was a plantation camp right around it [Haga Store], so people would come in and charge. On payday, they come in and pay. So we had to keep a record of all their charges. There were a lot of Filipino customers, so I learned how to speak a little Filipino, too, Ilocano [dialect].

I saved every bit of [my pay], and then when I came home, I gave some of it to my folks to help the family. Then New Year's, when I come home to spend the holidays with the family, I'd buy fireworks. I got all the fireworks, of course, wholesale from Haga's. I had to catch the taxi from Waialua all the way to town, and from there get onto another taxi out to Kahana. All the boys—my brothers—would be down on the main highway waiting for me. (Laughs.) And they used to be so happy with all the fireworks I brought home for them.

KAʻAʻAWA

[When I returned home to stay], we moved to Kaʻaʻawa. They found a place down here where the man was going to give up his [lease on his] farm. You see, when my father was farming [in the valley], he had to walk from his house to the farm, quite a distance. But over here, the house was right in the center of the farm.

I'll never forget when my father wanted to put the farm in the whole area all around the house. My brother wanted a little lawn where he could play football, so he got all the other younger brothers to go on a strike. (Laughs.) I was home when that happened and I saw my brothers all coming home, walking in from the farm, and then my father grumbling and walking in. (Laughs.) He had to give in. He was a loving man and so he felt, well, if that's what they want. So that's how we got the lawn in front of the house.

[In 1941] the Kualoa Ranch Company that owns the land decided to subdivide it and lease it for homes. So, they were going to subdivide our farm, too. If we gave up the farm, where would my father get the income? So that's when I decided to put up the store [Kaʻaʻawa Vegetable Stand].

At that time, there was no running water in the [nearby Swanzy Beach] Park. A lot of people used to come over to our house and ask for water. So I thought, "Oh, gee, if we had soda, that would be good." (Laughs.) So that's what got me started, too.

It [the store] was part of the lease that we had from the ranch company. We asked for that certain lot, where we can put up the store. The house would be on the other lot, so we had two lots there.

Mr. [George] Bennett, he was nice. He was with the Waimānalo Plantation, he was manager there. He sent the carpenters from the [sugar] plantation to build the store. So he really did a lot to help us get started on that.

Then we had the Fujishige trucking service. They used to go into town every day to pick up the groceries. That's how we used to get our supplies. Dairymen's, they used to deliver. [They'd come] with the milk and ice cream. Several soda companies used to come out and deliver the soda.

WORLD WAR II

Right after the war broke out, that's when they [the military] took over the whole park and all the houses on the ocean side where the officers used to live. Kahana Valley, they used that area for actual jungle training. We had one local outfit, the [370th] Engineers, in Kahana. The rest of them were mostly from the Mainland.

The military built the training camp right around the area. The GIs used to sleep in the [training] camp on the hill above the store. One outfit would come in one week and train. Then the following week, another group would come in. So every week, they had new people coming in.

I needed help, so they [her two brothers] came home and helped me in the business. So we became partners. My business really started booming.

Lines would form and the whole place would be packed. They would get all their sodas and ice cream. And after a while, we put in a pinball machine and a jukebox. Oh, that thing was going on all day!

We had one bad experience there at night. We had one furo in the back of the house, separate from the house. I went to take a bath and came out of the door. This guy just slugged me and I fell down. I think I must have passed out for a minute. But before I conked out, I screamed, so my brothers came running out. It wasn't anything serious. I just got a little cut on the side of my ear. [But] ever since that, the person who was in charge of the [training] camp posted guards—one in the front of the store and one in the back—near our house to protect us. I thought that was very nice of him to do that.

There was a company that used to make sandwiches. We used to buy them by the boxes, boxes! They used to deliver it way out here. The GIs probably got sick and tired of the food that they were getting at their mess hall. So they would come down and buy these sandwiches. One time, I'll never forget, the day they were going to bring in the new troops, they didn't come in. So, here we were, stuck with boxes of sandwiches. We took it out to the guards and said, "Anybody comes around, just hand it to them." (Laughs.)

TIDAL WAVE OF 1946

My father went out for a walk and he went down to the park. He saw the waves coming. So he ran home and told us, "Nigero, nigero (Run away, run away). Tidal wave, tidal wave!"

So we just ran up on the hill in the back where the GIs had their training camp. And we were watching the waves come in. The waves pushed some of the buildings that were in the park against each other. We couldn't see the road, it was all covered with water. Some of the houses along the highway, they were really damaged. But there was no damage whatsoever to our home or the store. The store was built a little bit high, so the water went all around [it].

These two men, they almost got drowned. They were out there in the boat, and the waves came and, oh, they said they had to fight to get in. They managed to get in, but [one] guy lost his wallet. He was carrying quite a sum of money. It was scattered all over. We found some in our yard, too. (Laughs.) We knew whose it was and we gave it back to him. He appreciated that.

BASEBALL AND MARRIAGE

We had a baseball team. Three or four of my brothers were playing on that team. This was before the war. My [future] husband used to live in Punalu'u

Valley. He came to play on our team, too. And he was a star pitcher. We would go out there and root for them.

I'll never forget, there were two of us [girls] who were really noisy. We'd yell at the umpire, yell at the pitcher, and all that. [My father] never scolded me, but my mother didn't like the idea of me yelling. (Laughs.) My mother would say, "Onna no kuse ni (A fine thing for a girl to do)!"

After the war, somebody told him [her future husband], "Eh, let's go down to Ka'a'awa Vegetable Stand, get [there's] one pretty girl over there." And he was thinking, "Oh, that pug-nose thing, that's not pretty." (Laughs.) [But] soon after that, we started dating. That's how we got married.

KA'A'AWA POST OFFICE

We used to get our mail from Hau'ula Post Office. They had this taxi driver that would pick it up and take it down to Hanta Store. They had a little box out in the front, and we used to stop there on our way home from school to pick up the mail. Then when I opened the store, he was nice enough to drop ours off at my store. Later, they had another driver that used to deliver it, but he delivered along the highway only. Every time there were packages or registered mail, we had to go all the way down there [Hau'ula] to pick it up.

So Mr. Humphrey, he approached me one day, "How about putting in a post office in the store?" I said, "Well, okay, that's all right." So he got a petition and that's how we were able to get the post office. They were paying something like twenty-three dollars a month. (Laughs.) It was a fourth-class post office and nobody [else] wanted the job.

I think by that time, we changed the [store's] name to Ka'a'awa Store. It [the post office] was in one corner of the building. It was a little one, oh shucks, not even ten-by-ten feet, I think. [We had] a small window in the front, with the little counter. We had chicken wire around the top. (Laughs.)

People would come in, talk story. About the farms and the ball games and their families. Lot of community affairs. Of course, some gossip, too. (Laughs.) That's how I was able to keep up with the latest.

CHILDREN

My mother took care of my [two] children, feeding them, and all those things. Then by the time she died, well, they were old enough to take care of themselves. My house was right next door to the store [and] to the post office, so the kids used to come in and visit me whenever they wanted to. I would play with them for a few minutes in between customers. So it was really nice, being close to your job and children.

[Looking back], I'm glad that I was able to get out, even for that short time, to see what the outside world is like. That's another reason why I sent my kids to Mid-Pac [Mid-Pacific Institute in Honolulu]. I wanted them to go out and see what the world is like and experience a lot of other things that they would never experience in the little community. I'm glad they're independent and they can support themselves. As long as they're doing things that are good, helping others, I'm happy about that.

GLOSSARY

aka mame	red beans
akule	big-eyed scad fish
furo	bath, bathhouse
haole	Caucasian
kaya	mosquito netting
miso	fermented soybean paste
obake	ghost
shōyu	soy sauce
tōfu	bean curd

APPENDIX: CENTER FOR ORAL HISTORY PROJECTS

COH TRANSCRIPTS AND PUBLICATIONS

Center for Oral History transcripts and publications are available at Hawai'i State Regional Libraries, University of Hawai'i system libraries, and the Hawai'i State Archives.

Businesses of 'A'ala: Oral Histories of Japanese Entrepreneurs in Honolulu, circa 1900–1960.

This project documents the history of 'A'ala Rengō, an early 20th-century center of Japanese-owned small businesses in the 'A'ala section of Downtown Honolulu. Interviews with business proprietors and family members focus on lifestyles, community, ethnicity, and entrepreneurship. Forthcoming.

Chinese Restaurateurs.

Eight Chinese restaurateurs discuss the beginnings, maintenance, successes, failures, and day-to-day operations of their restaurants. Forthcoming.

The Closing of Sugar Plantations: Interviews with Families of Hāmākua and Ka'ū, Hawai'i.

These are life history interviews conducted with displaced Hāmākua Sugar Company and Ka'ū Agribusiness Company workers and their families. The workers or their spouses were surveyed earlier for a University of Hawai'i Center on the Family research project on job loss. August 1997, 598 pages, 2 volumes, photographs.

An Era of Change: Oral Histories of Civilians in World War II Hawai'i.

Thirty-three civilians—reflecting Hawai'i's diverse occupations, lifestyles, and ethnicities—talk about World War II and how it affected their everyday lives. Published in cooperation with the National Park Service, U.S. Department of Interior. April 1994, 1807 pages, 5 volumes.

Families without Patriarchs: Oral Histories of Japanese American Families in World War II Hawai'i.

Life history interviews, covering the prewar and postwar years as well as the war years under martial rule, were conducted with spouses and children of issei incarcerated by the U.S. government. Forthcoming.

Farrington High School Class of 1959.

Four women and three men of the Farrington High School class of 1959 were interviewed to study how the 1950s affected them and how their aspirations were realized, altered, or unfulfilled over five decades. Forthcoming.

Five Life Histories.

Personal experiences and historical events are recalled by five individuals of various backgrounds: Ernest Malterre, Jr., Raku Morimoto, Yuzuru Morita, Charlie Santos, and Edith Yonenaka. June 1983, 279 pages, 1 volume, photographs.

Hawai'i Nisei Project.

Nisei veterans and spouses tell of their experiences before, during, and after World War II. A website featuring interview narratives and video clips is available at www.nisei.hawaii.edu. Forthcoming.

Hawai'i Political History Documentation Project.

Forty-two former office holders, aides, appointees, party organizers, union officials, lobbyists, and political observers share their perspectives on territorial and state politics. June 1996, 1618 pages, 3 volumes.

Hui Panalā'au: Hawaiian Colonists in the Pacific, 1935–1942.

Eight men who occupied the isolated Line Islands in the South Pacific in the late 1930s and early 1940s in order to establish territorial jurisdiction for the United States are interviewed. They talk about their experience and reflect on its significance in their lives and on history. July 2006, 298 pages, portable document format (.pdf) on CD-ROM, photographs.

I'i/Brown Family: Oral Histories.

Members of the I'i/Brown family discuss social and historical changes observed at the family property at Waipi'o, O'ahu, as well as their early childhood, schooling, family relationships, ethnic identity, work history, daily life, and activities. March 1999, 162 pages, 1 volume, photographs.

Ka Po'e Kau Lei: An Oral History of Hawai'i's Lei Sellers.

Eleven long-time lei sellers share their experiences on lei making; lei selling on downtown sidewalks, the waterfront, and at the airport; tourism growth; and relationships with wholesalers, the state government, and the military. June 1986, 439 pages, 1 volume, photographs.

Kalihi: Place of Transition.

In this community-focused project, longtime residents talk about their experiences in Kalihi, a multiethnic working-class area of Oʻahu. June 1984, 1120 pages, 3 volumes, photographs.

Kōloa: An Oral History of a Kauaʻi Community.

Thirty-three residents describe life, past and present, in Kōloa, the site of the first commercial sugar plantation in Hawaiʻi. September 1988, 1518 pages, 3 volumes, photographs.

Kona Heritage Stores.

Six women and seven men, lifelong Kona residents, describe their family and home life, community, childhood activities, cultural upbringing, schooling, coffee farming, and family businesses. August 2006, 508 pages, portable document format (.pdf) on CD-ROM.

Lānaʻi Ranch: The People of Kōʻele and Keōmuku.

These interviews contain detailed descriptions of the daily lives of cowboys, their spouses and children, and other ranch residents. July 1989, 934 pages, 2 volumes, photographs.

Life Histories of Native Hawaiians.

Nine individuals of Hawaiian ancestry, including a musician, nurse, entertainer, seaman, road worker, recreation organizer, cowboy, and schoolteachers, talk about their childhood experiences, cultural practices, and political involvements. November 1978, 488 pages, 1 volume, photographs.

The 1924 Filipino Strike on Kauaʻi.

The bloodiest confrontation in Hawaiʻi labor history cost the lives of sixteen Filipino strikers and four Hawaiian policemen at Hanapēpē, Kauaʻi on September 9, 1924. Visayan workers, their wives, plantation and government officials, and other observers talk about the strike and how it affected them. July 1979, 973 pages, 2 volumes, photographs.

Oral Histories of African Americans.

Three women and seven men discuss family life, education, employment, segregation, racial violence, community life, political activities, and experiences in Hawaiʻi. December 1990, 406 pages, 1 volume, photographs.

An Oral History of Robert Richards Midkiff.

Business leader and community builder Robert Richards Midkiff talks about his family, education, military service, business career, and community work. Appended to his interview transcript are copies of selected speeches and an article. July 2001, 99 pages, addenda, 1 volume, photograph.

An Oral History of Sidney Kosasa.

Entrepreneur Sidney Kosasa, the founder of ABC Stores, recalls his family, education, internment camp experience, pharmacy career, and drug and sundries retail businesses. February 2004, 123 pages, 1 volume, photograph.

The Oroku, Okinawa Connection: Local-style Restaurants in Hawai'i.

With ancestral roots in Oroku, Okinawa, first-, second-, and third-generation participants/observers of family-run restaurants talk about their lives in the restaurant business. Published in cooperation with the Japanese Cultural Center of Hawai'i. February 2004, 429 pages, 1 volume, photographs.

Perspectives on Hawai'i's Statehood.

Nine political leaders, aides, observers, and scholars discuss Hawai'i's statehood movement and the sociopolitical issues of post-World War II America which influenced it. June 1986, 186 pages, 1 volume. Videotape available.

Pioneer Mill Company: A Maui Sugar Plantation Legacy.

Eighteen former workers and residents of Pioneer Mill Company on Maui comment on such topics as childhood activities, family dynamics, camp housing, plantation employment, and union and community involvement. Also discussed are the decline of the sugar plantation and the closing of Pioneer Mill Company. December 2003, 508 pages, 1 volume, photographs.

Presidents of the University of Hawai'i: Fujio Matsuda.

A former University of Hawai'i president discusses his family, schooling, World War II service, postwar education, and career as an engineering professor, state transportation head, UH vice president, and president. July 1998, 236 pages, 1 volume, photographs.

Presidents of the University of Hawai'i: Harlan Cleveland.

A former University of Hawai'i president and U.S. ambassador to NATO talks about his family, education, and government, international, and university work. November 1998, 174 pages, addendum, 1 volume, photographs.

Public Education in Hawai'i: Oral Histories.

Former administrators and teachers discuss their backgrounds, training, careers, and educational philosophies, practices, and attitudes. September 1991, 612 pages, 2 volumes, photographs.

Reflections of Pālama Settlement.

Twenty-nine individuals recall their life experiences and articulate the significance the Pālama Settlement has had for themselves, Pālama residents, and others. August 1998, 852 pages, 2 volumes, photographs.

Remembering Kaka'ako: 1910–1950.

A controversial area undergoing redevelopment, Kaka'ako was once known as the toughest district in Honolulu. Twenty-six former residents discuss sports, community organizations, and the old neighborhood as it was when Kaka'ako was home to 5,000 of the city's working class. December 1978, 1252 pages, 2 volumes, photographs.

A Social History of Kona.

The changing lifestyles of Kona—at one time the largest community in Hawai'i outside of the sugar plantation system, and the only area in the United States to grow coffee commercially for over 100 years—are documented. June 1981, 1727 pages, 2 volumes, photographs. Slide/tape show on videotape available.

The State Foundation on Culture and the Arts: An Oral History.

SFCA executive directors, staff and commissioners, arts educators, and others talk about the origins and growth of the agency, its early goals and achievements, and the development and role of arts in the community. May 1991, 445 pages, 1 volume, photographs.

Stores and Storekeepers of Pā'ia and Pu'unēnē, Maui.

Individuals directly involved with stores serving the sugar plantation communities of Pā'ia and Pu'unēnē recall the social and economic roles these stores played and how these roles changed over seventy years. June 1980, 1433 pages, 2 volumes, photographs.

Tsunamis in Maui County: Oral Histories.

Interviews with Maui and Moloka'i residents were conducted in 1999 by the Pacific Tsunami Museum to collect the stories of tsunami survivors and to promote tsunami safety. The interviews followed a life history format with emphasis on recollections of tsunami experiences. March 2003, 501 pages, 1 volume.

Tsunamis Remembered: Oral Histories of Survivors and Observers in Hawai'i.

Thirty individuals, mainly residents of Hilo and Laupahoehoe, recall their experiences before, during, and after the destructive 1946 and 1960 tsunamis. April 2000, 980 pages, 2 volumes, photographs.

'Ualapu'e, Moloka'i: Oral Histories from the East End.

Thirteen interviewees talk about the 'Ualapu'e Fishpond project, the historical and cultural role of fishponds, and everyday life on Moloka'i's East End. Published in cooperation with the State of Hawai'i Department of Business, Economic Development and Tourism. June 1991, 576 pages, 2 volumes, photographs.

Uchinanchu: A History of Okinawans in Hawai'i.

The development of the Okinawan community in Hawai'i is chronicled in articles and essays. Highlighted are life history narratives based on oral history interviews with first-generation Okinawans. Published by COH in cooperation with the United Okinawan Association of Hawai'i. December 1981, 632 pages, photographs.

University of Hawai'i Diversity Project.

Students and faculty of the University of Hawai'i who studied or taught during the 1920s and 1930s talk about their lives and careers within the contexts of family background, culture, ethnicity, and gender. Forthcoming.

Waialua and Hale'iwa: The People Tell Their Story

The histories of Waialua, then one of O'ahu's few remaining sugar plantations, and Hale'iwa, a neighboring town, as told by Caucasian, Chinese, Filipino, Hawaiian, Japanese, Korean, Portuguese, and Puerto Rican senior citizens. May 1977, 1880 pages, 9 volumes. Slide/tape show on videotape available.

Waikīkī, 1910–1985: Oral Histories

This is a study of a community's transformation from taro fields, duck ponds, and bungalows to nightclubs, curio shops, and towering hotels, as observed by fifty long-time residents, workers, and business operators. June 1985, 1999 pages, 3 volumes, photographs.

Waipi'o: Māno Wai (Source of Life)

Old-timers recall taro farming and daily life in this remote Big Island valley and talk about the many changes that occurred in the first half of the century. Young residents and old discuss their visions for the future of Waipi'o and taro. December 1978, 1335 pages, 2 volumes, photographs. Slide/tape show on videotape available.

Women Workers in Hawai'i's Pineapple Industry.

Sixteen women field and cannery workers recall their daily work experiences in the pineapple industry and also talk about their domestic lives. June 1979, 1089 pages, 2 volumes, photographs. Slide/tape show on videotape available.

BIOGRAPHY MONOGRAPHS

The Center for Biographical Research of the University of Hawai'i at Mānoa is dedicated to the interdisciplinary and multicultural study of life writing through teaching, publication, and outreach activities.

In addition to *Biography: An Interdisciplinary Quarterly,* published since 1978, the Center sponsors the Biography Monograph series; a chronological list of previous monographs follows.

Anthony Friedson, ed. *New Directions in Biography* (1981).

Gloria Fromm, ed. *Essaying Biography: A Celebration for Leon Edel* (1986).

Frank Novak, Jr. *The Autobiographical Writings of Lewis Mumford: A Study in Literary Audacity* (1988).

Mari Matsuda, ed. *Called from Within: Early Women Lawyers of Hawaii* (1992).

Alice M. Beechert and Edward D. Beechert, eds. *John Reinecke: The Autobiography of a Gentle Activist* (1993).

Donald J. Winslow. *Life-Writing: A Glossary of Terms in Biography* (2nd ed., 1995).

Koji Ariyoshi. *From Kona to Yenan: The Political Memoirs of Koji Ariyoshi.* Ed. Alice M. Beechert and Edward D. Beechert (2000).

Leon Edel. *The Visitable Past: A Wartime Memoir* (2000).

Ruth Nadelhaft, with Victoria Bonebakker, eds. *Imagine What It's Like: A Literature and Medicine Anthology* (2008).

Philippe Lejeune. *On Diary.* Ed. Jeremy D. Popkin and Julie Rak (2009).

For further information about the Center or its publications, contact the Center for Biographical Research, University of Hawai'i at Mānoa, Honolulu, Hawai'i 96822 USA; telephone/fax: 808-956-3774; biograph@hawaii.edu; www.hawaii.edu/biograph.